W9-BEE-095

A Polity on the Edge

Harold D. Clarke

Allan Kornberg

Peter Wearing

a Polity *on the*

broadview press

Edge

Canada and the Politics of Fragmentation

Canadian Cataloguing in Publication Data

Clarke, Harold D., 1943–
  A polity on the edge : Canada and the politics of fragmentation

Includes bibliographical references and index.
ISBN 1-55111-240-X

1. Canada—Politics and government—1984-1993.*
2. Canada—Politics and government—1993-   .*
I. Kornberg, Allan, 1931–   .   II. Wearing, Peter.   III. Title.

FC635.c58 2000   971.064'8   C00-931015-0
F1034.2.c58 2000

Broadview Press Ltd., is an independent,
international publishing house, incorporated in 1985.

NORTH AMERICA
P.O. Box 1243,
Peterborough, Ontario,
Canada K9J 7H5

3576 California Road,
Orchard Park, NY 14127

Tel: (705) 743-8990;
Fax: (705) 743-8353

customerservice@broadviewpress.com
www.broadviewpress.com

AUSTRALIA
St. Clair Press,
P.O. Box 287, Rozelle, NSW 2039
Tel: (02) 818-1942; Fax: (02) 418-1923

UNITED KINGDOM
Turpin Distribution Services Ltd.,
Blackhorse Rd, Letchworth,
Hertfordshire SG6 1HN
Tel: (1462) 672555;
Fax: (1462) 480947
turpin@rsc.org

Broadview Press gratefully acknowledges the financial support of the Ministry of Canadian Heritage through the Book Publishing Industry Development Program.

Cover and interior pages designed by Zack Taylor,
Black Eye Design, Inc. Cover photograph by Zack Taylor.

PRINTED IN CANADA

Table of Contents

List of Figures

List of Figures

List of Tables

List of Tables

Preface

This is a book about events and conditions challenging the continued integrity of Canada, one of the world's oldest democracies. One of the authors, Allan Kornberg, initiated his research on this and related subjects nearly three decades ago in a series of élite-level studies of the roles that institutions, especially legislatures and political parties, play in the development, maintenance, and possible demise of democratic polities. Then, in the late 1970s, Clarke and Kornberg began to "look through the other end of the telescope" by investigating factors affecting the dynamics of citizen support for democratic political regimes and communities. For reasons made clear in the following pages, most of these studies have been conducted in Canada, a mature democracy where the experience of political life has long been both defined and constrained by the ongoing threat of system fragmentation. As a new millennium begins, the threat remains very real. In our judgement, the Canadian case is not unique. Rather, it offers important lessons for understanding the current statuses and future prospects of other democracies, new and old alike.

We wish to acknowledge the individuals and organizations that helped to make this book possible. The several large-scale surveys of the Canadian electorate that generated the data for our analyses were funded by generous research grants from the National Science Foundation (U.S.), with supplementary funding from the Canadian Embassy, Washington, D.C., the Provost's Fund, Duke University, and the University of North Texas. We especially wish to thank Frank Scioli, Political Science Program Director at the NSF, for his helpful advice and continuing interest in our "Political Support in Canada" research project. This project began in 1983, and the survey

13

data gathered in connection with it now provide a unique store of information concerning public political attitudes and behaviour during what has become one of the most dramatic and consequential eras in Canadian history. These data form the empirical core of the present volume. Thanks are due as well to the *Canadian Journal of Political Science*, the *Journal of Politics*, and *Party Politics* for permitting us to use some of our analyses that previously appeared in these journals.

We also wish to thank several other people who made important contributions to this project. In 1993, Tom Flanagan, University of Calgary, made many useful suggestions concerning how to study Reform Party activists. One of the most helpful was that we should enlist the services of Faron Ellis, then a Ph.D. candidate at the University of Calgary. Without Faron's assistance, our research on Reformers would not have been possible. Consonant with the significance of his contribution, Faron is designated as a co-author of Chapter Seven. In 1995, when we were working "around-the-clock" to conduct a study of the Quebec sovereignty referendum, Rollie Schafer, Vice-Provost for Research at the University of North Texas, helped us to make the grant application deadline. Two years later, Frank Scioli's then colleague at the NSF, Rick Wilson of Rice University, listened patiently as we enthusiastically discussed our plans for a study of the 1997 federal election campaign and then helped make that study a reality. Bob Burge of the Centre for the Study of Public Opinion, Queen's University, generously supplied us with public opinion data deposited at the Centre by the Decima organization.

The design and, until the early 1990s, execution of the surveys benefited greatly from the inputs of Mary Auvinen, who was Senior Project Director at Canadian Facts for many years. Mary shared her incomparable wealth of knowledge and experience with us, and invariably did much to improve the quality of our research. More recently, we have benefited from the contributions of our co-author, Peter Wearing, formerly Vice-President of Canadian Facts. Since 1993, Peter has played a key role in the development and execution of our studies of the Canadian electorate. Also deserving of recognition are several research assistants. Karl Ho, Matthew Lebo, JoAnn Lutz, Chris McIntyre, and Jonathan Rapkin of the University of North Texas worked assiduously to turn survey

Preface

responses into machine-readable data sets. We also wish to thank Eric Juenke who prepared the index.

Our intellectual debts are many, and we are pleased to acknowledge them. Over the years we have benefited greatly from opportunities to collaborate on varying combinations of articles, books, conferences, edited volumes, and research projects with Colin Campbell, Barry Cooper, David Falcone, Jane Jenson, Larry LeDuc, Allan McCutcheon, William Miller, William Mishler, Helmut Norpoth, Jon Pammett, Richard Price, Joel Smith, Marianne Stewart, and Paul Whiteley. They have taught us a lot. Important also were John Aldrich, Keith Archer, Samuel Barnes, Neal Beck, Ivor Crewe, Russ Dalton, Jack Dennis, Ray Duch, Euel Elliott, Frank Feigert, Tom Flanagan, Mark Franklin, Roger Gibbins, Jim Gibson, Michael Gillespie, Jim Granato, Paul Gronke, Gary King, Peter Lange, Robert Luskin, Neil Nevitte, Diana Owen, David Sanders, Peter Schmidt, Barry Seldon, Mildred Schwartz, Pat Seyd, Paul Sniderman, Norm Thomas, Ric Uslaner, and Cees Van der Eijk. Collectively, these people have provided the scholarly community with a rich set of insightful and stimulating ideas about the nature of political life in contemporary democracies and how to study it. Any errors are our fault, not theirs.

Thanks also are due to Michael Harrison and Barbara Conolly at Broadview Press. Michael's initial enthusiasm for the idea of doing this book encouraged us to proceed. Then, he and Barbara waited patiently as we wrote it. When it became apparent to us that a penultimate chapter on the 1998 Quebec provincial election and a detailed analysis of support for sovereignty since the 1995 referendum were needed to complete the story, they again waited patiently. We sincerely appreciate their willingness to do so.

Finally, we wish to thank Marianne, Patricia, and Sheilagh. We greatly value their encouragement and support, and we are very pleased to dedicate this book to them.

Harold Clarke
Allan Kornberg
Peter Wearing

ONE

A Mature Democracy at Risk

INTRODUCTION

On October 30, 1995, one of the world's oldest democracies came within the proverbial "eyelash" of disintegration. When the ballots in the Quebec provincial sovereignty referendum were counted, barely a percentage point (50.6 vs. 49.4—only 52,000 votes) was all that prevented the beginning of a process that might have ended Canada in its current form. The Parti Québécois (PQ) provincial government had asked Quebecers "Do you agree that Quebec should become sovereign, after having made a formal offer to Canada for a new Economic and Political Partnership, within the scope of the Bill respecting the Future of Quebec and of the agreement signed on June 12, 1995?" Fifteen years earlier, on May 20, 1980, an earlier PQ government had tried to convince Quebec voters of the wisdom of its sovereignty option. Like the 1995 proposition, the 1980 one had been rejected—but by a much wider margin (59.5 per cent vs. 40.5 per cent). Much had changed since then and, as the razor-thin 1995 decision indicated, the balance of federalist and souverainiste forces was much closer than it had been fifteen years earlier. The historic dream of "absolute freedom" (Cook, 1995: 106-07) remained alive in the hearts and minds of many Québécois nationalists.

It is true, of course, that Canada is not the only country in which the maintenance of its territorial integrity and form of government is a problematic exercise. Most notably, in recent years the former Soviet Union and Yugoslavia have experienced highly acrimonious controversies about the nature of emergent political communities and regimes. In both cases these disputes have degenerated into violent conflicts with heavy losses of life. Neither are controversies about the character of political regime and community settled in the new South Africa, nor unlikely to emerge in other states in Africa, Asia, and the Middle East. Moreover, there have been recurring, divisive debates over the structure of political regimes and communities in mature democracies as well: examples include countries as diverse as Belgium, France, Israel, Italy, Spain, and the United Kingdom. But among these latter countries it is Canada, a charter member of the democratic club and a country that has been described as "all in all, on the whole, the most admirable on earth" (Morris, cited in Gwyn, 1995: 51) for which the future viability of the political system in its current form is in most serious doubt. This book tries to explain why the continued integrity of the Canadian polity is problematic. The analyses focus on six pivotal events during a 10-year period (1988-1998) that both individually and, more importantly, *collectively*, have contributed to the precarious status of this mature democracy's continued viability.

The first of these events was the dramatic 1988 federal election in which the issue became whether Canada should strengthen its already close economic ties to the United States by entering into a free trade agreement (the FTA) with its giant southern neighbour. The FTA was championed by former Progressive Conservative Prime Minister Brian Mulroney, and vigorously resisted by the opposition Liberal Party and its then leader, John Turner. Mulroney viewed free trade as both good for the country and good for his party; it would be the key to Canada's future economic prosperity as well as a splendid example of how his government could "manage change." In contrast, Turner maintained that the agreement would pose grave threats to the country's economic and political independence, and would place its cherished social programs and culture at risk. In the event, the Conservative victory effectively ratified a potentially highly consequential shift in Canada's long-term relationship with the United States, and provided *de facto* endorsement of a broader neo-conservative project for restructuring Canada's economy and society.

Unfortunately for Mulroney and the PCs, the anticipated economic benefits of the FTA did not materialize—at least not in the short run. Soon after the prime minister and his party were returned to office, the recovery that had begun in the mid-1980s faltered and the economy spiralled downward into protracted recession. Although the slump was particularly serious in the country's industrial heartland, Ontario, economic distress was prevalent in all regions, and stories of plant closings, business downsizing, soaring budget deficits, and mounting unemployment became distressingly familiar features on the nightly news. Ignoring other possible causes of the problem, many people attributed the downturn to the recently implemented free trade agreement, and public support for the prime minister and his party fell sharply.

Although Mulroney seemed genuinely committed to trying to defuse the threat of Quebec separatism and resolve his country's long-standing constitutional problems, it is a plausible conjecture that the ongoing economic malaise and the decline in Conservative fortunes also figured in his decision to hold a national referendum in October 1992 on the Charlottetown Constitutional Accord. This referendum is the second critical event that we examine. Mulroney and the rest of the Canadian political establishment vigorously argued that public approval of the Charlottetown agreement was vital for the preservation of the country (Jeffrey, 1993). However, their pleas went unheeded, and the referendum proposal was soundly defeated.

The 1993 federal election is the third significant event considered. After the Charlottetown Accord was rejected, the economy remained in the doldrums, and Prime Minister Mulroney and PCs continued to be very unpopular with voters in all parts of the country. Conservative electoral prospects appeared so bleak, and the news from public opinion polls was so persistently bad, that Mulroney finally resigned in February 1993—much to relief of a number of Tory strategists. Their expectation was that his successor, Kim Campbell, a "fresh face" and Canada's first woman prime minister, would wipe the slate clean and give the PCs a fighting chance to win the upcoming federal election.

The strategy failed. On election day, the PCs suffered a massive defeat, and the electorate installed the Liberals led by Jean Chrétien as a new majority government. Like the Tories, the New Democrats were virtually eliminated from parliament as two new regionally based parties, the Reform Party in the West and the Bloc Québécois in Quebec, became the largest opposition parties. The presence of a large contingent of Bloc MPs as the official parliamentary opposition—whose avowed raison d'être was the independence of Quebec—signified Canada's deepening crisis of national integration, a crisis that certainly was not resolved by the subsequent 1995 Quebec sovereignty referendum.

This referendum is the fourth major event we study. The Parti Québécois proposal to initiate a process by which Quebec would become politically sovereign failed by an extraordinarily slim margin—less than the number of spoiled ballots. Moreover, the near-passage of the referendum did not provide the kind of salutary shock to bring Quebecers and persons in the rest of the country closer to consensus on constitutional options that might keep Quebec in Canada.

The fifth important event is the 1997 federal election. In this contest the need for, and the timing of, an election were themselves issues, as were national unity, the economy, and the honesty of Prime Minister Chrétien and the governing Liberal Party. Similar to the 1995 sovereignty referendum, the election appeared to change nothing and resolve nothing. Indeed, in many respects, it was yet another exercise in collective frustration. Its principal result seemed to be the perpetuation of a regionally splintered party system emblematic of Canada's fragmented polity.

As the twentieth century drew to a close, the threat to the integrity of the Canadian political system continued. The October 1998 Quebec provincial election is the sixth important event we consider. Both the Parti Québécois and its federalist adversaries recognized that this election was very important because its outcome would determine if the PQ would be in a position to continue its struggle for sovereignty by holding yet another referendum. When the ballots were counted, the PQ had won a second consecutive majority government, albeit without a majority or even a plurality of the popular vote. But, by keeping the reins of provincial power, the Péquistes retained their ability to mount another challenge to the continuation of Canada in its current form.

IMPRESSIVE STRENGTHS, PERSISTENT PROBLEMS

The crisis of national integration confronting Canada exists despite the fact that historically the country has shared many of the socio-political and economic strengths that characterize other mature democracies and that help maintain their viability and territorial integrity even in very difficult times. *Inter alia*, these countries are characterized by (1) political systems in which there is close congruence between the manner in which their constitutional orders prescribe how their component parts should work and their actual function; (2) heavy (and generally successful) reliance on voluntary public compliance with the authoritative edicts of government (but see Schwartz, 1983); (3) regular, free, competitive elections and representative institutions with stable national party systems that articulate and aggregate political demand; (4) market-oriented economies that are extremely powerful motors of wealth creation and technological innovation; (5) elaborate educational systems that develop human capital resources and promote relatively labile class systems; (6) dense networks of organized groups and voluntary organizations that generate social capital resources and facilitate political participation; (7) elaborate social safety nets to cushion the hardships associated with periodic economic downturns and that help narrow individual, group, and regional inequalities; and (8) mass communication and transportation networks that contribute to social, economic, and political integration and, together with the educational system, transmit system-supporting beliefs and values through subtle, but pervasive, political socialization processes.

Despite their formidable strengths, mature democracies may face periodically a cascade of problems generating crises that place very severe strains on the socio-political and economic fabrics holding them together. In the twentieth century, the most prolonged and widespread such crisis was the Great Depression. It began in the late 1920s, endured throughout the following decade and ended only with the outbreak of World War II. Before it was over, a variety of ideological "isms" such as Nazism, Fascism, and Marxism had gained strong public support in various countries. As the Depression also emphasized, the power of their market-oriented economies notwithstanding, democracies did not have sure-fire formulas for sustaining high levels of growth in competitive international marketplaces. The high tariff walls democracies erected against one another during the 1930s failed to revive their domestic economies and brought international trade to a virtual standstill. The deepening economic malaise enhanced the attractiveness of Marxism and

Socialism, which seemed to offer more equitable, effective, and humane ways of organizing a society's productive and distributive capacities.

In recent decades, technological advances in transportation and communications and the accompanying ability to store, analyse, and transmit information as well as to conduct financial transactions at speeds undreamed of even a generation ago have contributed to a complex, multi-faceted condition commonly labelled "globalization" (Friedman, 1998). And, since the best efforts of generations of Nobel prize-winning economists—Keynesians and neoclassicists alike—have failed to repeal the business cycle, reinvigorated market forces operating in an increasingly global context, have exposed the workforces of even the most prosperous democracies to threats to job security such as plant closings and relocations, reduced work hours, and caused private- and public-sector downsizing. Periodic recessions continue to occur and, although they now are euphemistically termed "dislocations" and "corrections," their attendant social and economic miseries remain unpleasant facts of life.

In addition to the persistently high unemployment that has plagued many mature democracies in the 1980s and 1990s (e.g., Bean, 1994), demographic trends—especially aging populations and the imminent retirement of the huge post-World War II, "baby boom" generation—have increased the demand for, and the costs imposed by, social safety nets. The tax burdens imposed by these escalating costs have had important political consequences. One such consequence has been to bolster the popularity of the complex of political ideas commonly labelled neo-conservatism (see, e.g., Clarke, Stewart, and Zuk, 1989; Cooper, Kornberg, and Mishler, 1988). In addition to a strong faith in the efficacious operation of domestic and international markets, neo-conservatives express a strong preference for smaller, less intrusive, and less costly governments. The need for deep spending cuts, particularly in social programs, to achieve these goals is a prominent part of neo-conservative rhetoric. Neo-conservatives couple these policy proposals with prescriptions for individual conduct—notably, people should accept personal responsibility for their actions, and focus on duty and service rather than on rights and entitlements. Accompanying these recommendations is the argument that individuals and individual rights must have primacy over groups and group rights, because the former rather than the latter are the fundamental building blocks of a free and just society.

Over the past decade, neo-conservative economic policies have had champions in political parties of both the traditional "right"and "left," and parties on both sides of the ideological spectrum have advocated "reinventing" government by making it smaller, more efficient, and less costly. However, advocacy and action are very different things and, after capturing the reins of power, governing parties often have found themselves caught between an "economic rock" and a "political hard place." They may want to reduce ballooning budgetary deficits by cutting spending on social programs but, at the same time, they feel great pressure to maintain and even increase funding for some of these programs because they are very popular, and a government that attacks them may seriously erode its public support. More fundamentally, by widening income inequalities that are inevitable in free societies with market-oriented economies, drastic reductions in major social programs would do violence to the norms of equity and fairness that are cornerstones of the legitimating belief systems on which contemporary democratic government and politics rest.

Democracies, particularly ones characterized by polycommunal societies and federal systems of government, also are subject to serious stresses caused by deep, persistent cleavages based on economic, ethno-linguistic, and religious differences, or simply historic grievances (Schwartz, 1974: ch. 1). When groups whose identities are based on such economic or cultural particularisms are regionally concentrated they can place enormous centrifugal pressure on national political systems and the societies of which they are a part. In this regard, it is important to recall that federal forms of government originally were justified in democratic theory as a means of accommodating and diffusing these pressures (e.g., Stevenson, 1989: ch. 1). Ironically, however, federalism provides the institutional locus for their organization and expression. And, as the Canadian case dramatically illustrates, dissident groups can use subnational governments as institutional levers to disrupt a national political system, perhaps even to fragment it.

Democratic theory has generated another unintended consequence for the maintenance of democratic government. One of the most fundamental precepts in democratic theory is that the state is the servant of the people. As such, its activities are justified as a means to the good life (e.g., Held, 1994). In contemporary mature democracies, this conception receives extremely broad, indeed almost unanimous, approval. Thus, when leaders of dissident groups in these polities articulate democratic ideological values and promise a political order that is more "democratic" than the existing one, their appeals constitute especially powerful threats. In the late twentieth century, the principal ideological challenge to the continued geographic and structural integrity of mature democracies comes not from communism, fascism, or other forms of authoritarianism, but from democracy itself. In contemporary Canada, this ideological challenge interacts with and reinforces long-standing, unresolved, constitutional and politico-economic problems to threaten the continuation of one of the world's oldest functioning democracies.

THE ROOTS OF FRAGMENTATION

Before there was a Canadian state there were provinces, one of which has origins that go back to the sixteenth century. On the one hand, the presence of provincial communities with strong, well-formed identities made Confederation possible. On the other, some of the same factors have contributed over the years to the difficulties the Canadian state has experienced in becoming a Canadian nation. The conditions under which Canada emerged and subsequently developed as a democratic state are well known (see, e.g., McNaught, 1969) and will be sketched briefly here. Confederation was a product of conscious decisions made by political leaders of Ontario, Quebec, New Brunswick, and Nova Scotia and the British government of the day. It brought together physically vigorous and reasonably literate populations residing in provinces in which the institutions and processes that provide the structural basis for a democratic polity were largely in place and already legitimized. In the generation that followed, the prospects of the new state appeared very promising. Reflecting the optimism, Prime Minister Sir Wilfrid Laurier is reputed to have predicted that the twentieth century would be Canada's. Even if this prediction has not proved to be fully accurate, nonetheless it is no great exaggeration to assert that for much of the past half-century Canadians have enjoyed a standard of living and a quality of life that is the envy of people in the great majority of the world's countries, regardless of their form of government or the organization of their economies.

If so, an inquisitive reader may ask, why does Canada—one of the freest and most affluent countries on earth—periodically appear to be on the brink of falling apart? Not surprisingly, perhaps, scholars frequently contend that Canada's current problems of national integration have their origins, at least in part, in the act of Confederation. For example, one student of Canadian federalism, Garth Stevenson (1989), has claimed that the process leading to Confederation was a profoundly élitist one in that all the key decisions were made by a handful of politicians rather than by a majority of the people in the four founding provinces. In addition, the provinces other than Quebec lacked the cultural cohesion and shared identity that derive from a common descent, language, religion, and established customs and traditions.

Others (e.g., Lipset, 1990; Preston, 1972) have argued that the thirteen colonies, which a century earlier had become the new United States of America, had some of the same problems but were able to overcome them because their citizens were united by the shared experience of participation in a successful revolution. It also is argued that the motives of Canada's founding fathers for entering into union differed markedly. Smith (1987: 3-29) claims they were motivated by political ambition as well as a preference for a strong defensible state that could foster commerce. Analyses of legislative debates in the parliament of the United Canada's before Confederation and of the new House of Commons for several years afterward indicate that some of Ontario's leaders viewed Confederation as a way out of political deadlock. Others were concerned with saving the West for the proposed new state from the potential predatory incursions of land-hungry Americans. Quebec's leaders viewed Confederation differently, as a mechanism that could best safeguard their cultural heritage and maintain their political autonomy. For their part, the leaders of Nova Scotia and New Brunswick anticipated that the new state could facilitate economic development and attract the kind of investment capital required to build an interprovincial railroad that, in turn, would fuel future prosperity (Kornberg and Hines, 1977).

A Polity on the Edge

Since there was no real agreement before or after Confederation on the *raison d'être* for the new state, no consensus ever developed regarding the defining character of the union that was forged, or of those who were parties to it. Was it a compact among the governments of the four uniting provinces, one between the four provinces and the new federal government or, perhaps, one between the two great ethno-linguistic communities? (see, e.g., Black, 1979; Bothwell, 1998; Lower, 1969). Since no one could say for certain what the rationale was for the state that was formed, over the years judicial interpretations of the British North America Act were able to vastly expand the power of the provinces and exacerbate decades of conflict between federal and provincial political leaders. Dual national and sub-national loyalties and identities thus are very deeply imbued in the Canadian political psyche (e.g., Bell and Tepperman, 1979; Black and Cairns, 1966; Cairns, 1971, 1983; Smiley, 1980; Stevenson, 1989).

As, or perhaps more, important than the legacies of Confederation in explaining the problem of keeping Canada together are factors that derive from, on the one hand, its geographic, social, and economic realities and, on the other, its political institutions and processes (see, e.g., Kornberg, 1970; Schwartz, 1974). Schwartz's observation (1974: 1) that "[n]ature and history have conspired to make geography central to an understanding of Canadian existence" perhaps best sums up two basic facts. In a continent-wide land mass second in size only to the former Soviet Union, the great majority of Canadians live in a narrow band north of the American border with two-thirds residing in Ontario and Quebec, the latter the home of four-fifths of the country's Francophones. Schwartz (1974: 1) argues that this "spatial makeup of Canada compounds every critical social and political problem the country faces." Some of the socioeconomic problems derive from the very significant differences in the size, value, and character of the natural resources and the level of industrialization and wealth of the ten provinces. The principal political difficulty is a national political system that combines a highly decentralized form of federalism with a British-style parliamentary government based on disciplined and cohesive political parties functioning in a popularly elected House of Commons and an appointed Senate. Add to these the centrifugal presence "next door" of the United States, the world's premier economic and military power, with an enormously influential mass media and popular culture.

This combination of geographic, socio-political, and economic conditions and the problems they generate have faced every generation of Canadians and their political leaders since Confederation. Those leaders have tried to deal with them in different ways and with varying degrees of success. Macdonald attempted to establish the legitimacy of the new federal government by demonstrating its effectiveness in dealing with the economic problems of the day. In addition to pressing for and facilitating the building of a transcontinental railroad, his "National Policy" of tariff protection for a protean Canadian industrial base was successful in that industry experienced significant growth during the last two decades of the nineteenth century and the first decade of the twentieth. Besides accentuating differences between the centre (Ontario and Quebec) and the peripheral regions of the country (the Atlantic provinces and the West), the National Policy's tariff walls encouraged American businesses to establish branch-plants in Canada. Indeed, Bliss (1991: 423-34) points out that one of the ironies of the 1911 national election in which Wilfrid Laurier's Liberal government proposed a relatively innocuous reciprocity agreement with the United States was that it was opposed both by protectionists and by local businessmen and politicians. The former argued it would undermine the economic foundations of an industrialized central Canada, and the latter maintained that a reduction in tariffs would largely remove the incentive American businesses had to establish Canadian subsidiaries—they would retreat across the border and take their capital and jobs with them.

Employment or, more precisely, the lack thereof was the principal socio-economic problem with which both the Conservative government of R.B. Bennett and the Liberal one of W.L. Mackenzie King were forced to deal in depression-ridden 1930s. Immigration policies promulgated by Laurier's Liberal government around the turn of the century had transformed the Prairie provinces by populating them with immigrants aggressively recruited from Ukraine and other Eastern and Central European locales. However, the promise of ongoing prosperity in their new homeland was not fulfilled. The Depression caused great hardship throughout Canada, but nowhere was the misery more widely felt than in the West. In the Prairies and elsewhere, the distress continued throughout the "dirty thirties," and "riding the rails" across the country in search of jobs became a way of life for thousands of unemployed young men.

Walter Young (1969) has argued that although the government's response was by no means adequate, the Depression demonstrated with tragic clarity the need for direct and permanent government intervention in the economy. Bennett's Conservative government initially strongly resisted extending additional federal assistance to the provinces or engaging the federal government directly in combating the worst effects of the slump. His position seemed to be that if the unemployed were given financial assistance it would merely encourage more people not to seek jobs. In short, "relief" or "the dole," as it was variously termed, actually worsened unemployment, or so he seemed to believe. However, the continuing and deepening crisis eventually forced the Tories to take action to ameliorate joblessness (Employment and Social Insurance Act), regulate monetary policy (Bank of Canada), and keep the country together (the establishment of Trans-Canada Airlines and the Canadian Broadcasting Corporation). These actions and the policies adopted by the King Liberal government, which came to power in 1935, may not have significantly alleviated the severe poverty and misery that afflicted so many thousands of Canadians for more than a decade. However, they may well have had other consequences since, despite dire predictions of massive unrest, there were only sporadic attempts to organize major political protests. The most serious such action was the aborted 1935 "March on Ottawa," which still had a considerable distance to cover when it was broken up by the police at Regina.

In the hard-hit western provinces, the misery of the 1930s did give rise to two new political parties—Social Credit and the Cooperative Commonwealth Federation Party, better known by its acronym, the CCF, and after 1961 as the New Democratic Party, the NDP (e.g., Young, 1969; Zakuta, 1964). The origins of both of these parties lie in the short-lived Progressive Party, which had roots in the United Farmers parties (Morton, 1950). These new parties, it can be argued, were organizational responses to the problems generated by the adoption at Confederation of both a federal system and Westminster-model parliament. Above, it was noted that there were reasons for adopting a federal system and combining it with a

Westminster-model parliamentary form of government, since these were systems with which the élites of the time had experience. It is probable that John A. Macdonald and the other founding fathers never anticipated a federal system in which the provinces would become major players, exercising substantially more power and importance than their counterparts in the United States. However, the powers of the provinces did grow and, as a consequence, there was (and remains) a tendency among their residents to rely on the provincial governments—regardless of their partisan composition—to represent provincial interests in the national political arena.

The tendency to rely on new parties and provincial governments for representation was especially strong in the West and the Atlantic provinces because of the political ramifications of the distribution of population between these regions, on the one hand, and Ontario and Quebec, on the other. Given that Canada's Westminster-model parliamentary system required disciplined, cohesive parties in order to function properly, the interests of Ontario and Quebec—regions with large populations and most of the Members of Parliament— typically prevailed over those of the West and the Atlantic provinces, regardless of whether a Conservative or a Liberal government was in office in Ottawa. Westerners became increasingly disgruntled with this state of affairs, and some concluded that their issues and concerns inevitably would be ignored or inadequately addressed by the existing parties or, indeed, by the larger political system. As noted above, the eventual result of this growing disaffection among Westerners was the formation of new parties including the CCF and Social Credit in the 1930s and Reform in the late 1980s. For different reasons disaffected Quebecers formed parties such as the Bloc Populaire, the Union Nationale, and, later, the Parti Québécois and Bloc Québécois. Their incentive to form new parties was heightened by the geographic concentration of the population to which they were appealing. This, in turn, gave new parties a reasonable chance of initial success and a defense against any claim that a vote for them would be "wasted."

The massive unemployment and widespread poverty that accompanied the Great Depression finally ended during World War II, which Canada entered in September 1939. In his magisterial study of the war, historian Gerhard Weinberg pays tribute to the Canadian armed forces "significant role in the war on land, sea, and in the air." He goes on to observe that during the war the country experienced dramatic internal changes in that "the economy was greatly stimulated by massive investments in new factories and means of transportation and communication" (Weinberg, 1994: 491-92). These investments, commentators note—some approvingly, others despairingly—were largely made by the United States. Indeed, as Granatstein (in Bliss, 1991: 710) concludes, by the end of the war "Canada was part of a continental economy." By 1945 American investment had risen to 70 per cent of the total foreign capital invested in Canada, Canadian exports to the United States had tripled, and imports from that country were ten times those from Britain. He acknowledges "that the war undoubtedly had distorted Canada's trade figures, but the direction was clear and it would be confirmed by the events of the reconstruction period."

The chief architect of postwar reconstruction was C.D. Howe, perhaps the most powerful member of the Liberal cabinet of Mackenzie King, both during and after the war. The American-born Howe, an engineer by profession, convinced King and other political and business leaders that a significantly expanded economic and industrial base and the prosperity this would bring could only be achieved by aggressively pursuing American investment capital. In retrospect, Howe probably did not have to twist too many arms to persuade the leaders of the time of the wisdom of such a policy. Given the physical devastation and economic condition of both financially strapped Britain and Western Europe, the United States was clearly the only possible source of large infusions of capital. In fact, Howe and his strongest supporters may have underestimated the extent to which Canada's economy and its industrial base would grow under the stimulus of American investment. Nor might they have anticipated how the resulting affluence would enable the federal government and the provinces to expand their respective bureaucracies and their panoplies of social programs. Equally important, Howe and his colleagues may not have realized how closely American investment would tie Canada's economy to that of the United States.

Canadian nationalists later would stigmatize this policy decision as the "great sell-out" (e.g., Laxer and Laxer, 1977; Lumsden, 1970; Watkins, 1968). But, even if the growth of American involvement in the Canadian economy began long before Howe came to Canada,

One :: A Mature Democracy at Risk

as Michael Bliss claims (Bliss, 1991: 433), nationalists still might contend that the levels American direct and portfolio investments had reached by the late 1970s and the influence this had on Canadian independence would not be tolerated by a third-world country, let alone by a mature democracy. More generally, nationalists argue that the giant presence of the United States and the shadow it casts over Canada's politics and culture as well as its economy have made it almost impossible to develop a national identity that could be assumed by all Canadians, regardless of their differences (see, e.g., Gwyn, 1995).

A second broad policy initiative pursued by the mostly Liberal governments (King, St. Laurent, Pearson, Trudeau) in the 40 or more years following World War II was to try to address the historic problem of regionalism based on cultural and economic particularisms (see, e.g., McRoberts, 1997). In the first instance, this decision was manifested in an assortment of federal programs intended to narrow regional and provincial economic disparities. In the second, it involved attempts to recognize, respond to, and diffuse the impact of reinvigorated Quebec nationalism and Western alienation. The result was the significant devolution of economic and political power to the provinces noted above, coupled with extensive bilingualism and biculturalism programs designed to recognize and reinforce "the French fact" throughout Canadian government, economy, and society. These "bi- and bi-" programs soon were followed by the promotion of multiculturalism as a "third force" in the sociocultural and political landscape. The latter initiative appealed to the West because a substantial proportion of the region's population was of other than Anglo-Celtic or French origins. Also, since many post-World War II immigrants to Quebec were neither of Anglo-Celtic nor French ethnicity, the emphasis on multiculturalism implicitly challenged the increasingly strident claims of Québécois separatists that their province "belonged" to persons of French descent, while simultaneously fostering a sense of Canadian, rather than Québécois, identity among the new arrivals.

However, according to critics (e.g., Flanagan, 1985; Gwyn, 1995; Knopff, 1985), the "bi- and bi-" and multicultural policies have had other effects as well. Specifically, they have contributed to the development of the kind of "identity politics" that loosens the ties that bind citizens together in a national political community. Such

31

architectonic attachments are particularly important in a socially heterogeneous country such as Canada. Critics also contend that since 1982 the presence of the Charter of Rights and Freedoms in the new Canadian constitution has legitimized and intensified this brand of politics.

Moreover, the long post-World War II boom did not obviate long-standing regional economic disparities, and the economy remained highly vulnerable to international events and conditions. Although, *circa* the late 1960s, many Canadians in every region enjoyed living standards that surpassed those of all but a handful of countries in the world, substantial inter-regional economic differences remained in such key indicators as industrial capacity, infrastructure development, and growth rates. Then, in the early 1970s, the country's continuing ability to sustain economic development and to fund the increasing costs of major social programs was called into question. Similar to many other Western countries, Canada suddenly found itself afflicted by "stagflation." Simultaneous surges in inflation and unemployment coupled with sagging growth were precipitated by the massive increases in energy costs that occurred in the wake of the 1973 Arab oil embargo and the rise of the Organization of Petroleum Exporting Countries (OPEC) cartel. Annual rates of inflation that had averaged only 2.2 per cent in the 1950s and 1960s, rose sharply in the 1970s, and peaked at 12.5 per cent in 1981. Joblessness, which stood at 4.4 per cent when the 1970s began, exceeded 7 per cent throughout the latter half of the decade, and then climbed into double digits in the early 1980s. Between 1972—the last year before the oil embargo—and 1982, the infamous "misery index," combining inflation and unemployment rates, nearly doubled, rising from 11.0 per cent to 21.8 per cent. There were political consequences as well, as the large increases in energy prices stimulated sharp conflicts between oil-rich Alberta and other energy-producing provinces, on the one hand, and central Canada and the federal government on the other.

Complicating these growing inter-provincial and federal-provincial conflicts was the dramatic intensification of the Quebec versus the Rest of Canada (ROC) struggle precipitated by the November 1976 election of a Parti Québécois government in Quebec. The PQ's avowed *raison d'être* was political independence for that province, and the party's presence posed a threat not only to the operation

One :: *A Mature Democracy at Risk*

of the federal system but also to the very existence of Canada's national community (e.g., McRoberts, 1988). However, subsequent events—the decisive defeat of the PQ's 1980 sovereignty association referendum, the adoption of a new constitution with a Charter of Rights and Freedoms in 1982, and the defeat of the PQ government in the 1985 Quebec provincial election—combined to give Canada the appearance of a new lease on life.

The election of a Brian Mulroney-led Conservative government in the 1984 federal election contributed to this appearance. Mulroney's leadership was symbolically important because he was both an Anglo and a fluently bilingual Quebecer—the "Boy from Baie Comeau" he sometimes was called, most often by himself. Although he had pledged during the 1984 campaign that protecting the social safety net was a "sacred trust," once in office the pledge was placed on a back burner. His attention was directed to getting a handle on the federal government's rising deficits by cutting spending—more specifically, by reorganizing the management of, and reducing spending for, social programs. Also, like his neo-conservative counterparts in the United States and Britain, Ronald Reagan and Margaret Thatcher, Mulroney became a strong advocate of free trade, which he contended was a key to invigorating Canada's economy and ensuring its future prosperity. As noted earlier, the re-election of the Mulroney-led Tories in the 1988 election was widely interpreted as de facto ratification of the use of free trade as a key instrument to secure Canada's position as a major player in the emerging global economy. Although Mulroney won the battle for free trade and the Canada-U.S. free trade agreement (FTA) was implemented, we will argue that his victory would become an instrument in his own and his party's undoing.

Nor were perceived negative consequences of the FTA the only problems that Mulroney and his government confronted during their second term. In the late 1950s, under the leadership of the charismatic John Diefenbaker, the West had become a loyal Conservative bastion and, when Mulroney led the party to victory in 1984, many Westerners believed that Ottawa finally would be responsive to their long-standing grievances. However, Mulroney needed to shore up Conservative support in Quebec since the latter province not only had the numbers to keep him and his party in office in the foreseeable future, it also was the key to the possible permanent resolution of the constitutional issue. Moreover, he and his advisers may well have assumed that West really had nowhere to go. Flanagan (1995) notes that initially neither the erosion of Conservative support in the West, nor the birth of the new right-of-centre party, Reform, were taken seriously by Tory strategists.

Accordingly, Mulroney, as he liked to say, "rolled the dice." In a widely publicized decision his government awarded a huge defense aircraft maintenance contract to a firm in Montreal rather than accepting a lower bid from a company in Winnipeg. This act was invested with great symbolic significance by Westerners, who interpreted it as akin to betrayal since it clearly favoured Quebec over their region. Tory support in the West dropped sharply. Although it recovered sufficiently in that region and in the rest of the country for the PCs to win re-election in 1988, it soon began another slide that eventually culminated in a PC electoral disaster in 1993.

We will argue that the prime minister's penchant for high-risk political activism played a key role in precipitating the renewed crisis of national integration of the 1990s and the dramatic decline in public support for him and his party after the 1988 election. Although many observers originally had characterized Mulroney as a quintessential political "trimmer," once in power he vigorously pursued highly controversial initiatives to resolve the country's economic and constitutional difficulties. Regarding the economy, in addition to the free trade initiative, his government instituted a new revenue-enhancing measure to trim the deficit and fund existing social programs. This was a tax of 7 per cent on virtually all goods and services, the so-called GST. The government proceeded to adopt the GST despite overwhelming evidence that it was massively unpopular among virtually every segment of the population. The GST must have been especially perplexing to many Tory neo-conservative "true believers" who were convinced that "their" government should be cutting taxes rather than raising them, just as Mulroney's counterparts in the United States and Britain were doing.

As for the constitution, Mulroney's intent was to broker a deal that could be embraced by Quebec and at least be acceptable to the rest of the country. Efforts to address the constitutional impasse led to what became known as the Meech Lake Constitutional Accord

One :: A Mature Democracy at Risk

(Monahan, 1991; Russell, 1992). The product of meetings in 1987 between the prime minister and the premiers of the 10 provinces, and signed by them, it was not, however, ratified by the provincial legislatures of Manitoba and Newfoundland within the required three-year period. The failure to ratify the agreement must have surprised and frustrated its architects who were skilled in the arts of élite accommodation. The process by which it was arrived at was fully in keeping with the traditional consociational practices of executive federalism and federal-provincial diplomacy by which prime ministers, provincial premiers, and senior federal and provincial bureaucrats bargained behind closed doors to devise mutually acceptable deals.

Although this élite-centred process was increasingly out-of-step with Canadians' growing desire for more direct involvement in political decision-making processes (Nevitte, 1996), we contend that the *content* of the agreement was crucial to its undoing. Particularly contentious was the clause that designated Quebec as a "distinct society." This clause gave constitutional sanction to the historic claim of Québécois nationalists that Quebec was a province "pas comme les autres," but outside of Quebec it generated widespread and vociferous public opposition. This opposition, in turn, stimulated outrage among many Quebec Francophones over insensitivity to Quebec's feelings in the rest of Canada and a seeming unwillingness by non-Quebecers to accept what was simply a fundamental statement of reality. The good intentions of its authors notwithstanding, the failure of the Meech Lake Accord precipitated a new constitutional crisis, which in Quebec produced a sharp upswing in support for the separatist Parti Québécois and its new federal counterpart, the Bloc Québécois. The latter party was founded by Lucien Bouchard, an erstwhile Conservative cabinet minister and long-time friend of the prime minister. According to Bouchard's analysis, the failure of Meech Lake represented a profound rejection of Quebec by the rest of Canada and the humiliation of Québécois in the eyes of the world.

In yet another attempt to resolve the country's constitutional difficulties, Mulroney and the provincial premiers negotiated what came to be called the Charlottetown Accord. Unlike the strategy he used to secure approval for the Meech Lake agreement, the prime minister decided that he would ask the public to ratify the

35

Charlottetown deal in a national referendum. By deciding to employ a national referendum, the federal government was moving in step with a trend towards the increasing use of the devices of direct democracy that has been gaining strength in a number of mature democracies (Butler and Ranney, 1994; Franklin, van der Eijk, and Marsh, 1995). Canadians were presented with a wide-ranging package of constitutional proposals, including recognition of Quebec as a distinct society, which they were requested to vote up or down. Despite demonstrating its virtuosity in crafting a referendum question that raised ambiguity to an art form (i.e., "Do you agree that the Constitution of Canada should be renewed on the basis of the agreement reached August 18, 1992?"), the Mulroney government's hopes of cutting the constitutional Gordian knot and thereby regaining its standing with the public went unrealized. The referendum was decisively rejected in every region of the country except Ontario where a razor-thin majority (50.2 per cent) endorsed it.

The rejection of the referendum package was partly a product of its multi-faceted nature (Johnston et al., 1996; LeDuc and Pammett, 1995). Designed to give everyone "something to like," it also gave everyone "something to dislike." However, our analyses also will demonstrate that the referendum proposal failed because of the political-economic context in which it was held. In the autumn of 1992, the country was in the throes of recession, and many voters held the prime minister and his government responsible for their straightened circumstances. In effect, the referendum took on many of the characteristics of an ordinary election and, by saying "No" so decisively, voters were sending a message that was not entirely addressed to the constitutional issues in question. Voting in the referendum also was influenced by more general negative assessments of all of the old-line national parties and their leaders, a topic that we will consider in subsequent chapters. For some observers, the failure of the Meech Lake and Charlottetown constitutional agreements signalled the end of "mega-constitutional politics" in Canada (Russell, 1993; see also McRoberts and Monahan, 1993). For Brian Mulroney it marked the effective end of his tenure as prime minister. However, his resignation did not diminish the threat to the country's continued integrity. Rather, we will argue that four subsequent events have established the context in which the political conflicts to determine Canada's future will be waged in the twenty-first century.

One of these events was the 1993 federal election. When the ballots were counted, PC parliamentary representation had been reduced to *two* MPs, fully 167 fewer than the party had elected only five years earlier. The NDP, which had entertained dreams of national power after its impressive victory in the 1990 Ontario provincial election, also was seriously weakened. The New Democrats elected only seven MPs in 1993, as compared to 43 in 1988. Amid the devastation, two new parties with strong bases in two disaffected regions, Reform in the West and the Bloc Québécois in Quebec, emerged as major players on the national political stage.

This profound shock to the existing party system did not take place in a vacuum. We will show that it represents the culmination of long-term negative trends in public support for the national parties. By the 1990s, Canadians had accumulated a veritable "laundry list" of grievances about how parties were performing. Our national survey data forcefully document the point. Moreover, the negativism was not confined to voters supporting one of the new parties or residents of disaffected regions. Instead, old-line party supporters and people in all parts of the country were very unhappy with the performance of the national parties.

In studying the growth of support for the new parties, we will focus on questions such as "Who joins political parties?" "What factors prompt participation in party organizations?" and "What difference does party organizational activity make?" These questions are of long-standing interest (see Kornberg, Smith, and Clarke, 1979) to students of political parties, and in recent years this interest has been reinvigorated by research demonstrating that the activities of local party organizations have important effects on their vote shares (e.g., Whiteley et al., 1994). This finding suggests that the short-term success and long-term prospects of new parties like Reform and the Bloc Québécois and the centrifugal forces they can exert on the political integrity of a country like Canada may be significantly affected by their ability to attract members and mobilize them to work on the party's behalf. Using survey data on 5,000 members of Canada's new Reform Party we will investigate who the Reformers are, how and why they joined their new party, and what they believe about government and politics. We also will consider the

37

kinds of party activities in which they engage, and investigate factors that influence their participation in the party organization. These analyses inform a discussion of forces influencing the development of new parties and of how such parties can facilitate or inhibit the integrity of a democratic political system such as Canada's.

The fragmentation of the national party system in the 1993 federal election was followed by the 1995 Quebec referendum, a contest that threatened to shatter the country itself. Recognizing the importance of the decision they were asked to make, voters came to the polls in droves, and the turnout rate was an unprecedented 93.5 per cent. Although the "no" side prevailed by a minuscule margin, the very ominous omen for the future of Canada was that a solid majority of Francophone Quebecers had voted for sovereignty. Our analysis of voting in the referendum begins by tracing major events and trends in public opinion in the "long campaign" leading up to the balloting. Then, after describing the political beliefs, attitudes, and opinions associated with Quebecers' support for the Canadian political system and the alternative of an independent Quebec, we analyse how various factors shaped voter choices. These factors included socio-political identities and support for Canada's national political regime and community, as well as projective assessments of the risks associated with alternative referendum outcomes. Also relevant were the alternative visions of democracy offered by proponents of a united Canada and a sovereign Quebec. In addition, consonant with our argument that important referendums take on many of the characteristics of federal or provincial elections, we consider people's feelings about the politicians and parties championing or opposing the referendum proposal. Our model of referendum voting is employed to investigate a series of "what if" scenarios concerning how changes in the values of key variables might have altered the referendum's outcome. The analyses conclude by considering public reactions to the result in Quebec and the rest of Canada, and why, in our judgement, these reactions could bode ill for a future Canada that includes Quebec.

The fifth event considered is the 1997 federal election. Four years earlier Jean Chrétien had led the Liberals to power after promising voters that he would reinvigorate Canada's economy and mend its tattered social safety net. By the spring of 1997 many Canadians believed that Prime Minister Chrétien and the Liberals, like former

One :: A Mature Democracy at Risk

Prime Minister Mulroney and the Conservatives before them, had failed to keep their promises and were not to be trusted. But, rather than trying to "throw the rascals out," many people simply stayed home. The 1997 election result affirmed what really had been only a possibility in 1993. The old "two-party plus" system (Epstein, 1964; see also Carty, 1995; Gagnon and Tanguay, 1989) that had dominated national electoral politics for some 60 years was history. In its place was a new, regionally based, multi-party system that reflected the deep-seated cleavages in Canadian society.

The sixth and most recent critical event was the 1998 Quebec provincial election, to which we turn in Chapter Nine. That the Péquistes had twice within a 15-year period used their statutory power as the government of Quebec to initiate a process that threatened to culminate in that province's separation from Canada was not lost on federalist forces. If the PQ could be defeated in the next provincial election and replaced by a majority Liberal government, there would be no more sovereignty referendums for several years. Moreover, it was possible that if the PQ were out of power for a substantial period, public support for the party and, more importantly, for its sovereignty project might erode significantly. Thus, a Liberal victory in the 1998 Quebec provincial election could seriously wound and might even slay the separatist dragon—or so it was hoped.

But how to do it? How to persuade Quebecers that they should turn out a reasonably popular governing party with a very popular leader? The answer, Liberal strategists and associated pro-Canada sachems decided, was to recruit an even more popular leader. And so they turned to Jean Charest, who only months before had led the national Progressive Conservative Party in the 1997 federal election, to be their saviour. Charest, they assumed—given his creditable showing in that election in comparison with federal Liberal leader Prime Minister Jean Chrétien and Bloc Québécois leader Gilles Duceppe—was just the one to lead federalist forces out of the political wilderness and thereby ensure that the near-disaster of the 1995 sovereignty referendum was not repeated. However, Charest was incapable of playing the heroic "Captain Canada" role in which he had been cast. Although the Liberals captured slightly more votes than the Péquistes in the 1998 Quebec election, Charest's pulling power with the voters was not nearly strong enough to keep a single-member plurality electoral system from awarding the PQ a handsome majority of parliamentary seats. The PQ's return to power ensured that the drama of Quebec's relationship with the rest of Canada—a drama that had occupied the attention of Quebecers and other Canadians for much of the last three decades of the twentieth century—would continue as the new millennium dawned.

In the concluding chapter, we return to the basic question that animates this study: "Can a contemporary, mature democracy disintegrate?" Could the concatenation of political, constitutional, and economic problems that produced the six critical events on which we focus in this book lead to yet another even more critical event, the outcome of which would leave Canada's continuation in its current form very much in doubt? Our answer enables us to consider another, even larger question. Does the Canadian experience offer any lessons for other democracies, mature and emerging?

TWO

The Dynamics of
Political Support

The heavy investments in Canada's economy made during World War II paid handsome dividends in the quarter century that followed. As the 1970s began, Canadians enjoyed a standard of living and a range of social services that were among the best in the world. This is not to say that all provinces were equally prosperous. Some were "more equal" than others. Perpetuating a well established pattern, central Canada, especially Ontario, was the clear winner in manufacturing, and the discovery of abundant oil reserves made Alberta a principal player in the energy field. Such economic differences were consequential; unemployment levels and average family incomes varied across the country and, as had been true for much of Canada's history, these and other indicators of the quality of life revealed that residents of the Atlantic provinces were disadvantaged in comparison with their fellow citizens in other regions. Although successive federal governments, both Liberal and Conservative, devised a variety of measures to narrow inter-regional and inter-provincial economic disparities, differences remained in industrial capacity, infrastructure development and growth rates. But, in terms of their influence on the lives of ordinary citizens, the impact of most of these differences were matters of degree, not kind. Indeed, as Canada entered the 1970s, it seemed that a virtuous spiral of economic growth and enlightened public policy was working to secure the happiness and well-being of the vast majority of people in all parts of the country.

There were, however, small clouds on the horizon foreshadowing the acrimonious disputes that were to ensue between the federal government and the provinces on the one hand, and between and among the provinces on the other, in their attempts to remake the federal system in a form more acceptable to them. For example, in 1959 long-time Quebec Premier Maurice Duplessis died and his Union Nationale party's hold on Quebec ended the next year with the election of a Liberal government led by the former federal Liberal cabinet minister, Jean Lesage. The "Quiet Revolution" had begun. Roger Gibbins (1994: 127) contends that the revolution was "not so much in the social and economic underpinning of Quebec, which had been in a state of transition since the 1930s, as it was in the province's state of mind." It can be argued that Lester B. Pearson, who became prime minister of a minority Liberal government in 1963, recognized the new reality in Quebec and acted accordingly. This is to say that both his personal inclination and long training and experience as a diplomat and his sympathy with Third World nationalist movements may well have led him to try to accommodate Quebec's aspiration to control its own destiny—to move forcefully and immediately from "*la survivance*" to "*la rattrapage.*" And, if that meant dealing with Quebec's political and bureaucratic élites much as if they were the leaders of a sovereign state and then extending similar treatment to the leaders of the other provinces—since fairness demanded no less—then so be it.

Not surprisingly, Pearson's willingness to consider sympathetically and, if possible, to accommodate the demands of Quebec and, if necessary, the other provinces, for a restructured federal system generated intense opposition within and outside his party from those who believed that the system was not broken and did not need fixing. And, among those who *did* recognize the need for change, Pearson's successor, Pierre Trudeau, and other powerful Quebec Francophones such as Trudeau's fellow "wise men," Jean Marchand and Gérard Pelletier, entertained an image of a Canadian national community and a federal system that differed markedly from Pearson's (McRoberts, 1997). Unlike Pearson, who thought of relationships between Quebec and the rest of Canada in terms of interactions between collectivities, Trudeau and those who shared his political vision wanted to make the "French Fact" manifest throughout Canada. After all, Francophones were Canadian citizens, not merely residents of Quebec. Therefore, they should—indeed must—enjoy the same language and other rights, irrespective of where they lived. According to this logic, individuals not collectivities were paramount. Thus, Quebec was the equal of, but not superior to, other provinces, and it followed that Quebec's aspirations for special status in confederation were unjustified. What was needed was not a series of ad hoc compromises among political élites representing the federal government, Quebec, and the other provinces, but rather a new constitution that entrenched the rights of all Canadian citizens. However, the profound differences between Pearson's and Trudeau's visions of what Canada was about were not fully apparent at the time. Rather, these and other important conflicts were submerged by the massive outpouring of pride and optimism about the country's future sparked by Canada's centennial celebrations in the summer of 1967.

Then, the world changed. As observed in Chapter One, in the early 1970s the country's ability to sustain economic development and fund the increasing costs of major social programs was circumscribed by unanticipated surges in inflation and unemployment and sagging growth sparked by the October 1973 Arab oil embargo and the rise of OPEC. As the decade wore on, the economics of stagflation became an unpleasant reality for Canadians in every region. On the political front, escalating energy costs stimulated sharp conflicts between oil-rich Alberta and other energy-producing provinces, on the one hand, and central Canada (Ontario and Quebec) and the federal government, on the other. In November 1976 these rancorous disputes were overlaid by the dramatic intensification of the Quebec versus the Rest of Canada struggle occasioned by the election of a separatist Parti Québécois government in Quebec.

The conflicts among federal and provincial political élites were reflected in public attitudes. National surveys conducted in 1974 and 1979 revealed sharp inter-regional and inter-provincial differences in people's perceptions of the costs and benefits of federalism, and the power that various provinces exercised in the federal system (Kornberg, Clarke, and Stewart, 1979). Perhaps most disquieting was the finding that, regardless of where they lived, many Canadians believed that *their* province incurred more costs than did other provinces, whereas *other* provinces received more benefits. Although this tendency to feel disadvantaged by the operation of existing federal arrangements was country-wide, it was particularly strong among residents of three western provinces (Alberta, Manitoba,

British Columbia), as well as among persons living in Ontario and Quebec. In addition, many people thought that the federal system was not a "level political playing field." There were large differences in the power of various provinces, with Ontario, Alberta, and Quebec exercising more than their fair share of clout.

Other surveys conducted during the period sketched similarly bleak pictures of mutual suspicion and generalized discontent. For example, a survey study in Trois Rivières, Peterborough, and Lethbridge conducted before and after the 1980 Quebec sovereignty-association referendum indicated that there was a substantial basis in public opinion for serious inter-regional and inter-provincial conflict which the outcome of the referendum did little to abate (Smith and Kornberg, 1983). Although people's images of Canada were largely favourable and structured in terms of the themes of social justice and energetic dynamism, many of those interviewed in the three cities declared that people in their own province were productive, co-operative "givers," but residents of other provinces were unproductive, unco-operative "takers" who were unconcerned about the welfare of the country as a whole. A combination of own-province chauvinism and other-province antipathy characterized the public mind. This negative climate of opinion undergirded and reinforced the ongoing, acrimonious conflicts among the provinces and the federal government. In turn, these conflicts inhibited efforts to reach agreement on constitutional initiatives that might secure the integrity of the Canadian state.

The dysfunctional character of these conflictive interprovincial and federal-provincial relations also is a theme pursued by Alan Cairns (1983) in his analysis of the strategies and tactics employed by four key actors (the federal government and the provinces of Quebec, Alberta, and British Columbia) during the long and arduous negotiations that led to the adoption of a new constitution in 1982 (see also Banting and Simeon, 1984). Cairns contended that throughout the protracted bargaining that was carried on solely by elected officials and senior federal and provincial bureaucrats, the operative principle of the contending parties was unabashed self-interest. Each government's position was to try to maximize its current power and influence and to minimize the possibility of any erosion in the future. According to Cairns, two factors explained this behaviour by first ministers and their bureaucratic advisors. One was the growth in size and scope of government, especially of provincial governments. After World War II, provincial governments steadily impinged on ever-broader areas of social, economic, and political life in response to, and aided by, important interest groups within their boundaries and the increasing numbers of people who directly or indirectly depended on these governments for their livelihood. In so doing, the provincial governments inevitably came into conflict with one another and the federal government, which, under the same set of pressures, did the same thing.

A second factor is what Cairns terms the "electoral imperative." Provincial political parties and their leaders discovered that representing themselves as the true champions of their provinces' interests was a recipe for electoral success. Thus, when they formed a government, they were driven to make self-serving demands on Ottawa and other provinces, and to reject compromises that might make them appear weak and vacillating in the eyes of their electorates. Since all the provincial governments played this game, the result was a politics of demand escalation that markedly enhanced the difficulty of devising political strategies and constitutional arrangements that could counter the threat posed by the election of a separatist Parti Québécois government.

The struggle between the Péquistes and their federalist adversaries culminated in the May 1980 Quebec sovereignty-association referendum. Despite the watered-down wording of the referendum question and the PQ government's attempts during the referendum campaign to represent the choice as either something less radical than complete Quebec independence from the rest of Canada or as simply one that would lead to an unblocking of the protracted constitutional impasse (*"deblocage"*), many Quebec voters believed that a "yes" majority would mean that the province would become a separate country. Some, of course, were very much in favour of such an outcome. However, many others, regardless of their level of dissatisfaction with the operation of the federal system, wanted Quebec to remain in Canada. And, although the latter group were in the majority and the referendum was rejected by a substantial margin, the fact that the question was posed and that a referendum on it went forward dramatized the point that in a democracy political arrangements—federal or otherwise—cannot long survive without broad public support.

The problem of securing adequate political support from the citizens of a democratic polity is not an easy one. Unlike dictators in authoritarian states, political leaders in democracies must eschew the frequent use of coercive measures and rely almost entirely on voluntary compliance to get people to obey laws and regulations and support the political system. Political support may be defined as a person's affective orientation, i.e., their feelings of "like" or "dislike," towards political objects (e.g., parliament, political parties, the judiciary) and processes (e.g., federalism, elections). These feelings can be positive, neutral, or negative. Following democratic theory, it is useful to distinguish among support for political authorities (i.e., elected and appointed political officials of varying power and importance), regimes (i.e., a political system and its component parts), and political communities (i.e., groups of persons "bound together by a political division of labour") (Easton, 1965: 177). Research has demonstrated that these distinctions are not simply scholarly abstractions; Canadians *do* distinguish support for political authorities from that for the regime and community, and support at all three levels varies over time. It is highest and most stable for "Canada in general," i.e., the national political community, lower and less stable for major regime institutions such as parliament, the civil service, and the judiciary, and lowest and least stable for prominent politicians such as leaders of federal and provincial political parties (Kornberg and Clarke, 1992: ch. 4).

Support at all three levels of the political system is dynamic; it waxes and wanes over time. And, although it is intertwined, in Canada at least, the dominant flow of support is upward—from political authorities, to regime, to community. By way of illustration, using "feeling thermometers," in 1974 average public support for "Canada in general" was 84 on a scale running from 1 to 100 with 50 designated as the neutral point, but only 63 for the "government of Canada." Five years later it declined to an average score of 80 for Canada and 59 for the government of Canada. On average, support for Canada and the federal government was lowest in Quebec in both years: 75 and 71 for Canada and 63 and 54 for the government. However, as Figure 2.1 illustrates, the overall Quebec scores hide substantial differences between Francophones and members of other language groups. Among Francophones, average support for Canada was 72 in 1974 and 70 in 1979, but among non-Francophones it was fully 90 and 85. The latter figures were even higher than those recorded in the rest of Canada (88 and 83, respectively).

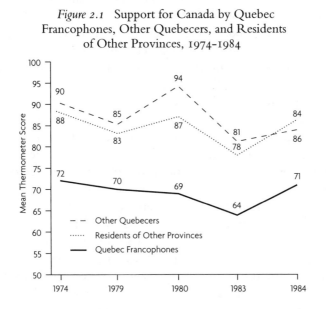

Figure 2.1   Support for Canada by Quebec
Francophones, Other Quebecers, and Residents
of Other Provinces, 1974-1984

Despite these differences in feelings about Canada and its political system between Francophones and other Quebecers, the decisive defeat of the Parti Québécois 1980 sovereignty association referendum, the adoption of a new constitution with a Charter of Rights and Freedoms in 1982, and the defeat of the PQ government in the 1985 provincial election seemed to give Canada relief from the crisis of confederation that had begun in the mid-1970s when the Péquistes came to power. But, the respite was only temporary. The complex economic and political problems the country had been experiencing had not been resolved. A renewed crisis of confederation was only a few years away.

THE 1984 FEDERAL ELECTION:
THE BOY FROM BAIE COMEAU COMES TO OTTAWA

The retirement of Pierre Trudeau in early 1984 signalled a sea change in Canadian politics. The "Trudeau era" was over, and the

"Mulroney years" were about to begin. In the 1984 federal election, Brian Mulroney, the fluently bilingual, self-styled "Boy from Baie Comeau," led the Progressive Conservative Party to a smashing victory. The PCs routed the governing Liberals by capturing 50 per cent of the popular vote and fully 75 per cent (211 of 282) of the seats in parliament. Reflecting a widespread, if frequently tacit, assumption that somehow the federal Liberals were Canada's "natural governing party" (Whitaker, 1984), most election post-mortems initially focused on why the Liberals had lost so badly rather than on why the Conservatives had won so handsomely. Observers pointed to the tactical and personal errors made by John Turner during his short tenure as prime minister after he became Liberal leader in the spring of 1984 (see, e.g., Frizzell and Westell, 1985). The list of Turner's sins of omission and commission was lengthy. Among his principal errors were his lack of political "smarts" in agreeing to a number of high-level patronage appointments foisted on him by Trudeau, who was intent on rewarding faithful party allies before stepping down as prime minister. Turner also was castigated for dismissing several of his top operatives during the middle of the campaign and replacing them with old guard pols prominently associated with Trudeau. His willingness to engage in a televised debate in French (which he spoke somewhat less than fluently) with his bilingual Tory opponent was viewed in some quarters as an act of idiocy, as was his widely publicized gaffe of patting the derrière of Iona Campanolo, the president of his party's national organization, during a Liberal campaign rally.

Analyses reveal that neither the extent of the Liberal defeat nor the magnitude of the Conservative victory could be explained in any great part by these or other specific tactical errors on Turner's part. Rather, as is typical of federal and provincial elections, in 1984 voters were strongly influenced by varying combinations of perceptions of which party was closest to them on important election issues, feelings about the party leaders, and the direction and intensity of identifications with political parties. In these regards, our 1984 national post-election survey reveals that Mulroney and his party easily won the struggle for the hearts and minds of Canadians. With respect to their hearts, feeling thermometers show that the average voter had a much higher regard for Mulroney and the Conservatives than for the Liberal and New Democratic parties and their respective leaders, John Turner and Ed Broadbent, respectively. Mulroney was rated five points ahead of Broadbent (61-56) and 14 points (61-47) ahead of Turner. Mulroney's party did even better, topping the NDP by 14 points (60-46) and the Liberals by 15 (60-45). As for their minds, a recession-ridden economy and the high levels of unemployment it had produced were the principal issues on which voters focused. Many of them had endured the pain of the recession and concluded that the Tories were more likely to address these issues effectively than were either the Liberals or New Democrats. Mulroney's campaign rallying cry of "Jobs! Jobs! Jobs!" was heard throughout the land by a receptive audience eager for political change.

Ties That Do Not Bind

The Conservatives' crushing 1984 victory was very impressive, but it bears emphasis that the potential for substantial instability in voting behaviour and election outcomes long has been characteristic of Canadian politics. For example, the 1984 federal election was the third successive such contest to produce a turnover of government in Ottawa. In 1979, a majority Liberal government had been replaced by a minority Progressive Conservative one holding a precarious 48 per cent of the seats in Parliament. Only nine months later, the new PC government was forced from office, and the ensuing 1980 election produced a majority Liberal government with a 52 per cent parliamentary seat share. As discussed above, four years later, the Liberals' again were driven into the political wilderness. The electoral volatility of the 1970s and early 1980s is not unique. It also was evident in the late 1950s and throughout the 1960s, and it demonstrates, among other things, that many Canadians do not have strong, stable attachments to political parties.

Students of politics long have recognized the importance of psychological attachments to parties (see, e.g., Wallas, 1981), and in the 1950s the concept of party identification—a sense of belonging to and affection for a political party analogous to one's sense of membership in an ethnic, religious, or other social group—was introduced to students of voting behaviour by researchers at the University of Michigan (Belknap and Campbell, 1952). Studies conducted during that era in the United States (Campbell et al., 1954, 1960; see also Converse, 1976) indicated that most voters identified with a political party and, that once formed, these identifications tended to be stable and to strengthen over time. The inertial properties of party identification and its operation as a perceptual screen filtering perceptions of issues, candidates, and the political world more generally made it a powerful long-term force on voting behaviour in successive elections. By working to anchor party systems in the minds of the electorate, party identification promoted the stability of the larger political order (Campbell et al., 1966). Although many scholars accepted the reality and significance of stable partisan attachments in the United States, subsequent studies questioned the generality of the American findings, and a number of researchers disputed the applicability of a "Michigan-style" social-psychological concept of party identification in other political settings (e.g., Budge, Crewe, and Farlie, 1976).

Canada was one such locale. Here, pioneering studies of voting behaviour in the 1965 and 1968 federal elections by John Meisel and associates (e.g., Meisel, 1975; see also Jenson, 1976; Stevenson, 1987) suggested that many Canadians did not have strong, stable party identities of the kind described by the authors of *The American Voter* (Campbell et al., 1960). National panel surveys (i.e., surveys where the *same* individuals are interviewed two or more times) conducted between 1974 and 1980 confirmed Meisel's findings (e.g., LeDuc et al., 1984), and subsequent surveys revealed that partisan instability continued apace throughout the 1980s. Between 1980 and 1983, 30 per cent of those participating in our national panel survey either switched their party identifications or moved between being identifiers and non-identifiers.[1] Comparable figures for 1983-84 and 1984-88 national panels are 31 per cent and 30 per cent. All of these studies also indicated that there is substantial *inconsistency* in party identification across levels of the federal system. Unlike the United States, where the vast majority of voters identify with the same party in national and state politics, sizable minorities of Canadians in every region either identify with different parties in national and provincial politics, or identify with a party at one level of the federal system but do not identify with any party at the other level.

Individual-level mutability in party identification creates the potential for large swings in parties' aggregate shares of partisan supporters. This potential was not realized in the 1970s, but it was in the 1980s. As Figure 2.2 shows, between 1965 and 1980 the Liberals always held a substantial lead over the Conservatives in the percentage of federal party identifiers, and the NDP always trailed far behind both of its major party rivals. The average percentage of federal Liberal identifiers was 43 per cent, whereas the Conservative and NDP averages were 30 per cent and 14 per cent, respectively. However, between 1980 and 1984 the incidence of Liberal identification declined from 45 per cent to 32 per cent, whereas the Conservative share rose from 28 per cent to 40 per cent. The volatility of party identification in Canada is further underscored by the fact that only 14 months after their 1984 electoral triumph, the Conservative portion of federal party identifiers declined by 10 per cent, and the non-identifier group increased by the almost the same amount—from 9 per cent to 20 per cent.

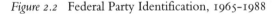

Figure 2.2 Federal Party Identification, 1965-1988

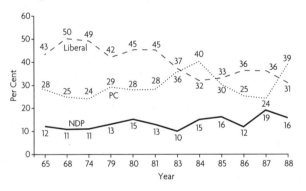

This erosion of Conservative partisanship was accompanied by a precipitous decline in the percentage of persons who said that they intended to vote for the party in the next federal election. Indeed, by early 1987 the PCs trailed both the Liberals and New Democrats in monthly CIPO (Gallup) polls, and they had lost the support of nearly 40 per cent of the electorate (Figure 2.3). The New Democratic Party, in particular, profited handsomely, at least in the short run, from the disaffection with the Tories. By 1987 the New Democrats led the field with what for them was an unprecedented 37 per cent vote intention rating. However, their lead was very short-lived. By the spring of 1988, they again had fallen to third place in the polls and PC support was on the upswing.

Figure 2.3 Liberal, PC, and NDP Voting
Intentions, October 1984–November 1988

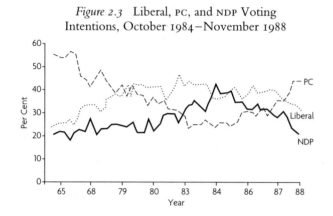

In addition to the decline of NDP support, the Tories also benefited from the internecine warfare being waged in the Liberal Party over the leadership of John Turner. For years after his 1975 resignation from the Trudeau cabinet and his return to private life in Toronto, hundreds of Liberal party insiders had treated Turner as a kind of "emperor in exile." When, in 1983, Pierre Trudeau announced his intention to resign as prime minister, Turner's many ardent supporters pleaded with him to enter the leadership fight. He did so, and his subsequent victory was hailed by them as the beginning of a new era in which the country would be led by a man who combined finely-honed political acumen with extensive private business experience. Turner, it was argued, was a man who knew all the right people and knew how to tap their expertise to make the kind of smart, solid policy decisions that would get the economy and the country on the right track and keep it there. Given their great expectations, it perhaps is not surprising that disappointment in and disaffection from his leadership were equally great after the party's disastrous loss in the 1984 election.

Subsequent attempts to dump Turner by Liberals disenchanted with his leadership certainly helped Mulroney retain his grip on his party, despite its aforementioned steep slide in the polls. Often, a governing party's loss of public support is rooted in economic difficulties. That was certainly the case in the 1970s and early 1980s when unemployment and inflation were the principal problems facing the country. But, a time series analysis of CIPO monthly vote intentions data indicates that neither unemployment nor inflation levels significantly affected the Tory government's popularity between 1984 and 1988 (Clarke et al., 1992: ch. 5). Instead, the decline in Conservative support was strongly influenced by a seemingly endless number of scandals involving high-ranking cabinet members (Gratton, 1988). In addition, the government's support in the West plummeted because of its decision to locate a major maintenance facility for military aircraft in Montreal rather than in Winnipeg. The decision was interpreted by many of the party's staunchest western partisans as both a substantive and symbolic slap in the face, since it involved several hundred jobs and a preference for the "Johnny-come-lately" support of Quebec over the long-time loyalty of the West.

THE 1988 FEDERAL ELECTION: GAMBLING ON FREE TRADE

Early in the 1980s the country's persistent economic problems had led the Trudeau Liberal government to appoint a Royal Commission chaired by Donald Macdonald, a former senior Liberal cabinet minister and successful businessman, to conduct an inquiry and present the government with a strategic plan to secure Canada's favourable position in the emerging global economy. The Macdonald Commission's principal recommendation, when it reported in 1985, was to seek a free trade agreement with the United States. Although he had been opposed to such an agreement when he was campaigning for his party's leadership, Brian Mulroney permitted himself the luxury of a change of mind and now declared himself in favour of free trade. The Macdonald Commission report must have been a persuasive (and politically useful) reason to switch. In addition, he also must have estimated that if history were any guide, changing his position on a broad policy issue such as free trade would not incur significant electoral costs. He undoubtedly recalled, for example, that during World War II the Mackenzie King Liberal government had changed its policy on the use of conscript troops to fight outside of Canada and been easily re-elected. Another, more recent example was the Liberal government's widely publicized opposition during the 1974 federal election campaign to a program of wage and price controls proposed by the Conservatives to combat inflation. Campaign rhetoric notwithstanding, soon after it was re-elected that same Liberal government proceeded to adopt a wage and price control policy as the centrepiece of Prime Minister Trudeau's effort to "wrestle inflation to the ground." However, a more important consideration for Mulroney may well have been that free trade and privatization were the cornerstones of a neo-conservative agenda for which the most vigorous and vociferous champions were U.S. President Ronald Reagan and British Prime Minister Margaret Thatcher, leaders of the two countries with which he and his country were deemed to have a "special relationship." Accordingly, a team of skilled negotiators under the leadership of a veteran bureaucratic mandarin, Simon Reisman, was appointed to hammer out an agreement with the United States on free trade between the two countries. The agreement was duly reached and presented to parliament by the Mulroney government in the summer of 1988. When it was blocked by a Liberal majority in the Senate, Mulroney used the action as a pretext for calling an election.

One Issue Only

Free trade thus became an election issue in 1988, although it is doubtful that the prime minister and his advisers intended it to become *the* issue. Initially, their strategy was to soft-pedal free trade and instead focus public attention on and claim credit for the improved economy. However, the dynamics of the campaign soon overturned this strategy because Liberal leader John Turner, under attack within his party for its lacklustre showing in early polls, seized on free trade as an issue that might repair his fortunes within his party and enable him to lead it to victory. There were several reasons why Turner and his advisers may have decided to emphasize the free trade issue. First, in contrast to *valence* issues such as inflation and unemployment that virtually everyone agrees are "bad things," free trade was a *positional* issue on which Liberal strategists reasonably could surmise public opinion would be deeply divided. Given historic fears of economic domination by their giant southern neighbour, it could be assumed that many Canadians, a majority perhaps, would agree with the Liberals that the free trade agreement posed dangers for their country's economy. Second, and relatedly, Turner and company could contend that the agreement would have a variety of negative *non-economic* consequences, the most important being that free trade eventually and inevitably would lead to the erosion of Canada's political autonomy. By casting the FTA in this way, Mr. Turner could represent himself and his party as the champions of national independence struggling to save their country from the rapacious Americans and their Tory "running dogs." A third advantage for the Liberals was that by representing themselves as the leaders of the anti-free trade forces they would largely marginalize the NDP, which, as noted above, had risen in the polls in 1987, so much so that they constituted a threat to replace the Liberals as the principal opposition party in Parliament. In this regard, the Liberals' strategy of stressing their opposition to the FTA was facilitated by the NDP's indecision about how much emphasis to give free trade as compared to other issues.

The nationally televised leadership debates offered Turner the opportunity to articulate his party's opposition to the free trade agreement. He did so very effectively; indeed, so effectively that one post-debate survey reported that more than twice as many people (50 per cent vs. 23 per cent) stated that Turner had impressed them "most favourably" as made that judgement of the prime minister. And, underscoring the NDP problem on the issue, only 12 per cent said that they had been particularly impressed by Ed Broadbent, the New Democratic leader (Frizzell, Pammett, and Westell, 1989: 95). Equally important, Turner's performance in the leader debates was followed by a significant increase in Liberal support, with some polls showing the party had surged ahead of the PCS.[2] As a consequence, insofar as the volume of campaign rhetoric and media coverage were concerned, free trade effectively became the *only* issue until election day. The extent to which the heat generated by the debate over free trade focused the attention of Canadians on the issue is indicated by their responses to the "most important issue" question in our 1988 post-election survey. Fully 89 per cent cited free trade, and less than 2 per cent cited any other issue.[3] Such dominance of the issue agenda is unprecedented for any federal election for which national survey data are available.

The certainty with which the Conservatives predicted posi-tive—and the Liberals, negative—outcomes notwithstanding, our

Figure 2.4   Perceived Consequences of the Free Trade
Agreement, 1988 Pre- and Post-Election Surveys

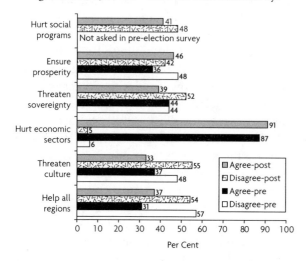

national surveys indicate that public opinion on the consequences of free trade remained deeply divided.[4] There was only one exception—that it would hurt some sectors of the economy. On that score, there was a strong consensus; in our pre-election survey 87 per cent stated that it would harm some economic sectors, and 91 per cent did so after the election (see Figure 2.4). In sharp contrast, before the election 48 per cent disagreed with the proposition that free trade would ensure Canada's future prosperity, whereas 36 per cent agreed. After the election, the comparable percentages were 42 per cent and 46 per cent, respectively. Opinions about non-economic effects also were divided, but consistently favoured the pro-free trade position. Moreover, summary judgements for and against the FTA were quite volatile, but ultimately moved in the government's direction. A survey taken before the leadership debates showed support for and opposition to the agreement evenly divided at 41 per cent. Turner's strong performance increased opposition to 50 per cent immediately after the debate, with pro-free trade sentiments declining to 35 per cent. Thereafter, however, public opinion moved in favour of the pact, especially during the last week of the campaign. In our national post-election survey, 50 per cent supported the agreement and 40 per cent were opposed.

Two :: The Dynamics of Political Support

An analysis of the socio-demographic and political characteristics of those supporting or opposing free trade demonstrates that people who had a favourable impression of the Conservative government's handling of the economy and its competence in other policy areas, and those who believed the political system was operating equitably and fairly, were more likely to discount both economic and non-economic problems associated with the agreement. So, too, were people who felt good about the country's and their own economic prospects and the government's ability to affect them. Also, persons identifying with the federal Conservative Party and residents of the West, the region historically most in favour of free trade, were less likely to find problems with the FTA. In addition, Canadians with higher incomes, who were less likely to be adversely affected by job losses or other negative economic consequences of the pact, also were less likely to find problems with it.

Cool Receptions

Voters' feelings about party leaders can vary substantially over relatively brief time periods. Figure 2.5 illustrates the point by showing that affection for Prime Minister Mulroney as measured by a 100-point thermometer scale[5] had dissipated from a relatively warm average of 61 points in 1984 to a decidedly cool 41 points in 1987. However, as his party's fortunes improved in the polls prior to the 1988 election, so too did public feelings about him. Although voters certainly did not warm to Mulroney as they had four years earlier, when he had recorded a thermometer score second only to the 68 points recorded by Pierre Trudeau in the "Trudeaumania" election of 1968, Mulroney's 1988 thermometer scores were 48 before, and 50 immediately after the election. As for The New Democratic chief, Ed Broadbent, he was more popular than either of his rival party leaders. Broadbent's thermometer rating of 54 before and after the election was 8 and 10 points higher, respectively, than Turner's despite the latter's strong performance in the leadership debates. If Broadbent's party had been as well liked as he was, the New Democrats might have fared much better.

Differences in public feelings about them notwithstanding, it was clearly the case that voters were not enchanted with *any* of

Figure 2.5   Feelings about Party Leaders, 1984-1988

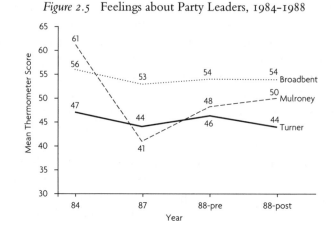

the party leaders in 1988. Perhaps particularly important, Liberal leader John Turner did not receive high marks from any segment of the electorate. Even persons who identified with his party were noticeably unenthusiastic. For example, whereas 70 per cent of Conservative identifiers preferred Mulroney and 87 per cent of NDP identifiers rated Broadbent higher than rival party leaders, only 40 per cent of Liberal identifiers ranked Turner ahead of his counterparts. Again, when asked to evaluate the party leaders in terms of "character" and "competence," voters gave all three leaders mediocre rankings. Across the electorate as a whole, average scores for the party leaders on 10-point "performance" and "honesty and

Figure 2.6 Party Leaders' Character
and Competence Ratings, 1988

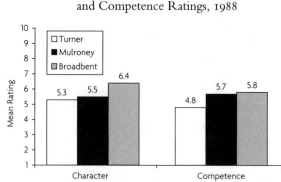

ethics" scales ranged only from 4.8 to 6.4 (see Figure 2.6), and in no region did voters accord the leaders high marks for their probity and wisdom. Once more, however, although he did receive marginally higher honesty and ethics scores than Mulroney in Ontario, British Columbia, and among non-Francophone Quebecers, Turner had the lowest performance rating of any leader in all parts of the country.

At the Polls

Above, we have observed that voting in Canadian elections is strongly influenced by voters' feelings about party leaders, their judgements of which party is closest to them on currently salient issues, and their identifications with federal and provincial parties. Accordingly, we employ variables measuring these feelings, judgements, and identifications in a multivariate model of voting behaviour in the 1988 federal election. Since we consider Liberal, PC, and NDP voting in three separate analyses, model parameters are estimated using a binary probit specification (Long, 1997: ch. 3). The model is:

$$\Pr(\text{VOTE}) = \Phi(\beta_0 + \Sigma\beta_{1-3}\text{LEADERS} + \beta_4\text{ISSUE} + \beta_5\text{FPID} + \beta_6\text{PPID})$$

where: $\Pr(\text{VOTE})$ = probability of voting for either the Liberal, PC, or New Democratic parties; LEADERS = party leader thermometer scores,[6] ISSUE = perception of party closest on the issue designated as most important in the election weighted by the perceived importance of that issue for the vote;[7] FPID and PPID = federal and provincial party identifications (measured at t-1),[8] β_0 = constant; β_{1-6} = coefficients measuring the impact variables influencing the vote; Φ = cumulative density function for the standard normal distribution.

Analyses reveal that, as in 1984, issue perceptions, feelings about party leaders, and partisan attachments with federal and provincial parties significantly affected electoral choice (Table 2.1). Measures of the goodness-of-fit of the models (estimated R^2 and percentage of cases correctly classified) indicate that, jointly, these effects were very powerful. Regarding individual variables, issue effects were predictable in all three analyses, with the probability of supporting

A Polity on the Edge

Table 2.1   Probit Analyses of Voting in the 1988 Federal Election

Predictor Variables	Vote		
	Liberal	PC	NDP
	b	b	b
Constant	− 0.40	− 1.05▲	− 0.34
Region/ethnicity:			
Atlantic	− 0.04	0.14	− 0.08
Quebec-French	− 0.88◆	− 0.20	0.39▲
Quebec-Non-French	0.29	− 0.11	− 0.14
Prairies	− 1.01◆	0.42▲	0.06
British Columbia	− 0.77✚	− 0.14	0.59▲
Age	0.00	0.00	− 0.01
Education	− 0.21✚	− 0.04	− 0.07
Gender	0.33▲	− 0.17	− 0.29▲
Income	0.15▲	− 0.07	− 0.20✚
Federal party identification, 1984	0.25◆	0.19◆	0.20◆
Provincial party identification, 1984	0.07	0.02	0.06
Party leader affect			
Turner	0.02◆	− 0.01▲	− 0.00▲
Mulroney	− 0.02◆	0.02◆	− 0.01✚
Broadbent	− 0.01▲	− 0.01	0.03◆
Party closest, most important issue	0.44◆	0.54◆	0.38◆
McKelvey R^2	.79	.79	.67
% correctly classified	90.6	91.6	90.9
Proportional reduction in error (λ)	.69	.82	.41

◆ p ≤ .001;   ✚ p ≤ .01;   ▲ p ≤ .05; one-tailed test.

a particular party increasing if a voter favoured that party on an issue as opposed to favouring another one or no party at all. Leader influences also operated as anticipated, with the probability of voting for a party being positively related to how much a voter liked the leader of that party, and negatively related to how much a voter liked the leaders of other parties. Federal party identifications worked as expected as well; persons who identified with a federal party were more likely to vote for it than were non-identifiers or persons who identified with another party. However, provincial party identifications were not influential.

Since free trade was effectively the only issue in 1988, it is useful to examine the electoral impact of opinions on the issue

Two :: The Dynamics of Political Support

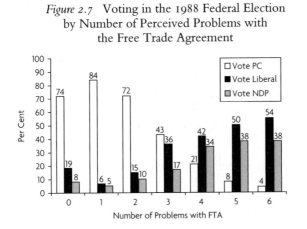

Figure 2.7 Voting in the 1988 Federal Election
by Number of Perceived Problems with
the Free Trade Agreement

more closely. For this purpose, we created an index that measures the number of problems our survey respondents saw with the agreement.[9] As might be anticipated given the publicity the FTA received and the opposing positions the competing parties took on the issue, this free-trade problems index is strongly correlated with voting behaviour. The direction of the relationship is as expected; the more problems voters saw, the less likely they were to cast a PC ballot (see Figure 2.7). Thus, among voters who saw no problems at all with the agreement, fully 74 per cent voted for the Conservatives, but among those who saw the maximum number of problems (six), only 4 per cent did so. Paralleling this sharp erosion of Tory support as the number of perceived problems with the FTA increased, Liberal and NDP support escalated dramatically. Among persons who saw no problems with the FTA, 19 per cent voted Liberal and 8 per cent cast an NDP ballot, but among those who saw six problems, these numbers were 54 per cent and 38 per cent, respectively. The importance of attitudes towards the FTA remains evident when the free-trade problems index is substituted for the party closest on most important issue variable in our multivariate model of the vote. Controlling for feelings about party leaders and federal and provincial party identifications, the FTA problems index has the expected (negative) sign in the Conservative vote model, and the expected (positive) signs in the Liberal and NDP models.

What If?

It is evident that short-term forces generated by reactions to party leaders and key issues strongly influenced voting behaviour in 1988. To determine the magnitude of these effects, we calculated the probabilities that people would vote for a party as their perceptions of free trade and feelings about the party leaders changed. Regarding the free trade issue, we found that Conservative identifiers with average feelings about the three leaders had a .86 probability of casting a PC vote if they did not perceive any problems with the free trade agreement. However, this probability declines to .55 and .20 as the number of perceived problems increased. In contrast, the probability of voting Liberal or NDP rose sharply when people saw more problems with the agreement.

In assessing the impact of attitudes towards the party leaders on voting choice, we focused our attention on John Turner. We considered a scenario in which voters perceived an average number of problems with the free trade agreement and had average feelings (on the 100-point thermometer scales) for Mulroney and Broadbent. We then varied Turner's thermometer score and calculated the probabilities of a Liberal vote. The results show that a more popular John Turner would have had his strongest positive influence by boosting Liberal voting among his own party's identifiers. Non-identifiers with a party also would have been more likely to have voted Liberal if they had held Turner in greater esteem. However, the increases in these probabilities were not great. For example, even if Turner had been as popular as his predecessor, Pierre Trudeau, had been at the height of "Trudeaumania" in 1968, the probability of voting Liberal in 1988 still would have less than .5 among persons who did not identify with a political party, and much less than that among persons who identified with the Conservatives or the New Democrats.

In sum, these scenarios indicate that although leader images mattered in 1988, the issue of free trade mattered more. The Conservatives' strenuous arguments on behalf of the merits of the FTA ultimately convinced enough voters to enable Mulroney and his colleagues to be returned to office. Throughout the campaign the prime minister and his party had coupled these arguments with the claim that they were the only ones who were competent to "manage change" as Canada entered the last decade of the twentieth century. Soon after the Conservatives' electoral victory, these arguments were questioned and this claim was tested. The conclusions drawn by many voters were to spell disaster, first for Mulroney, and then for his party.

CONCLUSION: CRUCIAL CHOICES

Elections in Canada and other mature democracies perform a variety of instrumental and expressive functions that are critically important for the maintenance of democratic societies and democratic political orders. However, survey data show that in 1988 Canadians gave elections as a process mixed reviews. On the one hand, many people believed that elections facilitate the accountability of politicians and give people choices among competing policy alternatives. On the other, they questioned how effective elections are in educating voters about public affairs. They also questioned the usual claim by winning parties that they have received a "mandate" from the people. Analyses of factors associated with the Brian Mulroney-led Conservative Party victories in the 1984 and 1988 federal elections show that short-term factors—voters' perceptions of which party is closest to them on salient issues and their feelings about party leaders—largely determined the Conservatives' winning these contests. Economic issues were very important in both elections, but there were big differences between the specific economic issues at play in the two contests. In 1984, a recessionary economy and the high rate of unemployment that it generated were classic valence issues. Virtually everyone agreed that jobs and economic growth were good things, and many voters believed that Brian Mulroney and the PCs could deliver them. In sharp contrast, in 1988 the free trade agreement was a classic position issue. Although Mulroney and his party portrayed the FTA as a routine economic deal that could be abrogated if, at some future date, it should not prove to be in Canada's interests, Turner and the opposition Liberals vigorously argued that the country's very future would be jeopardized should the agreement go into effect. Faced with these sharply contradictory claims and armed with precious little evidence with which to evaluate them, the electorate was divided and uncertain.

A Polity on the Edge

In important respects, the 1988 federal election resembled another significant political event of the 1980s, the 1980 Quebec sovereignty-association referendum. In both cases, an opposition Liberal Party represented the issue at stake as one that went to the heart of what Canada is about. In both cases, it was argued that Canada's future as a political community was on the line. In 1980, the Liberals argued Quebecers faced a choice between a Canada that ultimately would or would not include Quebec. In 1988 they contended the choice was equally momentous; it was between a politically independent Canada, on the one hand, and the country's subordination and eventual absorption by the United States, on the other. In contrast, in both instances the governing parties downplayed what was at stake. In 1980 the Parti Québécois represented the referendum as an opportunity for voters to demonstrate support for the Quebec government and its intention to negotiate with Ottawa to change Quebec's historically unsatisfactory relationship with the rest of Canada. And, as observed above, in the 1988 federal election the governing Conservatives portrayed a PC vote as an opportunity to voice support for a government that had the foresight and competence to use economic devices such as a free trade agreement to deliver continued, and even greater, prosperity in the years ahead.

In short, in both 1980 and 1988 the contesting parties tried to invest the electorate's choice with dramatically different meanings. In the first case, the Péquistes failed in their effort to minimize the significance of the decision, and sovereignty-association was soundly defeated. In the second, the Conservatives were successful in allaying voters' fears about the free trade agreement, and they were returned to office and the pact was implemented. Both decisions were critical. In subsequent chapters we will argue they set in motion a series of events that influenced not only the course of Canada's political affairs, but also its integrity as a state and its prospects as a nation.

NOTES

1. The parties referenced in the federal and provincial party identification question sequences vary by province and over time. For example, in 1984 and 1988, the federal party identification sequence was: (a) "Still thinking of *federal* politics, do you usually think of yourself as a Liberal, Conservative, NDP, Social Credit, or what?" (b) [If a party was named in (a)] How strongly [party named in (a)] do you feel—very strongly, fairly strongly, or not very strongly?" (c) [If "refused," "don't know," "independent" or "none" in (a)] "Well, do you generally think of yourself as being a little *closer* to one of the *federal* parties than to the others?" (d) [If "yes" in (c)] "Which party is that?"

2. For detailed analyses of the nature and extent of the impact of the leader debates on attitudes towards the FTA, the leaders and vote intentions, see Johnston et al. (1992).

3. Respondents were asked "In your opinion what was the *most* important issue in the election." Those mentioning an issue or issues were then asked: "Which party was closest to *you* on this issue?" and "How important was that issue to you in deciding how to vote in the election—very important, fairly important, or not very important?"

4. Respondents were asked if they "agreed" or "disagreed" with the following statements: (a) "The free trade agreement ensures Canada's future prosperity;" (b) "The free trade agreement threatens Canada's political independence;" (c) "Economically, the free trade agreement helps some industries but it hurts others;" (d) "The free trade agreement threatens Canadian culture and the arts;" (e) "The free trade agreement benefits all of Canada, not just certain regions or provinces;" (f) "The free trade agreement could threaten important social programs such as unemployment insurance and medical care." Items (a)-(e) were asked in both the pre- and post-election interviews, and item (f) was asked in the post-election interview only. The question sequence concluded by asking: "Overall, are you in favour of the free trade agreement or opposed to it?"

5. The thermometer scale question sequence was: "Think for a moment about a thermometer scale, which runs from 1 to 100 degrees. Fifty is the neutral point. If your feelings are warm towards something, give it a score higher than 50, the warmer your feelings, the higher the score. If your feelings are cool towards something, give it a score less than 50. The cooler your feelings, the lower the score." After this preamble, respondents were asked to rate each of the federal parties and their leaders.

6. See note 5 above.

7. The scoring of this variable varies according to whether Liberal, PC or NDP voting is being analysed. For example, in the Liberal case, voters selecting the Liberals as closest on the most important election issue were scored 1, those selecting another party, -1, and those selecting no party or saying there was no important issue, 0. These scores were weighted by

multiplying them by a variable assessing the perceived importance of the issue in the vote decision (see note 3 above). The latter variable is scored: "very important" = 3; "fairly important" = 2; "not very important," "no important issue," or "don't know" = 1. The resulting index ranges from +3 (Liberal Party was closest on most important issue and issue was very important to vote) to -3 (other party was closest on most important issue and issue was very important to vote). The measures used in the PC and NDP vote analyses substitute PC and NDP, respectively, for Liberal as party closest.

8. The measures of federal and provincial party identification in these analyses vary depending on which party's vote is being analysed. For example, in the PC vote analysis, the measure is: "very strong" Conservative = +3; "fairly strong" Conservative = +2; "not very strong" Conservative or leaning Conservative = +1; non-identifier = 0; "not very strong" other party or leaning other party = -1; "fairly strong" other party = -2; "very strong" other party = -3. For Liberal voting, the measures run from very strong Liberal (+3) to very strong other party identifier (-3), and for NDP voting, from very strong New Democrat (+3) to very strong other party identifier (-3).

9. The free trade problems index is an additive measure based on responses to the six statements concerning the perceived consequences of implementing the free trade agreement listed in note 4 above. The index ranges from 0 (no perceived problems) to 6 (six perceived problems). For statements (a) and (e) "disagree" responses are scored 1 and other responses, 0; for items (b), (c), (d), and (f) "agree" responses are scored 1, and other responses, 0.

THREE

Taking the Blame

Certain political leaders, Winston Churchill is alleged to have said, have a veritable genius for snatching defeat from the jaws of victory. The rapid and precipitous decline in the fortunes of Prime Minister Mulroney and his Progressive Conservative government after their victory in the November 1988 federal election lends force to this famous dictum. Indeed, by the end of 1990, media pundits were joking that the prime interest rate soon would exceed the government's popularity. Soundings of the public mood conducted at the time indicate that their cynical humour was not far off the mark. Our 1988 post-election survey showed that Canadians gave the prime minister an average score of 50 and the PCs 54 on a 100-point thermometer scale. Moreover, 39 per cent of the electorate identified themselves as Conservative—only 1 per cent less than the figure recorded immediately after the "Tory tide" had swept the PCs to power in 1984. However, by the autumn of 1990 Mulroney's score had declined to 28 and his party's to 35, and the percentage of people willing to accept a Conservative Party label had fallen to 24 per cent, 8 per cent less than for the opposition Liberals and only 1 per cent more than that for the perennial third-party New Democrats. Public opinion polls painted an equally bleak picture for the Tories. As Figure 3.1 shows, in December 1988, one month after the PC electoral victory, 49 per cent of those answering Gallup's monthly vote intention question said they would vote Conservative in the next federal election. One year later, that figure had been cut in half, and by December 1990 a mere 14 per cent stated that they would cast a PC ballot.

Figure 3.1 PC, Liberal, and NDP Voting Intentions,
November 1988 - December 1992

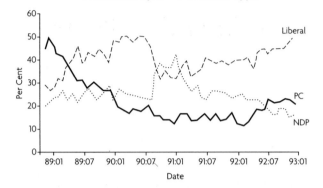

Observers have attributed this dramatic erosion of Conservative support to three factors. One was the failure of the Mulroney government to secure ratification of its major constitutional initiative, the Meech Lake Accord. A second was the government's insistence on going ahead with the imposition of a major value-added tax (the Goods and Services Tax—GST) in the face of massive public opposition. A third factor was a decline in support for the free trade agreement, the PCs' principal economic policy initiative and the issue that had dominated the 1988 election campaign. In this chapter we will argue that although each of these explanations of the spectacular slide in Conservative popularity has merit, a more basic consideration was the widespread public perception that Canada's economy was in very poor shape, their economic futures were bleak, and that the government was to blame for these unhappy circumstances.

The government's failure to perpetuate the prosperity that Canadians had enjoyed in the mid- and late-1980s was not for a lack of trying. As observed in Chapter One, in mature democracies such as Canada governments of all ideological hues and policy persuasions constantly monitor economic trends, and strive to thwart the "twin evils" of inflation and unemployment, while trying to promote stable and vigorous growth. However, despite their best efforts, governments have discovered to their chagrin that there are instances when they are unable to achieve these laudable goals. In particular, they have been unable to eliminate the periodic recessions that long have been characteristic of market-oriented economies. Soon after returning to office in late 1988, the Conservatives confronted this and other unpleasant economic facts of life. Mounting budget deficits that appeared on the verge of spiralling out of control compounded the difficulties brought about by an economic slowdown and rising unemployment.

A good case can be made that the personality of the prime minister played an important role when the government decided how to address these problems. We noted earlier that although some observers had described him as a quintessential political "trimmer," once in office Mulroney belied his reputation for caution and demonstrated a marked preference for high-risk political activism. In his own words, he was willing to "roll the dice" to support his claim that he could address the country's historic constitutional and economic problems and "manage change" successfully. In what was undoubtedly a politically "dicey" economic measure, he willingly pushed ahead with the Goods and Services Tax, the yield from which was earmarked to ameliorate the increasingly worrisome federal budget deficits. Particularly distressing to the prime minister and his economic advisors must have been the observation that these deficits were proportionately much larger than those being run by the United States where public alarm about the federal government's ability to pay its bills was becoming widespread. Although value-added taxes have been employed as a major revenue-generating device for many years by a number of Western democracies, the choice of such a fiscal measure was somewhat surprising for as astute a politician as Mulroney. We may assume that the then Minister of Finance, Michael Wilson, and his advisers tried to convince the prime minister that for a variety of economic and political reasons a significant increase in personal or corporate taxes was an even worse choice.

Notwithstanding the possible merits of such arguments, it is hard to conceive of a measure with greater potential for generating negative political reactions than one that daily and with virtually every purchase they made reminded Canadians that they were being heavily taxed. Moreover, the new tax would be imposed precisely at a time when many Canadians were beginning to suffer the income losses and attendant economic insecurities of an incipient recession. No stranger to the use of public opinion surveys, Mulroney's own polls must have revealed—as did our own 1990 national survey—that the GST was hugely unpopular in every region and among every major demographic group in the country. Overall, less than one person in four (26 per cent) said that they favoured the new tax, and fully seven in 10 (70 per cent) were opposed to it. Nor were Canadians buying the reasons the prime minister and his colleagues offered to justify the tax. Fully 62 per cent of them disagreed with the statement that the GST would help fund important social programs, and a majority (52 per cent) refused to believe that revenues from the tax would reduce the size of the federal deficit (see Figure 3.2). Moreover, almost three-quarters (73 per cent) thought that the GST would spark a new round of inflation, and nearly two-thirds (65 per cent) concluded the tax was unfair since rich and poor alike would be taxed at the same rate.[1]

Figure 3.2 Opinions Regarding the GST, 1990

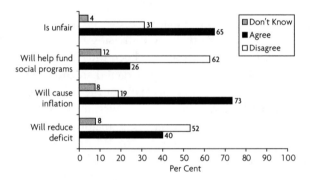

Adding to the government's woes was growing public disenchantment with the newly implemented free trade agreement with the United States. Prime Minister Mulroney had invested a great deal of political capital in the agreement, arguing that it would be good for the country and was a prime example of his ability to "manage change" successfully. Although many Canadians were uncertain about the prime minister's claims, many eventually accepted them. Recall that, with the exception of a strong consensus that the agreement would hurt some sectors of the economy, public opinion on the economic consequences of the FTA was divided, but moved in a pro-free trade direction over the course of the 1988 election campaign. Opinions regarding the non-economic consequences of free trade also revealed deep divisions in the electorate and similar movements in favour of the agreement.[2] Overall, the percentage of people supporting the pact increased from 39 per cent before the election to 50 per cent immediately afterwards, whereas the percentages of opponents and undecideds declined by 5 per cent and 6 per cent, respectively.

By 1990, pronounced changes in public opinion concerning the FTA had occurred. Comparing the results of our 1988 post-election and 1990 national surveys reveals that there was an 18 per cent decline in the number of people agreeing that the agreement would ensure future prosperity, and a 14 per cent drop in the number agreeing that it would benefit the entire country. The belief that even though free trade might help certain industries it would hurt others had become virtually unanimous. Growing reservations about its non-economic consequences also were apparent. In 1990 majorities (54 per cent and 57 per cent, respectively) agreed that the pact was a threat to both the country's independence and important social programs, and over 40 per cent concluded that it posed dangers to Canadian culture and the arts. Finally, as Figure 3.3 shows, overall opposition to the agreement had increased by 17 per cent (to 57 per cent), whereas support declined by almost as much (to 35 per cent).

Figure 3.3 Opinions Regarding FTA, 1988-1990

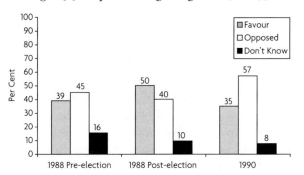

Diminished enthusiasm for free trade and strong opposition to the GST were grounded in Canadians' increasingly negative views of the economy. Many people had concluded that the economy was in bad shape because of its mismanagement by government, and both the country's and their own future well-being left much to be desired. In turn, these concerns about the condition of the economy and its prospects had corroded public support for the governing Tories, over and above the effects of increasingly negative attitudes towards free trade and the GST. In support of the contention that Conservative support was driven downward by negative evaluations of the state of the economy and perceptions of its mismanagement by the federal government, we employ data on these topics gathered in our 1990 national survey. We place these data in comparative perspective using information from several other national surveys conducted since 1983. All of these studies include questions asking Canadians about their evaluations of national and personal economic conditions, their attributions of responsibility to government for these conditions, and their opinions about salient economic issues such as free trade and the GST.

EVALUATING THE ECONOMY, BLAMING THE GOVERNMENT

In his classic study of how public reactions to economic conditions affect voting behaviour in the United States, the late V.O. Key Jr. argued that although voters are unlikely to be awarded Nobel prizes in economics, they are "not fools" (Key, 1968: 7). Canadians' responses to our survey questions about the state of the economy testifies that the wisdom of his argument transcends the American case. After experiencing a deep recession in the early 1980s following a decade of "stagflation" characterized by varying combinations of high inflation and unemployment and mediocre growth rates, only 2 per cent of the participants in our 1983 national survey said Canada's economy was doing "very well," 42 per cent said it was doing "fairly well," and 54 per cent said "not very well." As the economy subsequently improved across much of the country, so, too, did public evaluations of it—the percentage stating that the economy was doing "very well" or "fairly well" reached 61 per cent in 1987, and fully 81 per cent in 1988 (see Figure 3.4). However, by late 1990, the country was falling into another recession, and there was another dramatic shift in opinion. The percentage now saying the economy was in fairly or very good shape fell to 16 per cent, whereas the percentage offering negative assessments skyrocketed to 83 per cent. Reflecting the continuing economic malaise, negative

Three :: Taking the Blame

Figure 3.4 Evaluations of the Performance
of the National Economy, 1983–1992

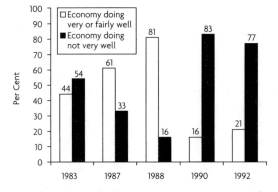

judgements remained very high in our 1992 survey, with 77 per cent concluding that the economy was not performing very well.

As judgements about the economy turned decidedly negative after 1988, opinions concerning its stewardship by the federal government did so as well. Although only a minuscule number of people in any of our surveys ever reported that the government was doing a "very good" job managing the economy (the maximum being 7 per cent in 1988), between 1983 and 1988 there was a steady increase in the percentage stating that the government was doing a "good" job and a decrease in the percentage who said it was doing a "poor" or "very poor" job (see Figure 3.5). In 1990, however, this trend was sharply reversed. Persons judging the government was doing either a "very good" or "good" job declined from 71 per cent to 20 per cent, whereas those believing the opposite increased from 22 per cent to 77 per cent. Canadians' feelings about their personal economic situations and their assessment of the extent of the government's influence on their material well-being also became more negative between 1988 and 1990, although the changes were not as marked as judgements about national conditions. The largest difference concerned the future, with the percentage believing that their standard of living would be better in three or four years decreasing from 34 per cent to 21 per cent. There also was a decline (from 41 per cent to 32 per cent) in the percentage who believed they were better off than they had been in the past, as well as a drop in the number who said they were "very satisfied" with their current financial circumstances (from 25 per cent to 22 per cent).

73

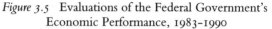

Figure 3.5 Evaluations of the Federal Government's
Economic Performance, 1983–1990

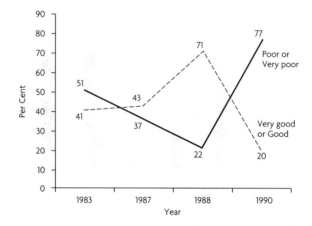

Public opinion data gathered in quarterly Decima polls reveal that the pronounced negative dynamic in national and personal economic evaluations observed in our periodic national surveys commenced very soon after the 1988 election (see Figure 3.6). National and personal economic evaluation indices ranging from a maximum of +100 to a minimum of -100 stood at 5.9 and 32.5 points, respectively, in the quarter immediately prior to the election.[3] Although these figures show that Canadians did not hold wildly positive views of the state of the economy or their personal financial situations at that time, their opinions were much more sanguine than those that would be recorded subsequently. Less than a year after the election, in the third quarter of 1989, national economic judgements had turned decidedly negative at -22.1 points, and personal ones, although still positive, had fallen to 22.6 points. The free fall continued. By the end of 1992, the national index had tumbled to -85.9 points and the personal evaluations index, although not quite as dismal, had dropped to -46.3 points (see Figure 3.6). The slide in economic evaluations closely paralleled the sharp decrease in Conservative voting intentions discussed above. Over the 1988–92 period, the correlation between Tory electoral support and the national economic evaluations index is very strong (r = +.84), and the correlation with the personal version of the index is even stronger, (r = +.87).

There are good reasons to conclude that these impressive statistical relationships are not accidental. Like citizens of other

Three :: Taking the Blame

Figure 3.6 Evaluations of National and Personal
Economic Conditions, 1980-1992

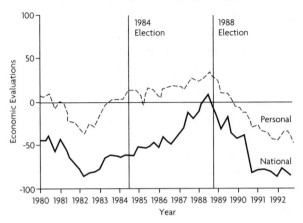

mature democracies, many Canadians believe that government bears
responsibility for the state of the economy. A smaller, but still
substantial, group also think that the government influences their
personal material circumstances. However, unfortunately for any
Canadian government, the responsibility attribution process is very
one-sided—the more sanguine people are about national or personal
economic conditions, the less likely they are to credit government
for the happy state of affairs.[4] Conversely, when people make
negative economic assessments, they are much more likely to hold
government culpable. In 1988, for example, among persons who
believed the economy would improve in the future, 49 per cent
attributed a "great deal" of responsibility to government, but 57 per
cent of those who thought it would deteriorate did so. Regarding
their personal situations, only 24 per cent of those who said they
were "very satisfied" with their standard of living credited government for their good fortune. However, the percentage who held
government responsible increased to 38 per cent among those who
said they were a "little dissatisfied" with their material condition and
to 62 per cent among those who were "very dissatisfied."

The 1988 figures are not atypical. Similar asymmetric attributions
of responsibility to government for economic conditions are made
by persons participating in all of our other national surveys—blame
is always more prevalent than praise. Thus, in 1990, among persons
who thought the national economy would improve in the future,

34 per cent stated that government would have a great deal of responsibility for the anticipated upturn (see Figure 3.7). Among those who believed conditions would remain the same the percentage rose to 40 per cent, and it reached fully 70 per cent among those who believed the economy would deteriorate. Regarding personal economic prospects, the comparable progression is even more dramatic, with the percentages attributing responsibility to government increasing from 12 per cent, to 23 per cent, to 74 per cent. This evidence that Canadians are more apt to blame than to praise government for national and personal economic circumstances did not augur well for Mulroney and his colleagues, given that many voters had concluded that there was very little to cheer about economically after the PCS had been returned to office in the 1988 election.

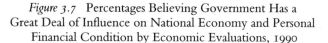

Figure 3.7 Percentages Believing Government Has a Great Deal of Influence on National Economy and Personal Financial Condition by Economic Evaluations, 1990

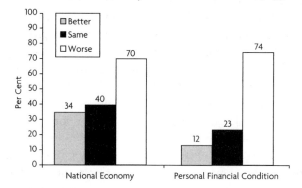

Studies of public economic evaluations and their impact on support for governing parties typically categorize economic evaluations in terms of referent (self versus society), and time horizon (past, present, and future) (see, e.g., Clarke et al., 1992; Lewis-Beck, 1988; Norpoth, Lewis-Beck, and Lafay, 1991). Our survey data enable us to determine the extent to which these analytic categories correspond with how Canadians actually think about the economic world and their place in it. Confirmatory factor analyses[5] (e.g., Bollen, 1989: ch. 7) of variables corresponding to the six types of evaluation[6] consistently show that people's economic judgements are structured along three dimensions. One of these dimensions concerns past (retrospective) and present (contemporaneous) evaluations of the national economy. A second dimension concerns retrospective and contemporaneous judgements about one's personal economic condition. However, when thinking about the future, the self versus society distinction blurs. Thus, a third dimension structures expectations (prospective evaluations) about both national and personal economic prospects.

The Economy, Free Trade, and the GST

Recall our contention that the public's attitudes towards free trade and the GST were based, in part, on evaluations of national and personal economic conditions and attributions of responsibility to the federal government for these conditions. We tested this hypothesis by performing binary probit analyses (Long, 1997: ch. 3) in which attitudes towards free trade and the GST are the dependent variables,[7] and national and personal retrospective and contemporaneous economic judgements are independent variables.[8] (We did not include judgements about future economic conditions in the models since, logically, such judgements might reflect people's assessments of the consequences of free trade and the GST). The analyses also include measures of federal and provincial party identifications[9] and several socio-demographic variables (age, education, gender, income, region/ethnicity)[10] as controls for other factors that might affect attitudes towards the two economic issues. We find that both personal and national economic judgements have statistically significant, positive effects on attitudes towards free trade and the GST (see Table 3.1). So, also, does regional residence; Quebec Francophones are more supportive of free trade than are other Canadians. In addition, younger people, better-educated individuals, men, higher-income earners, and both federal and provincial Conservative identifiers are significantly more supportive of free trade. Older persons, the better-educated, men, higher-income earners, and federal Conservative identifiers are the most favourably disposed towards the GST.

Table 3.1 Probit Analyses of Support/Opposition
to the FTA and the GST, 1988-1990 National Panel

Predictor Variables	FTA		GST	
	b	*t*	*b*	*t*
Region/ethnicity				
Atlantic	.11	.65	.07	.39
Quebec-French	.59	4.63◆	.71	5.52◆
Quebec-Non-French	.24	.78	− .26	− .70
Prairies	.23	1.77▲	.14	1.02
British Columbia	.25	1.55	− .11	− .62
Age	− .01	− 1.92▲	.01	2.49✚
Education	.12	2.97◆	.14	3.28◆
Gender	− .43	− 4.81◆	− .49	− 5.32◆
Income	.12	4.97◆	.07	3.00◆
Party Identification, 1988:				
Federal	.17	6.33◆	.13	4.41◆
Provincial	.09	2.98◆	.02	.52
Economic evaluation:				
Personal retrospective	.10	1.98▲	.14	2.79✚
National retrospective	.30	6.23◆	.26	5.62◆
Constant	− .48	-1.73▲	− 1.32	− 4.59◆
McKelvey R^2	.39		.31	
% correctly classified	72.5		77.1	
Proportional reduction in error (λ)	.33		.15	

◆ $p \leq .001$;   ✚ $p \leq .01$;   ▲ $p \leq .05$; one-tailed test.

We gauged the magnitude of the effects of economic judgements on attitudes towards free trade and the GST by conducting
simulations in which these judgements were allowed to vary while
other variables were fixed at empirically plausible or theoretically
interesting values. To gain insights into the ability of economic
evaluations to affect support for the governing PCs, we assumed
that judgements about the economy were being made by someone
who, other things being equal, might be predisposed to support a
Conservative policy initiative. Specifically, we considered a 46-year-
old woman who lives in Ontario, has a university education,
enjoys a moderately high income, and identifies (weakly) with the
Conservatives in both federal and provincial politics in 1988. This

person would have a 37 per cent probability of supporting free trade in 1990 and a 26 per cent probability of supporting the GST if she had made average national and personal economic judgements about the economy and government's impact thereon. However, if her economic judgements were more favourable than those of the average person, the probability that she would support the FTA and GST increases dramatically. For example, if her economic judgements are one standard deviation above average, the likelihood that she would support free trade increases to 52 per cent, and if they are two standard deviations above average, the probability rises to 68 per cent. Conversely, if her economic judgements were one or two standard deviations below average, her probability of supporting the agreement would decline to 23 per cent and 13 per cent, respectively.

The GST was opposed so widely that all probabilities of supporting it are shifted in a negative direction. However, changes in economic evaluations still have large effects. If the person described above had economic evaluations that are a standard deviation more positive than average, her likelihood of supporting the GST would have increased to 41 per cent. If they were two standard deviations more positive than average, the probability of support would have climbed to 56 per cent. If they were negative by these amounts, the prospects that she would support the tax would have declined to 15 per cent and 7 per cent, respectively. These are large differences, and they reinforce the point that Canada's post-1988 economic slump had major negative effects on the public's reception of the two major policy initiatives—the FTA and the GST—that were the centrepieces of the Conservative government's economic strategy.

CONSTITUTIONAL CRISIS: THE MEECH LAKE ACCORD

The Conservatives' post-1988 woes were not confined to the political fallout caused by an ailing economy. Prime Minister Mulroney's attempt to (at the very least) "get a handle" on the constitutional issue had been precipitated by the defeat of the Parti Québécois in the 1985 Quebec provincial election and its replacement by a Liberal government led by Robert Bourassa. Mulroney, not unreasonably, assumed that it was time to seize the moment—that a unique opportunity existed to reach agreement on a variety of matters that would result in Quebec's becoming the final signatory to the 1982 constitution.[11] Accordingly, meetings were held on April 30 and June 3, 1987, between the federal government and the 10 provinces at the Meech Lake federal conference centre. The prime minister and the provincial premiers reached agreement on a number of long-standing contentious issues. These included the constitutional status of Quebec; provincial representation in the nomination processes for members of the Senate and Supreme Court; compensation to the provinces by the federal government for shared-cost programs in which a province did not wish to participate; and a provision for amending the constitution through annual federal-provincial conferences. The most controversial items were the first two, Quebec's status and Senate reform. The agreements reached on these matters were compromises; although Quebec would not have the power to veto the constitutional formula, it would be recognized as a "distinct society." As for the Senate, nominations to that body would be made by provincial rather than federal cabinets and additional Senate reforms could be on the agenda of future constitutional conferences. However, the regional distribution of Senate seats would remain unchanged, and the actual power to make Senate appointments would be retained by the federal cabinet.

Although the Meech Lake Accord was signed by the prime minister and the 10 provincial premiers, it failed to be ratified by the Manitoba and Newfoundland provincial legislatures within the prescribed three-year period that ended June 22, 1990. This, in turn, sparked a new constitutional crisis that Mulroney would attempt to resolve through a 1992 national referendum on yet another package of constitutional reforms—a topic we will consider in the next chapter. For the present we observe that even though the prime minister and the provincial premiers had endorsed the Accord it was not received with overwhelming enthusiasm. Some critics contended that the concept of a distinct society was unclear and had the potential to generate new problems. For example, it could enable a Quebec government desiring such a goal enhanced powers to override minority language rights in the province. For their part, Westerners complained that the compromise on Senate reform was a far cry from instituting the "triple E" Senate (a politically effective body with enhanced legislative powers, an elected membership, and

Three :: Taking the Blame

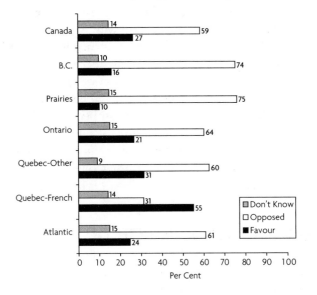

Figure 3.8 Opinions Regarding Meech
Lake Accord by Region/Ethnicity, 1990

equal representation for each of the five regions) that was essential
to give their region a strong voice in Ottawa. Spokespersons for
Aboriginal peoples and for women joined the chorus, complaining
that the Accord would do little, if anything, to secure the rights
of these groups.

Meech Lake did not strike a responsive chord in the Canadian
public, and concerns about the Accord were clearly evident in
responses to questions posed in our 1990 national survey. When
asked whether the agreement would help unify the country with
Quebec becoming a full partner, 39 per cent of those participating
in the survey agreed, 51 per cent disagreed, and 10 per cent said
they were unsure or did not know. Support for the Accord was
highest among Quebec Francophones (63 per cent) and lowest (25
per cent) among Westerners. In the West, it was strongly criticized
by the new Reform Party. Reflecting their party's opposition, only
13 per cent of Reform identifiers viewed the agreement favourably
whereas 81 per cent were opposed to it. In particular, Reformers
disliked the provisions for Senate reform, which they viewed as
inadequate, and the clause that recognized Quebec as a distinct
society, which they claimed would divide rather than unify the

country. Reformers were not alone in criticizing the distinct society clause. Nationwide, 62 per cent shared the opinion that it was divisive, and only 31 per cent believed otherwise. Opinions about the clause sharply divided Quebecers, with 56 per cent of non-Francophones but only 31 per cent of Francophones stating that they were pessimistic about the prospects of the Accord's ability to unify the country if it included recognition of Quebec as a distinct society. Overall, as Figure 3.8 shows, only 27 per cent of Canadians reported that they favoured the Accord, 59 per cent said they were opposed, and 14 per cent were unsure (see Figure 3.8). Quebec Francophones were the most supportive (55 per cent), and residents of the Prairies (75 per cent) and British Columbia (74 per cent), the most opposed.

ECONOMIC DECLINE AND POLITICAL FREE FALL

We began this chapter by observing the precipitous decline in support for the Conservative government of Prime Minister Brian Mulroney that began almost immediately after the Tories were re-elected in 1988. We went on to observe that some explanations of the erosion in Conservative support focus on the prime minister's attitudes and personality characteristics, namely, his willingness to employ politically risky initiatives in pursuit of his goals of addressing and resolving the country's economic and constitutional problems. More specifically, he was the driving force behind the hotly debated free trade agreement with the United States, he forged ahead with a Goods and Services Tax although he knew it was widely detested in all parts of the country, and he tried to bring Quebec back into the Canadian political community by promoting a constitutional agreement, the Meech Lake Accord, which recognized Quebec as a "distinct society," although he knew the phrase set off alarm bells among non-Francophone Quebecers, Westerners, and many other Canadians. We acknowledged that each of these three initiatives—the FTA, the GST, and the Meech Lake Accord—generated widespread opposition and worked to erode support for the Mulroney government. However, we argued that even when these three factors are taken into consideration, indeed, when they are held constant, the slumping economy and people's perceptions that the government was responsible for its deterioration and the negative impact this had on their own material conditions were the most important reasons support for the prime minister and his government declined so precipitously.

To test the hypothesis that voters' economic evaluations were key factors in an explanation of the collapse of Conservative popularity, we employed our 1990 national survey data and performed a multiple regression analysis in which support for the federal Conservative government was the dependent variable. Conservative support was measured by averaging the thermometer scores for the federal PC Party and Prime Minister Mulroney.[12] The independent variables in the analysis included those in the FTA and GST models discussed above, as well as public attitudes toward the Meech Lake Accord[13] and future-oriented economic judgements. The model is:

$$\text{PC} = \beta_0 + \beta_1 \text{NATEC} + \beta_2 \text{PEREC} + \beta_3 \text{FUT} + \beta_4 \text{FTA} + \beta_5 \text{GST}$$
$$+ \beta_6 \text{MEECH} + \beta_7 \text{FPID} + \beta_8 \text{PPID} + \Sigma \beta_{9\text{-}18} \text{DEMO} + \varepsilon$$

where: PC = Progressive Conservative support; NATEC = national retrospective-contemporaneous economic evaluations; PEREC = personal retrospective-contemporaneous economic evaluations; FUT = future economic evaluations; FTA = attitude towards the free trade agreement; GST = attitude towards the GST; MEECH = attitude towards the Meech Lake Accord; FPID = federal provincial party identification 1988; PPID = provincial party identification, 1988; DEMO = socio-demographic characteristics (age, education, gender, income, region/ethnicity); ε = error term; β_0 = constant; $\beta_{1\text{-}k}$= regression coefficients. Model coefficients are estimated using ordinary least squares (OLS) regression methods.

Estimating the model coefficients reveals that all three economic evaluation factors have statistically significant, positive effects on Conservative government support, net of controls for the demographic variables, prior party identifications and attitudes toward Meech Lake, the FTA, and the GST (see Table 3.2). This finding is noteworthy because individual-level analyses of economic evaluations and governing party support conducted in non-Canadian settings have tended to emphasize the importance of national retrospective judgements and most have reported that personal retrospective and prospective evaluations (national or personal) do

Table 3.2   Multiple Regression Analysis of Support for the Federal
Progressive Conservative Government, 1988-1990 National Panel

Predictor Variables	b	Std. b	t
Region/Ethnicity:			
Atlantic	− .41	− .01	− .22
Quebec-French	7.60	.15	5.09◆
Quebec-Non-French	1.57	.01	.45
Prairies	1.21	.02	.83
British Columbia	.41	.01	.23
Age	.02	.02	.65
Education	− 1.06	− .06	− 2.28▲
Gender	1.65	.04	1.66
Income	− .23	− .02	− .89
Economic evaluations:			
Personal retrospective	3.52	.15	6.88◆
National retrospective	7.53	.33	14.05◆
Future (personal & national)	5.03	.22	9.39◆
Free Trade Agreement	2.46	.10	3.87◆
Goods and Services Tax	3.32	.13	4.88◆
Meech Lake Accord	1.85	.07	2.97◆
Party Identification, 1988:			
Federal	1.80	.16	5.71◆
Provincial	.89	.08	2.58✚
Constant	27.18		8.52◆

$$R^2 = .46$$

◆ p ≤ .001;   ✚ p ≤ .01;   ▲ p ≤ .05; one-tailed test.

not have significant effects. In the Canadian case, in contrast, although retrospective and contemporaneous assessments of the state of the national economy have the strongest effect of any of the independent variables in our model (standardized b = .33), future-oriented judgements, which have personal as well as a national component, have the second strongest impact (standardized b = .22). Additionally, while the impact of retrospective and contemporaneous evaluations of personal economic circumstances is somewhat weaker (standardized b = .15), it is highly significant (t = 6.88, p < .001), controlling for the two other types of economic evaluations and all other independent variables in the model.

Although the regression analysis indicates that the economic variables are important, it also reveals that attitudes towards the

FTA, the GST, and the Meech Lake Accord affected Conservative support. As anticipated, people who were positively disposed to the FTA, the GST, and the Meech Lake Accord were stronger supporters of the Conservatives. As for the other variables in the model, as expected, federal and provincial PC identifiers were more supportive than identifiers with other parties or non-identifiers, but most of the socio-demographic variables were not influential. The two exceptions show that Quebec Francophones and persons with lower levels of formal education exhibited higher levels of support for the Conservatives than did other Canadians. Together, the several predictors explain a healthy 46 per cent of the variance in support for the government and its leader.

To comprehend the relative explanatory power of economic evaluations and economic issues (the FTA and GST), we conducted two regression analyses in which we reversed the order of entry of the three types of economic evaluations and the two economic issues, respectively. The results reveal that economic evaluations have stronger explanatory power. Specifically, all of the demographic variables, entered first, explain only 8 per cent of the variance. Federal and provincial Conservative party identifications (measured in 1988) explain an additional 12 per cent, and favourable attitudes towards the Meech Lake Accord add 2 per cent to this total, bringing it to 22 per cent. The entry of the economic evaluations then doubles the proportion of explained variance to 44 per cent and people's attitudes to both free trade and the GST increase it to 47 per cent. Thus, free trade and GST attitudes together can uniquely explain only 3 per cent of the variance in 1990 Conservative support. Reversing the order of entry of economic evaluation and economic issue variables shows that the former uniquely explain 15 per cent of the variance in Conservative support, with 7 per cent of the variance being shared between the two sets of variables.

These findings, together with those concerning the determinants of attitudes toward the FTA and GST reported above, indicate that economic evaluations had important direct and indirect effects on Conservative support and, thus, on the likelihood of voting for the party in a forthcoming election.[14] As Figure 3.9 shows, the percentage of respondents in our 1990 survey stating that they would cast a PC ballot in the next federal election increased dramatically as support for the party moved from negative to positive. Overall, slightly less than 10 per cent of those with negative support scores (0-49) stated that they would vote Conservative, whereas nearly 50 per cent of those with positive scores (51-100) said that they would do so. Unfortunately for the Tories, and a harbinger of the electoral disaster that they would eventually suffer, less than one voter in five was in the latter group, whereas over seven in 10 were in the former one.

Figure 3.9 Vote Intention in Next Federal Election, by Feelings about PC Party and Prime Minister Mulroney, 1990

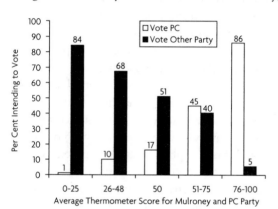

CONCLUSION: FROM FLOOD TIDE TO EBB TIDE

In the September 1984 federal election, the Mulroney-led Conservatives enjoyed spectacular success—gaining 50 per cent of the popular vote and 75 per cent (211 of 282) of the seats. One of the principal forces propelling the PC victory was the public's unhappiness with the former Liberal government's stewardship of the economy and its feeling that the Conservatives might do better. Analyses presented in this chapter strongly indicate that Mulroney's Conservative government would share the fate of its Liberal predecessor in the 1993 federal election—and for the same reasons. Since the 1988 election there had been a precipitous decline in the electorate's support for the party and its leader, coupled with significant increases in negative evaluations of national and personal economic conditions and the government's capacity to manage the economy effectively.

Three :: Taking the Blame

In this regard, analyses demonstrate that unhappiness with national and personal economic conditions had large adverse effects on Conservative support, over and above attitudes towards the free trade agreement, the GST and the Meech Lake Accord. Moreover, negative economic evaluations had indirect effects as well, influencing attitudes towards free trade and the GST, both of which also influenced Conservative support. Attitudes towards free trade had moved strongly in a negative direction since immediately after the 1988 election, and the GST was massively unpopular. In the face of widespread dissatisfaction with the state of the economy, the Conservatives had difficulty convincing voters of the wisdom of either of these highly salient economic policy initiatives.

Adding to the Mulroney government's woes were voters' tendencies to make asymmetric judgements about government's responsibility for national and personal economic conditions. This finding is not unique to the post-1988 period; rather, surveys conducted over the past two decades consistently reveal that many people tend not to credit government when they perceive economic good times and satisfactory personal living standards, whereas they do tend to blame government when they believe conditions are worsening. In the context of what appeared to many to be a steadily worsening economy, this tendency to blame the government provided the psychological underpinnings for a massive erosion of Tory support.

Thus, long before it occurred, there were very good reasons to conclude the Conservatives would lose the next (i.e., 1993) federal election. Except for a relatively brief period surrounding the 1984 election, neither the PC leader, his party, nor their policies when in office, had inspired any great affection and enthusiasm among Canadians. In the run-up to the 1988 election, feelings about the Conservatives and Prime Minister Mulroney were at best lukewarm, and attitudes towards the party's major issue, free trade, were decidedly mixed. The volatility in public opinion polls conducted during the campaign suggested PC support was very soft, even as the party was securing the votes needed to form a second consecutive majority government. And, as we have seen, that support went downhill soon thereafter. That is on the one hand.

On the other, it is highly unlikely that Mulroney, astute politician and student of the Canadian electoral history that he is, was ready to throw in the proverbial towel. He was aware of the general volatility of Canadians' political attitudes and behaviour. He certainly knew that in the wake of his 1984 victory, support for the Conservatives had eroded rapidly, only to bounce back sufficiently in the run-up to the 1988 election to enable them to win again. And, being a realist, he knew that even if he did not inspire any great affection or trust in the electorate, he had demonstrated that he was a leader who could skilfully employ the considerable patronage and other resources at his command when he needed them most, on election day. Moreover, he knew that Meech Lake and free trade were more popular in Quebec than in other parts of the country and that even the heartily disliked GST had somewhat more support among Quebec Francophones than among other Canadians. That support might still be the base on which he could construct another winning coalition, if the economy improved and if he could cobble together a constitutional deal that would satisfy Quebec and be at least minimally acceptable in the rest of Canada. Admittedly, these were two very large, but not impossible, "ifs" given the mutable nature of Canadians' party support patterns. The demonstrated importance of short-term forces generated by party-leader images and party-issue linkages in deciding elections and the fact that he did not have to face the electorate until late 1993 undoubtedly were additional factors in the prime minister's political calculus, as he considered how to reverse his party's misfortunes and thereby salvage his political career. As we will argue in the next chapter, he judged that a national referendum on constitutional reform had the potential to accomplish these goals.

NOTES

1. The "agree–disagree" statements posed about the GST include: (a) "The GST will reduce the size of the federal deficit;" (b) "The GST will start a new round of inflation;" (c) "The GST will help pay for important social programs like medical care and unemployment insurance;" (d) "The GST is unfair because poor people will pay the same rate as the rich."
2. For the text of the statements measuring perceptions of the consequences of the free trade agreement, see Chapter Two, note 4.
3. The Decima economic evaluation indices are computed by subtracting the percentage of respondents making a negative evaluation from the

percentage making a positive one. Accordingly, the indices can vary from -100 (everyone makes a negative evaluation) to +100 (everyone makes a positive evaluation). For additional details, see Clarke and Stewart (1996).

4. The hypothesis that responsibility attributions for economic evaluations are asymmetric, i.e., that voters are much more likely to blame a government for bad or deteriorating conditions than to credit it for good or improving conditions, often has been articulated in the contemporary literature on political economy. For an early statement of the hypothesis, see Bloom and Price (1975).

5. Unlike exploratory factor analysis (EFA), confirmatory factor analysis provides goodness-of-fit tests of theoretically specified models, inter-factor correlations that are parameter estimates (rather than arbitrary values as in an obliquely rotated EFA, and error covariances can be specified. See, e.g., Bollen (1989: chs. 6, 7). Here, CFA is implemented using LISREL 7's weighted least squares (WLS) estimation procedure. WLS relaxes the assumptions of interval-level measurement and multivariate normality and, therefore, suits attitudinal data that involve dichotomous or ordinal measures and skewed distributions. See Joreskog and Sorbom (1988: 192–93).

6. The six economic evaluation indices were constructed as follows: (1) *Past Self:* Respondents were asked: (a) "Do you think that you are financially better off now than you were four years ago, worse off, or are things about the same?" (b) "Do you think that government has had a great deal, something, or not much at all to do with this?" Responses were scored: "better off" = +1, "same" = 0, and "worse off" = -1; "great deal" = +2, "something" = +1, "not much" = 0. Scores for (a) and (b) were multiplied to yield an index ranging from +2 to -2. (2) *Present Self:* An index ranging from +4 to -4 was constructed by multiplying responses to (a) "Now let's think about the things you can buy or do, all the things which make up your material standard of living. Would you say that your are very satisfied (+2), fairly satisfied (+1), a little dissatisfied (-1), or very dissatisfied (-2) with the material side of your life right now?" (b) "Do you think government has a great deal (+2), something (+1), or not much at all (0) to do with this?" (3) *Future Self:* An index ranging from +2 to -2 was constructed by multiplying responses to: (a) "Still thinking about the material side of things and looking ahead over the next three or four years, do you think that you will be better off (+1) or worse off (-1) or will things stay about the same (0)?" (b) "Will government have a great deal (+2), something (+1), or not much at all (0) to do with this?" (4) *Past National:* "Would you say that the federal government has done a very good job (+2), a good job (+1), a poor job (-1), or a very poor job (-2) in handling the economy?" Qualified answers, e.g., "depends," were scored 0. (5) *Present National:* Unlike the other categories no question referring explicitly to the federal government is available. The following is used as a proxy: "Think generally about how the Canadian economy is doing these days, would you say it is doing very well (+2), fairly well (+1), or not very

well (0)?" Qualified answers were scored +1. (6) *Future National*: An index ranging from +2 to -2 was constructed by multiplying responses to (a) "Do you think the Canadian economy will get better (+1), worse (-1), or stay about the same (0) over the next year or so?" (b) "Will the government have a great deal (+2), something (+1), or not much at all (0) to do with this? For all six indices "don't know" responses were scored 0.

7. Persons in favour of the FTA were scored +1; those opposed are scored 0. "Don't knows" and "no opinions" were removed from the analysis. Opinions about the GST were scored the same way.

8. Factor scores provided by a three-factor principal components analysis model were used to build indices measuring sociotropic, egocentric, and future-oriented economic evaluations.

9. The federal and provincial party identification measures were scored: very strong Conservative = +3, fairly strong Conservative = +2, not very strong or leaning Conservative = +1, non-identifier = 0, not very strong or leaning other party identifier = -1, fairly strong other party identifier = -2, very strong other party identifier = -3.

10. Age is measured in years; annual family income has nine categories ranging from under \$10,000 per year = +1 to \$80,0000 per year or more = +9; gender is scored women = +1, men = 0; formal education is elementary or less = +1, some secondary = +2, completed secondary or technical, community college = +3, some university = 4, completed university (B.A., B.Sc. or more) = +5. Region/ethnicity is a set of 0-1 dummy variables with Ontario as the reference category.

11. For an account of the political process leading to the Meech Lake Accord and the events leading to its eventual failure, see Monahan (1991). See also Russell (1992: ch. 9).

12. The correlation (r) between the thermometer scores for the PCs and Brian Mulroney is +.79. CFA analyses of the 1983, 1988, and 1990 survey data indicated the utility of the governing party and governing party leader thermometers for measuring support for an incumbent federal government. These analyses show that Canadians distinguish among their feelings about incumbent political authorities, the national political regime, and the national political community. See, e.g., Kornberg and Clarke (1992: ch. 4).

13. Respondents were asked: "Overall, were you in favour of the Meech Lake Accord or opposed to it?" Those stating that they were in favour were scored +2, those opposed were scored 0, and "don't know's" were scored +1.

14. The vote intention question sequence is: (a) "If a *federal* election were held today, which party do you think you would vote for?" [If "refused," "undecided" or "don't know,"] (b) "Well, are you leaning in any special direction? Which party do you favour right now?" Persons mentioning a party in response to (a) or (b) were considered as intending to vote for that party. Those not mentioning a party were included in the base for calculating the percentages displayed in Figure 3.9.

FOUR

Last Chance?

Referendums, as Butler and Ranney (1978) observe, are almost as old as democracy itself. In the past two decades, the use of national referendums in democracies—new and old alike—has increased. In several countries, governments have employed them to enable citizens to decide important issues concerning constitutional change and political sovereignty. Canada is a case in point. In 1980, and again in 1995, the very future of the country was at stake in Quebec's two sovereignty-association referendums. Constitutional change also was at issue in the 1992 national referendum on the Charlottetown Accord. The latter was not Canada's first national referendum; indeed, the history of such events began in 1898 when a national "plebiscite" was held on the prohibition of the sale of alcoholic beverages (Boyer, 1992: 16-26). In that referendum, a very narrow majority (51 per cent) of those voting opted for prohibition, but the sale of alcoholic beverages continued because the federal government decided that the matter should be left to the provinces. A second national referendum occurred in 1942 as a result of the country's involvement in World War II. At that time Canadians were asked to vote "yea" or "nay" on the question of whether Mackenzie King's Liberal government should be released from its pledge not to send troops conscripted for military service to arenas of conflict outside of Canada. Quebec voted overwhelmingly (by a four-to-one margin) against using conscripts for duty overseas, but voters in all of the other provinces endorsed the proposal by equally large margins. Although Quebec's rejection of the referendum proposal made it difficult for the federal government to abandon its earlier promise, it eventually did so, and conscription for overseas service was instituted in 1944 (Boyer, 1992: 36-42). The 1992 vote on the Charlottetown Accord was Canada's next national referendum.

This referendum was the product of two crises of political support that confronted Prime Minister Brian Mulroney and the governing Progressive Conservative Party. The first of these involved the continued integrity of the Canadian political community; the second involved the massive erosion of public support for the prime minister and his party. We concluded the previous chapter by arguing that the two crises were intertwined in that the dire predicament Mulroney's government and party faced because of their enormous loss of popularity in the early 1990s might be overcome if the constitutional problems that bedeviled the country could be resolved. Recall that the Mulroney government's unpopularity was caused by several factors. These included fallout from the failure of the prime minister's earlier constitutional initiative, the Meech Lake Accord, growing discontent with the Canada-U.S. free trade agreement that his government had championed, and intense opposition to the new national value added tax (the GST) that had been instituted to generate the revenues needed to pay down the ballooning national deficit. However, more important was the widespread perception that the Canadian economy was in terrible shape and that the government was responsible.

Taking a page from history, Mulroney decided (as had Prime Minster Mackenzie King a half-century earlier) to get himself and his party "off the hook" by letting the public provide a solution to a crisis largely of his making. In King's case it was his failure to understand that Canada's military commitments could not be fulfilled through the employment of armed forces composed solely of volunteers. Hence, a national referendum that could provide "political cover" was needed to let him renege on his earlier com- mitment not to use conscripts outside of Canada. If the referendum proposal passed, King could argue that the public had endorsed the use of conscripts for overseas service. In Mulroney's case, it was his failure—when he negotiated the Meech Lake Accord with the provincial premiers—to appreciate the development of a climate of opinion favouring greater public involvement in making important political decisions (see, e.g., Nevitte, 1996). There was growing support for the position that major constitutional changes could no longer be made by a small group of federal and provincial political leaders and senior bureaucratic advisors closeted in the cosy confines of a well-appointed government conference centre. So, even if he could not produce a quick fix for the country's ailing economy (just as King could do almost nothing to affect the course of World War II), there were both strategic (i.e., legitimating a resolution of the constitutional crisis sparked by Meech Lake) and tactical (i.e., heightening the prospects of his government's re-election by a grateful electorate) reasons for deciding to "toss the dice" one more time by holding a national referendum on constitutional renewal.

The chain of events leading up to the Charlottetown Accord and the national referendum designed to legitimate it began in the fall of 1990 with a series of public hearings, the Citizens' Forum on Canadian Unity. In these hearings and other settings, it became clear that additional concessions would have to be made to Quebec and the West if majority support for constitutional change was to be obtained in these regions. Hence, in addition to recognizing Quebec as a "distinct society," as had the Meech Lake Accord, the Charlottetown agreement included a provision that Quebec, regardless of the future size of its population, would be guaranteed 25 per cent of the seats in the House of Commons. To secure support in the West and the Atlantic provinces, a provision was made for equal provincial representation in the Senate. Other groups, notably those representing women and Aboriginal peoples, also were concerned that their interests be addressed. Hence, a provision for Aboriginal self-government was included, although for a variety of reasons, no provision focusing on the concerns of women was added to the package that would be offered to the electorate. During the referendum campaign Constitutional Affairs Minister Joe Clark recognized that this omission might cause a problem, and suggested that changes to the legal text of the Accord might be made after it had secured public approval (Jeffrey, 1993: 71). The two other provisions included in the Accord were more seats for the House of Commons—which presumably would find favour in large provinces such as Ontario and British Columbia—and greater powers to all provinces. The latter provision undoubtedly was designed to win support in Quebec, but the Mulroney government, not without reason, hoped that Canadians, regardless of their region of residence, would find the idea of enhanced power for their province an attractive one.

The wording of the question actually put to the voters, "Do you agree that the constitution of Canada should be renewed on the basis of the agreement reached August 18, 1992," neither specified the content of the Accord nor asked voters to express their opinions on its various provisions. The reasons for this were several. The leaders of both Reform and the Bloc Québécois were strongly opposed to the Accord. Since the great majority of their supporters were concentrated in the West and Quebec, it was hoped that phrasing the question very generally and asking voters for a simple "yes" or "no" verdict on the entire package would diminish the possibility of generating a coalition of negative minorities (who disagreed strongly with one or more specific proposals) that would be large enough to defeat the Accord. This prospect may well have induced the government not to release the "legal text" of the agreement until the referendum campaign was well under way, and to suggest the text was not cast in concrete by labelling it a "best efforts draft." Not surprisingly, this tactic also opened the government up to the charge that it was a "phoney" referendum because voters were being asked to approve something that could be changed afterwards.

The referendum campaign received heavy coverage in the mass media, and evidence from a national survey conducted in a 16-day period surrounding the event[1] indicates that most Canadians were very much aware of it. Indeed, only 15 per cent of those interviewed stated that there was "not enough" coverage, and more than one-third (36 per cent) thought that media coverage was excessive. Not surprisingly, television was the most important source of information about the referendum for almost half (47 per cent) of the public. Only 8 per cent cited literature generated by the opposing sides as the most important source of their knowledge of events. Opinions regarding the quality of media coverage were deeply divided—only a bare majority (51 per cent) judged the media's work was good, and slightly over four in 10 (42 per cent) concluded that the media had done a poor job. For the most part, these disagreements about the quality of media coverage did not concern questions of bias; two-thirds believed reporting of the referendum campaign was "fair and unbiased." Of the minority (27 per cent) who felt otherwise, Quebecers were by far the most likely (96 per cent) to regard the media's coverage as slanted in favour of a "no" vote. In other regions, large majorities of those perceiving media bias judged that it ran in the opposite direction.

The attention given by the media to the referendum meant that most Canadians were aware that important questions of constitutional choice were at stake. Our survey data indicate that voters were not indifferent to the decision they were being asked to make. Across the country, nearly half of the electorate (ranging from a high of 58 per cent in British Columbia to a low 41 per cent in the Atlantic provinces) said they were "very interested" in the referendum. An additional 35 per cent said they were "somewhat interested." Such expressions of interest were corroborated by actual behaviour; nearly 75 per cent of those eligible to cast a ballot in the referendum actually went to the polls. Although media coverage may have stimulated voter interest, relatively few of our survey respondents indicated that they had been influenced by what they had learned about the arguments made and positions taken by the leaders and activists of the opposing sides. Only one in five acknowledged such influence and, despite the enormous publicity given to former Prime Minister Pierre Trudeau's statements opposing the agreement,[2] only 18 per cent said that their vote had been affected by his arguments. Also, despite the fact that Prime Minister Mulroney had led the campaign for a "yes" vote, only 15 per cent of those stating their vote had been influenced by a political figure said that it was the prime minister's strident arguments on behalf of the Accord that had affected their voting decisions.

Mulroney's inability to sway the electorate was symptomatic of the more general failure of the Canadian political establishment to convince voters of the wisdom of a "yes" vote. Despite endorsements from both the Liberal and New Democratic parties and many of "the Great and the Good" in Canadian public life, and despite a massive government-led public relations effort, 55 per cent voted "no" (see Figure 4.1). Opposition to the proposal was widespread—negative majorities were registered in British Columbia, Alberta, Saskatchewan, Manitoba, Quebec, and Nova Scotia. In Ontario, the vote was "yes," but only by an extraordinarily slim (.2 per cent) margin. Larger "yes" majorities were recorded in the three smaller provinces of New Brunswick, Newfoundland, and Prince Edward Island, but only in the latter did more than two-thirds of the voters (74 per cent) endorse the Accord. Overall, the public verdict on the proposed constitutional agreement was both quite clear and decidedly negative.

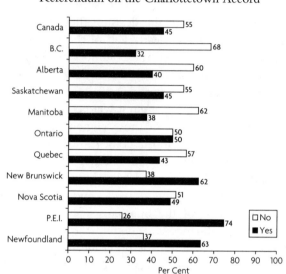

Figure 4.1 Vote in the 1992 National Referendum on the Charlottetown Accord

EXPLAINING THE VOTE

Attitudes towards the Proposal

The most obvious explanation for the failure of the Charlottetown Accord to secure public approval was that many voters either disagreed with at least some of the proposed constitutional revisions or believed that they did not satisfy the concerns of various groups (see Dion, 1993; Johnston et al., 1996). Reactions to the proposal were, in fact, very mixed. Although a large majority (70 per cent) of those participating in our national survey agreed with the provision for equal representation of the provinces in the Senate, much smaller ones supported self-government for Aboriginal peoples (55 per cent) or the expansion of the powers of the provinces (56 per cent). Other provisions received even less support[3] (see Figure 4.2). Only 45 per cent were willing to recognize Quebec as a distinct society, 31 per

Figure 4.2   Attitudes towards the
Provisions of the Charlottetown Accord

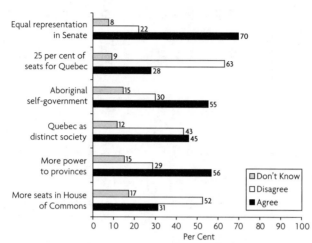

cent wished to enlarge the House of Commons, and just 28 per cent agreed that Quebec should be guaranteed at least one-fourth of the seats in that body. Regionally, only equal representation in the Senate was endorsed by majorities in all parts of the country (see Table 4.1, Panel A). The provision for enhanced provincial power gathered majority support in four regions, whereas Aboriginal self-government received support in three. Outside of Quebec, no regional majority favoured recognizing that province as a distinct society or allocating it a minimum of 25 per cent of the seats in the House of Commons, and majorities in every region (Quebec included) did not want the size of the House to be increased.

Perhaps the most difficult problem the supporters of the referendum faced was that only 12 per cent of the public agreed with all six proposals, whereas nearly half (48 per cent) disagreed with three or more provisions, and fully 70 per cent disagreed with at least two of them. Regionally, Westerners were the least, and Quebecers the most, enthusiastic about the several provisions in the Accord—a condition also reflected in the finding that identifiers with the Reform Party were on average the most likely (mean = 3.2), and Bloc Québécois identifiers the least likely (mean = 2.1), to see problems with the agreement. The larger story, however, was the lack of strong regional variation in reactions to the Accord. On

Table 4.1   Attitudes towards the Constitutional Referendum: Provisions and Group Concerns by Region

	Atlantic		Quebec		Ontario		Prairies		B.C.	
	Agree %	Disagree %	Agree %	Disagree %	Agree %	Disagree %	Agree %	Disagree %	Agree %	Disagree %
A. Referendum Provisions										
Equal representation, Senate	**76**	18	**55**	35	**71**	21	**82**	10	**79**	13
Quebec, 25% of seats	29	**64**	**58**	34	21	**67**	9	**82**	12	**82**
Aboriginal self-government	**61**	26	**52**	34	**61**	25	**54**	28	43	43
Quebec, distinct society	42	47	**71**	20	41	45	25	**64**	31	**59**
More power to the provinces	**54**	33	**69**	18	**50**	33	49	33	**57**	30
More seats, House of Commons	33	45	38	46	29	**54**	21	**58**	31	**52**
B. Referendum Satisfies Concerns of:										
Western Canadians	24	40	31	34	29	43	20	**59**	25	**61**
Quebec	**55**	25	**56**	37	**53**	30	**52**	25	**54**	28
Atlantic Canada	41	40	44	23	35	39	34	34	28	41
Ontario	41	21	**50**	30	49	30	47	20	**52**	23
Aboriginal peoples	**64**	16	**55**	28	48	30	49	25	48	37
Women	36	37	41	38	30	44	32	32	24	42
Francophones outside Quebec	41	26	49	28	32	35	35	31	33	37
Anglophones inside Quebec	17	**51**	**50**	32	18	**55**	24	48	14	**56**

Note: "Pro–con" and "don't know" responses not shown but included in calculation of percentages. Boldface percentages indicate positive or negative majority.

Figure 4.3   Does the Charlottetown Accord
Satisfy the Concerns of these Groups?

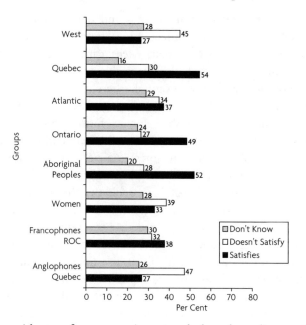

average, residents of every region stated that they disagreed with two or three of its provisions.

A lack of enthusiasm for the Accord also is suggested by responses to questions about its ability to satisfy the concerns of regional and other groups.[4] Substantial minorities were uncertain about how it would affect the interests of various groups and, for only two of them (Quebec; Aboriginal peoples) did even small majorities agree that its effects would prove satisfactory (see Figure 4.3). For the most part, these perceptions did not vary sharply across the country. Majorities in all five regions agreed that the proposal would satisfy Quebec's concerns but did not believe that it would satisfy those of women, Westerners, Francophones outside of Quebec, or residents of the Atlantic provinces (see Table 4.1, Panel B). Similarly, except in Quebec and the Prairies, majorities did not agree that the interests of Anglophone Quebecers would be well served, and only in Quebec and British Columbia did majorities believe that the agreement was satisfactory for Ontario. Reflecting the nearly even split in their vote, 49 per cent of Ontarians concluded that the Accord satisfied the concerns of their province.

A Polity on the Edge

Opinions About the Referendum and Its Consequences

Reactions to the referendum process and beliefs about its possible consequences also may have affected how voters behaved. Regarding the former, we can assume that, *ceteris paribus*, people who were negatively disposed towards the process would express that negativism by voting against the proposal, thereby "sending a message" to the government élites who had negotiated the constitutional agreement and strongly pushed for its ratification via a national referendum. The potential for such an anti-referendum protest vote was substantial. Although a majority (62 per cent) of those in our national survey thought that the referendum gave "ordinary people" an opportunity to participate in deciding the country's future, majorities also expressed reservations about the utility of holding it.[5] Specifically, 60 per cent judged that the referendum would *not* settle the important issues facing the country, 77 per cent believed that it was diverting attention from pressing economic problems and, despite the aforementioned public relations campaign and nationwide mailing concerning the contents of the agreement, fully 81 per cent believed that most people did not understand what it was about. As Table 4.2 shows, these opinions did not vary markedly from one part of the country to the next. However, this was not the case for other opinions. Residents of the Prairies and British Columbia were considerably more likely than other Canadians to disagree with the idea that important political questions should be decided by the federal and provincial governments rather than by referendums, and Quebecers were more likely to conclude that the referendum would do more to divide than to unify the country. Nationally, opinion on these matters was deeply divided—49 per cent thought that important questions should be decided by governments not referendums, and 46 per cent thought that the referendum would have a divisive, not a unifying, effect.

It also can be hypothesized that perceptions of the consequences of the referendum for the future of the country also might influence voting behaviour. Early in the campaign, Prime Minister Mulroney argued that the Charlottetown Accord was Canada's "last, best chance" for survival, and that rejection of the package would markedly enhance the prospect of Quebec separating from the rest of the country. Raising the spectre of Quebec separatism was

Table 4.2 Attitudes towards the Referendum Process by Region

	Atlantic		Quebec		Ontario		Prairies		B.C.	
	Agree %	*Disagree* %	*Agree* %	*Disagree* %	*Agree* %	*Disagree* %	*Agree* %	*Disagree* %	*Agree* %	*Disagree* %
The referendum won't settle any of the important issues facing the country.	**54**	41	**63**	34	**58**	35	**63**	30	**56**	40
The referendum gives ordinary people a chance to help decide Canada's future.	**66**	26	**60**	33	**61**	34	**64**	29	**65**	29
Rather than holding a referendum we should be concentrating on solving the country's economic problems.	**73**	22	**79**	19	**77**	20	**78**	20	**73**	25
Important political questions should be decided by federal and provincial governments, and not by a referendum.	**59**	33	**56**	39	**50**	40	44	47	30	**61**
Most people don't really understand what the referendum is all about.	**83**	14	**78**	16	**83**	12	**81**	16	**75**	21
The referendum will do more to divide the country than bring it together.	36	49	54	37	45	39	42	47	45	46

Note: "Don't know" responses not shown but included in calculation of percentages. Boldface percentages indicate positive or negative majority.

Table 4.3   Anticipated Consequences of
Defeat of the Referendum Proposal by Region

	Atlantic %	Quebec %	Ontario %	Prairies %	B.C. %	Canada %
A. Most Likely Outcome						
Breakup of Canada	8	9	8	5	4	7
Further constitutional negotiations	46	48	44	42	47	45
Maintenance of constitutional status quo	38	34	42	49	42	41
B. Probability of Quebec Separating						
More likely	20	31	25	14	19	23
Less likely	16	12	15	13	16	14
No difference	54	50	53	69	59	56

Note: "Don't know" responses not shown but
included in calculation of percentages.

decried by opponents of the agreement as a blatant scare tactic, and our survey evidence indicates that most voters did not buy the prime minister's argument—nationally, only 7 per cent forecast that a "no" vote would lead to the breakup of the country, and large pluralities thought that the consequence would be further constitutional negotiations (45 per cent) or maintenance of the status quo (41 per cent).[6] As Table 4.3, Panel A shows, these opinions were shared by residents of every region. Similarly, Panel B shows that large majorities in every region (ranging from 62 per cent in Quebec to 82 per cent in the Prairie provinces) rejected the argument that a "no" vote would make it more likely that Quebec would separate. Indeed, large numbers in every region (ranging from 50 per cent in Quebec to 69 per cent in the Prairies) thought that defeat of the referendum proposal would have no effect on the probability that Quebec would sever its ties with the rest of Canada. *Pace* the prime minister, the large majority of Canadians believed that their country would survive if the Accord were repudiated. For them, the risks of a "no" vote were minimal.

Four :: Last Chance?

Economic Evaluations and Attitudes towards the PC Government

Although it is reasonable to expect that the several factors discussed above had important effects on referendum voting, it also may be argued that attitudes towards the federal Progressive Conservative government and, especially, evaluations of its stewardship of the economy were consequential. After all, *this* government and its leader, Prime Minister Mulroney, had negotiated the Charlottetown Accord and called a national referendum to seek public approval for it. The prime minister then had assumed a highly visible role in the referendum campaign, travelling back and forth across the country to secure passage of the proposal.

Recall that analyses presented in Chapter Three demonstrated that voters' disaffection with the prime minister and his government were strongly influenced by reactions to the country's faltering economy. In the 1988 federal election campaign, the PCs had touted their ability to "manage change" and deliver the prosperity that Canadians desired. However, soon after their triumph in that contest, the economy fell into a deep and protracted recession. Public support for the newly implemented Canada-U.S. free trade agreement declined, and voters' evaluations of national economic conditions and their personal economic circumstances turned profoundly negative. Moreover, forecasts about the future were pessimistic; when the 1992 referendum was held, nearly three-quarters of those participating in our national survey thought that "hard times" would continue, or become even harder. The referendum thus was held in a context of pervasive public discontent with a government that had presided over and, many believed, was responsible for, their economic misery. As just observed, that government had negotiated the Charlottetown Accord, had called the referendum on the Accord, and its leader had campaigned vigorously on its behalf. These several widely publicized actions forged a link between the federal government and the referendum proposal in the public mind. This link, in turn, transformed the proposal into a convenient lightning rod for voters discontented with the PC government. Canadians dissatisfied with the government—and there were very many of them—now had an opportunity to express their hostility by rejecting its referendum proposal.[7]

Although the PCs led the campaign for a "yes" vote, the other old-line federal parties, the Liberals and the New Democrats, also supported the proposal. But this was probably a mixed blessing since public sentiments towards these parties were far from sanguine. Our 1992 national survey indicates that only 10 per cent identified with the NDP and, although 35 per cent identified with the Liberals, survey data collected since the 1988 federal election indicated that Liberal support was both lukewarm and volatile. More generally, as will be discussed in Chapter Five, support for all three old-line parties had eroded significantly over the quarter-century preceding the 1992 referendum. The most obvious indicator of public unhappiness with the existing party system was the presence of two new parties, Reform and the Bloc Québécois, which were poised to become major players on the national political stage. For different reasons, both advocated rejecting the Charlottetown Accord; therefore, it could be expected that people supporting either of these parties would demonstrate that support and their accompanying unhappiness with the old-line parties by voting "no" in the referendum.

Support for the National Political Regime and Community

If implemented, the Charlottetown Accord would have effected major changes in the institutional components of Canada's national political regime. The principal justification for the proposed changes was that they would enhance and solidify public support for the Canadian political community. The problematic nature of that support was obvious during the course of the Meech Lake crisis and, as observed, Prime Minister Mulroney had argued that failure to approve the new agreement would pose a grave threat to the continued integrity of that community. Thus, it was hypothesized that people who were strong supporters of the Canadian political community would be more likely to favour the proposal, viewing it as an instrument that would promote the integration and perpetuation of Canada. However, since the price of community was substantial change in *existing* regime institutions, we also hypothesized that persons who supported those institutions would be less likely to approve the proposal.

Four :: Last Chance?

Social Cleavages

Other factors aside, it could be expected that support for the referendum would vary across region/ethnicity and other important divisions in Canadian society. Regarding region/ethnicity, one may treat Ontarians as a convenient (if arbitrary) baseline group for purposes of statistical analysis. Given the resurgence of separatist sentiments in Quebec following the failure of the Meech Lake Accord, we anticipated that, despite the aforementioned concessions to Quebec in the Charlottetown agreement, support for the referendum proposal would be lower among Francophone Quebecers than Ontarians. However, since a "no" vote might strengthen separatist forces in the province, we also expected that non-French Quebecers would be more likely to vote "yes" than residents of Ontario. Because support for Reform was concentrated in the Prairies and British Columbia, and (with the exception of Senate reform) the proposal was widely viewed in these regions as designed primarily to satisfy the demands of Quebec, we also anticipated that support would be lower in these regions than in Ontario.

As for other demographic variables, the vocal opposition of women's rights groups to the agreement suggested that women would be less likely to favour it than men. In addition, age and socio-economic status might play a role. Recalling the argument that a "no" vote threatened the continued integrity of the country, we reasoned that persons in higher socio-economic categories might feel that they had a strong stake in preserving Canadian unity and thus would be more likely to vote "yes." Similarly, fear of the consequences should the country disintegrate might have be greater among older Canadians, since many of them depended heavily on social programs funded by the federal government. Thus, we expected older people would be more likely than younger ones to cast a "yes" ballot.

ANALYSING REFERENDUM VOTING

We employed a probit analysis, in which the dependent variable is a dichotomy (vote yes = 1, vote no = 0), to test our hypotheses about factors affecting voting in the referendum.[8] Predictor variables

included: (a) four factor-score variables (constitution-Quebec, consti-
tution-Senate, Aboriginal peoples, groups general) that summarize
reactions to the referendum proposal and its ability to satisfy group
concerns;[9] (b) three factor-score variables (process-general, Quebec
separation, public competence) that capture judgments about the
referendum process and the event's possible consequences;[10] (c) levels
of support for the governing Progressive Conservative Party and Prime
Minister Mulroney;[11] (d) attitudes towards the free trade agreement;[12]
(e) three factor-score variables that measure voters evaluations of
the impact of government performance on the past, present, and
future status of the national economy and their personal financial
condition;[13] (f) federal party identification;[14] (g) national regime
and community support;[15] (h) region/ethnicity and other socio-
demographic characteristics (age, education, gender, income).[16]

Collectively, a model of the vote that included these several
variables had considerable explanatory power. It correctly predicted
the referendum vote for 77.9 per cent of the cases—a substantial
improvement (53.5 per cent) over a prediction made absent knowledge of the independent variables (see Table 4.4). Similarly, another
measure of the goodness-of-fit of the model, the McKelvey R^2 (see
Aldrich and Nelson, 1984: 58), was sizable, .56. Regarding individual
predictors, with one exception, the several variables measuring
attitudes towards the proposal and its possible consequences behaved
as anticipated. All four "provisions and group concerns" factors had
significant effects. Thus, persons favouring the provisions to change
Quebec's constitutional status, those favouring the proposed reforms
of the Senate, and those believing that the proposal would positively
affect Aboriginal peoples or other groups, all were more likely to
vote "yes" than were people who did not hold these beliefs. Persons
who accepted the proposition that a "no" vote might enhance the
probability of Quebec separation and those who endorsed the utility
of a referendum also were more likely to vote "yes." However, the
variable tapping opinions about the competence of the public to
make important constitutional decisions was not influential.

Referendum voting was affected by other factors as well. As
argued above, the federal government was very closely associated
with the referendum proposal. Prime Minister Mulroney and his
colleagues had negotiated the Charlottetown Accord, called the
referendum, framed the wording of the proposal, and campaigned

Four :: Last Chance?

Table 4.4   Probit Analysis of Voting
in the 1992 Constitutional Referendum

Predictor Variables	b	t
Region/Ethnicity:		
Atlantic	0.09	0.48
Quebec-French	− 0.65	− 3.39◆
Quebec-Non-French	0.65	2.83✚
Prairies	− 0.37	− 2.35✚
British Columbia	− 0.46	− 2.74✚
Age	0.02	5.59◆
Education	− 0.01	− 0.09
Gender	− 0.03	− 0.27
Income	0.07	2.87✚
National community support	0.01	1.81▲
National regime support	− 0.01	− 1.77▲
Federal party identification:		
PC	0.12	0.69
Liberal	0.09	0.62
NDP	0.15	0.78
Reform	− 0.72	− 2.29▲
Bloc Québécois	− 0.97	− 3.15◆
Other	− 0.24	− 0.74
Federal PC government support	0.01	4.53◆
Economic evaluations:		
National–retrospective	0.02	0.43
Personal–retrospective	0.05	0.85
Future	0.01	0.10
Free Trade Agreement	− 0.06	− 0.93
Referendum provisions and group concerns:		
Constitution–Quebec	0.48	7.58◆
Constitution–Senate	0.10	1.85▲
Aboriginal peoples	0.28	5.42◆
Groups general	0.28	5.22◆
Referendum process/consequences:		
Process general	0.24	4.17◆
Quebec separation	− 0.15	− 2.89✚
Public competence	− 0.05	− 0.90
Constant	− 1.42	− 3.33◆

McKelvey R^2 = .56

% correctly classified = 77.9

Proportional reduction in error (λ) = .54

◆ p ≤ .001;   ✚ p ≤ .01;   ▲ p ≤ .05; one-tailed test.

hard for a "yes" vote. When doing so, they had argued strenuously that the defeat of the proposal would threaten the continued integrity of the country. These actions were consequential—people who were favourably disposed to the PC government were more likely to cast a "yes" ballot, as were those who were most strongly supportive of Canada as a political community. However, but also as expected, persons who were most supportive of *existing* regime institutions—some of which would have to change if the referendum were successful—were more likely to vote "no." Partisanship made a difference as well. As expected, people who identified with one of the two new parties (Bloc Québécois, Reform) were significantly more likely to vote "no" than were people who not identify with any of the federal parties (the baseline party identification category). Finally, and again as anticipated, Francophone Quebecers and Westerners were more likely to vote "no" than were Ontarians (the baseline region/ethnicity category), whereas non-Francophone Quebecers, older people, and those with higher incomes were more likely to vote "yes." Gender and level of formal education were not influential. However, contrary to our hypotheses, economic evaluations, attitudes towards the free trade agreement and identification with the three old-line parties were *not* significant predictors of the vote.

Additional probit analyses in which subsets of the predictors were added sequentially to the vote model helped us to gauge the relative strength of various determinants of referendum voting. These sequential analyses started with socio-demographic characteristics. When these variables were entered into the analysis, they were collectively significant but did not have much explanatory power, the McKelvey R^2 being only .13. Adding attitudes towards the national political regime and community increased R^2 to .21, party identifications boosted it to .28, and feelings about the PC government (entered together with economic evaluations and attitudes towards the free trade agreement) raised it to .35. The latter figure indicates that slightly more than three-fifths of the vote models' overall explanatory power could be obtained using variables that had nothing directly to do with either reactions to the provisions of the referendum proposal or assessments of the referendum process and its possible consequences. These latter variables were influential, however; adding assessments of the proposal's provisions and its ability to satisfy group concerns increased R^2 to .51, and evaluations of the referendum process and the forecast consequences of the referendum outcome raised it to .56. By way of comparison, an analysis using only the "referendum-specific" variables yielded an R^2 of .37—two-thirds of the explanatory power provided by the model that included all of the predictor variables. Taken together, these results suggest that referendum voting was the product of a complex and diverse set of forces. Orientations towards the referendum *per se* were important, but other variables mattered as well.

The (Hidden) Political Economy of Referendum Voting

As just observed, evaluations of national and personal economic conditions and attitudes towards the Canada-U.S. free trade agreement did not have significant effects in a multivariate model of factors affecting referendum voting. However, this does *not* mean that these evaluations and attitudes were unimportant. Rather, we hypothesized that they exerted *indirect* effects on voting behaviour in the referendum by influencing attitudes towards Prime Minister Mulroney and his government. We tested this hypothesis by analysing a multivariate model of factors affecting PC government support. The independent variables in this model included the three economic evaluation variables, attitudes towards the FTA, party identification, region/ethnicity, age, education, gender, and income. To control for the possibility that feelings about the government when the referendum was held were largely driven by attitudes towards the proposal rather than by economic evaluations, the referendum process, and its possible consequences, the variables measuring these attitudes also were included in the model. Multiple regression analysis was used to estimate model parameters.

Paralleling results presented in Chapter Three, the regression analysis of our 1992 survey data revealed that national-retrospective, personal-retrospective, and future-oriented economic evaluations had significant positive effects on PC government support. In each case, persons who made positive, rather than negative, judgements about the national economy or their personal economic circumstances were more likely to be relatively strong government supporters. Attitudes towards the free trade agreement were signifi-

A Polity on the Edge

Table 4.5 Multiple Regression Analysis of Support for the Federal Progressive Conservative Government, 1992 National Survey

Predictor Variables	b	Std. b	t
Region/Ethnicity:			
Atlantic	− 1.50	− .02	− 0.77
Quebec–French	4.00	.07	2.09▲
Quebec–Non-French	− 2.25	− .03	− 1.04
Prairies	− 1.23	− .02	− 0.75
British Columbia	0.85	.01	0.46
Age	− 0.06	− .04	− 1.71▲
Education	0.53	.01	0.53
Gender	2.98	.07	2.77✚
Income	0.07	.01	0.26
Federal party identification:			
PC	13.51	.25	8.21◆
Liberal	− 0.31	− .01	− 0.35
NDP	− 6.11	− .09	− 3.02◆
Reform	− 2.80	− .03	− 1.00
Bloc Québécois	− 2.99	− .03	− 1.03
Other	3.18	.02	0.96
Economic evaluations:			
National–Retrospective	5.24	.24	9.37◆
Personal–Retrospective	3.05	.15	5.47◆
Future	2.05	.10	3.66◆
Free Trade Agreement	2.99	.10	3.49◆
Referendum provisions and group concerns:			
Constitution–Quebec	1.66	.08	2.62✚
Constitution–Senate	1.27	.06	2.25▲
Aboriginal peoples	0.83	.04	1.51
Groups general	2.26	.11	4.09◆
Referendum process/consequences:			
Process general	1.59	.07	2.75✚
Quebec separation	− 0.23	− .01	0.43
Public competence	− 1.84	− .09	− 3.38◆
Constant	28.85	—	7.99◆

$$R^2 = .34$$

◆ p ≤ .001;   ✚ p ≤ .01;   ▲ p ≤ .05; one-tailed test.

cant as well and, as anticipated, persons who favoured the agreement tended to be stronger government supporters. Collectively, the effects of economic evaluations and attitudes towards the FTA were quite powerful. For example, if all three economic evaluations had been one standard deviation more positive than average, PC support

Four :: Last Chance?

(as measured on a 100-point thermometer scale) would have been more than 10 points higher and, if they had been two standard deviations more positive, PC support would have been more than 20 points higher. Having a positive, rather than a negative, attitude towards the FTA would have raised that support by an additional three points. These figures clearly indicate that the referendum proposal would have met with a more favourable reception had the vote been held in a context in which the electorate's economic evaluations were more sanguine. Attitudes towards the PC government significantly affected the vote, and those attitudes, in turn, were strongly affected by voters' economic judgements.

How much difference did these unfavourable economic evaluations make for the referendum outcome? Would the proposal have passed had the referendum been held at a time when the economy was booming, Canadians were pleased with its performance, and optimistic about the country's economic future and their own financial prospects? The probit analysis of referendum voting presented above helps us to answer these intriguing questions. Since probit coefficients do not have a straightforward interpretation similar to those for OLS regression (Long, 1997: 61-69), we assessed the impact of changing economic evaluations in counterfactual scenarios in which the values of other variables in the referendum vote model were fixed at theoretically interesting or typical values.

Although there are many possibilities, we constructed scenarios in which the voter was a woman who did not identify with any of the federal parties. Since there were major regional differences in support for the referendum proposal in different parts of the country, we successively considered the possibilities that she was a resident of Quebec, the Prairies, British Columbia, and either Ontario or the Atlantic provinces.[17] Her scores on all of the other variables in the probit model were set to their average values. We then computed the probabilities that this hypothetical voter would cast a "yes" ballot, assuming that she was a resident of various regions. Then, to take into account the very large negative shifts in national and personal economic evaluations that occurred after 1988, we recomputed the probabilities of a "yes" vote, assuming that the voter's judgements about economic conditions were one and two standard deviations more positive than was actually the case in 1992.

A Polity on the Edge

These calculations show that initially the probability of a "yes" vote exceeded .5 only in Ontario and the Atlantic provinces (see Figure 4.4). However, if economic evaluations had been one standard deviation more positive, the probability of a "yes" vote would have reached a majority level (.52) in the Prairies and almost would have done so in British Columbia (.48). If economic assessments had been two standard deviations more positive, the probability of a "yes" ballot would have exceeded .5 by comfortable margins everywhere but in Quebec. In the Atlantic provinces and Ontario, where majorities actually endorsed the agreement, such markedly more positive economic evaluations would have resulted in ringing endorsements, with a "yes" probability climbing to fully .74. In Quebec, however, the possibility of a "yes" majority would have remained in doubt—even with such highly favourable economic judgements, the likelihood of a "yes" vote was exactly .50.

Figure 4.4 Probability of a "Yes" Vote in Referendum
if Economic Evaluations Had Been More Positive

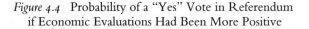

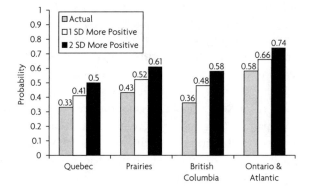

These scenarios assume that our hypothetical voter did not identify with one of the federal political parties. Since identification with one of the old-line federal parties (PC, Liberal, NDP) did not have significant direct effects on referendum voting (see Table 4.4), this assumption provides a reasonably accurate basis for assessing economic effects for much of the electorate. However, since identifications with the Reform and Bloc Québécois parties were associated (negatively) with the vote, and most Reform identifiers reside in the Prairies and British Columbia whereas all Bloc

Four :: Last Chance?

Québécois partisans are Quebecers, we considered how varying economic evaluations would have affected such persons. If our voter had been a Reform identifier living in the Prairies, her probability of voting "yes" actually would have been only .17. Assuming her economic judgements had been one or two standard deviations more positive, this probability would have risen to .23 and then to .31. The comparable figures for a British Columbia Reform identifier were .14, .20, and .27, respectively. Probabilities of a "yes" vote for a Bloc Québécois identifier were even smaller, with an initial .07 probability increasing to .11 and then to .15 as economic evaluations became increasingly positive.

What, then, do these scenarios suggest about the political economy of the referendum result? Clearly, a vigorous economy would have substantially raised the paper-thin "yes" margin in Ontario, and enhanced the already sizable "yes" majority in the Atlantic provinces. In the West, the presence of Reform identifiers in the Prairies and British Columbia (14 per cent and 8 per cent of these electorates, respectively), would have diminished the effects of a healthy economy. However, since Reform support was partially a product of economic discontent, the party likely would have had fewer adherents in these two regions if the economy had not faltered so badly after 1988.[18] Also, since most Reformers were erstwhile federal PCs, the "yes" forces would have enjoyed greater strength in both regions. In Quebec, Bloc Québécois identifiers (20 per cent of that electorate in 1992) strongly opposed the referendum proposal and, as shown, their opposition was largely impervious to a more prosperous economy. Moreover, since Bloc Québécois partisanship was very largely a product of non-economic forces, i.e., the reinvigoration of secessionist sentiments stimulated by the Meech Lake crisis, a stronger economy likely would have done little to erode BQ support. Although our basic scenarios (see Figure 4.4) do suggest that persons who were not Bloquistes would have responded favourably to a better economy, the sizable proportion of BQ supporters in the Quebec electorate suggests that achieving a "yes" majority still would have been an uphill battle.

In sum, these scenarios clearly indicate that the referendum result would been have different if economic conditions had been better. However, whether improved economic circumstances could have produced the regional unanimity in support that many observers believed was crucial for legitimizing the proposed constitutional changes is problematic. Indeed, one plausible outcome of holding the referendum when the economy was booming is that there would have been a national "yes" majority, accompanied by "yes" majorities (of quite different sizes) in every region but Quebec.

CONCLUSION: THE CONTEXT OF CONSTITUTIONAL CHOICE

Like other forms of politics, direct democracy is not an arid exercise in Cartesian logic. The political-economic context in which a national referendum is held can do much to shape the result. Certainly that was true of the 1992 Canadian referendum on constitutional reform. It was the product of a political crisis precipitated by the failure of an earlier effort at constitutional renewal, the Meech Lake Accord. The context also was one in which the federal government was highly unpopular not only because of its failed Meech Lake initiative, but also because of its sponsorship of the highly controversial free trade agreement with the United States and its imposition of a widely detested value-added tax. More important, however, the economy was in a severe recession, and many Canadians had concluded that the governing Conservatives and their leader, Prime Minister Mulroney, were to blame for the unhappy state of affairs.

Given these political and economic circumstances, it is plausible that the Mulroney government's decision to hold a national referendum on a new package of constitutional reforms that it had negotiated might have yielded beneficial consequences both for the country and for that government. The benefits for the country were obvious—assuming the proposal received public endorsement, the Charlottetown Accord might resolve a variety of long-standing problems of crucial importance for the maintenance of the Canadian polity. The payoffs for Mulroney and his colleagues were straightforward as well. Obtaining approval for the Accord would assist in erasing memories of the government's earlier failure to revise the constitution, while helping to restore an image of competence that had been badly tarnished by a sputtering economy. Winning the referendum thus had the potential to bolster the government's public standing and give it a fighting chance to be returned to power—especially if the economy improved.

Four :: Last Chance?

To increase the probability of a successful outcome, the government's strategy was to request approval for the entire constitutional package, rather than to ask voters to pass on each of its six provisions. By bundling the six provisions into a single question, it was hoped that voters who were aware of the contents of the package would *like* one or more of the proposals enough to cast a "yes" ballot. That expectation proved unfounded. Although a large majority favoured the proposal for Senate reform, and smaller ones endorsed the provisions for devolution of power to the provinces and Aboriginal self-government, other aspects of the agreement met with widespread disapproval, either nationally, in particular regions, or both.

Indeed, almost half the electorate found problems with three or more of the proposals and only just over one voter in ten agreed with all six. In addition, reactions to the referendum proposal and process and its possible consequences had significant effects on voting behaviour. However, other important forces, such as those associated with feelings about the prime minister and his government, also were at work. A protracted recession shaped people's economic evaluations which, in turn, strongly affected their non-support for the Mulroney government. Feelings about that government had significant direct effects on referendum voting.

In retrospect, it is apparent that the referendum campaign and its outcome were replete with ironies. First, the ill-fated Meech Lake Accord had been designed explicitly "to bring Quebec in from the cold" and resolve Canada's long-standing constitutional impasse. The federal government's post-Meech attempts at damage control paved the way for the 1992 referendum, some provisions of which were specifically aimed at satisfying Quebec. Nonetheless, Quebec still voted "no," and the unpopularity of these provisions among non-Quebecers eroded support for the proposal in other parts of the country.

Second, if the referendum had been held in a more hospitable economic climate, it would have had a better chance of passing. However, the impact of a healthier economy would have been smallest in Quebec. But, as noted, satisfying Quebecers' demands for constitutional change and thereby defusing the threat posed by separatist forces was a primary rationale for negotiating the Charlottetown Accord, which was the subject of the referendum. Ironically, insofar as the maintenance of Canadian unity is concerned, if there was an "upside" to the referendum outcome, it is that the Bloc Québécois and its allies could not fan the flames of separatism by claiming that the referendum showed that Quebec and the rest of Canada were hopelessly deadlocked concerning the proposed constitutional changes. A majority of Quebecers had rejected the deal, but so, too, had majorities in British Columbia, the Prairies, and the country as a whole. Their reasons for doing so varied, but the result did not pit a pro-Accord majority in the ROC against an anti-Accord majority in Quebec.

Third, had the referendum passed, it likely would have significantly improved the Mulroney government's dismal standing with an electorate that blamed it for the painful recession. But, again, it did not pass, and ironically, one of the reasons it didn't was, on the one hand, the electorate's negative evaluation of the government's stewardship of the economy and on the other, the government's close association with the referendum in the eyes of the public. In a very real sense, the government was in a box of its own making. Having committed themselves to a national referendum on a constitutional deal that they had negotiated, the prime minister and his colleagues were forced to campaign strenuously to secure its passage. But, as they did so, they strengthened the linkage between the proposal and themselves in the public mind, thereby enhancing the likelihood that support for the proposal would be eroded by their massive unpopularity.

The 1992 national referendum on the Charlottetown Accord teaches an important lesson about the exercise of direct democracy. Referendums, like elections, can provide opportunities for citizens to register their opinions on pressing political issues. However, voters may use referendums for purposes other than those anticipated by the governments that called them. In situations where disgruntled electorates are unable for the time being to "throw the rascals out" for perceived mismanagement of the nation's economy or other sins, they may use government-sponsored referendums to "send the rascals a message" by "throwing out" their proposals. This does not mean that holding a referendum is a convenient and surefire way for an unpopular government to avoid retribution at the polls by allowing voters to vent their spleen on a government-sponsored referendum proposal. As we will see in the next chapter, the wrath of an angry electorate may be difficult to deflect. A year after they had soundly rejected the federal government's referendum proposal, Canadian voters ousted the governing Progressive Conservatives from office and drove them deep into the political wilderness.

NOTES

1. The interviews were conducted during the seven days before the referendum and during the nine days afterwards. Differences between the reported vote intentions of the pre-referendum respondents and the reported votes of the post-referendum respondents are not statistically significant (χ^2_{21} = 2.51, p = .113). Also, reported vote shares closely match the actual results for the country as a whole (difference = 2.0 per cent), with regional differences ranging from a low of 2.2 per cent for the Atlantic provinces to a high of 5.9 per cent for the Prairies.

2. In an article in the news magazine *Maclean's* published in late September and in an October 1 speech in Montreal, Trudeau attacked the Accord as an ill-conceived attempt to appease Quebec separatists who were "blackmailing" Canada.

3. The question was: "Some people have said they are in favour of, or against, specific parts of the constitutional agreement. I'd like to know if you agree or disagree with some specific provisions of the agreement. First, do you agree or disagree with the proposal for: (a) equal representation of the provinces in the Senate? (b) the guarantee that Quebec will always have 25 per cent of the seats in the House of Commons? (c) the establishment of self-government for Native and Aboriginal peoples? (d) the recognition of Quebec as a distinct society? (e) giving more powers to the provinces in specific areas? (f) the addition of extra members to the House of Commons?"

4. The question was: "Would you agree or disagree that the constitutional agreement answers most of the concerns of the following specific groups? (a) western Canadians? (b) Quebec? (c) Atlantic Canada? (d) Ontario? (e) Aboriginal peoples? (f) women in Canada? (g) French-speaking people outside Quebec? (h) English-speaking people in Quebec?"

5. The question was: "People have different opinions about the referendum. I'd like to know if you agree or disagree with some of the following views. For example: (a) The referendum won't settle any of the important issues facing Canada; (b) The referendum gives ordinary people a chance to help decide Canada's future; (c) Rather than holding a referendum we should be concentrating on solving the country's economic problems; (d) Important political questions should be decided by federal and provincial governments and not by referendums; (e) Most people don't really understand what the referendum is all about; (f) The referendum will do more to divide the country than bring it together."

6. Respondents were asked if they thought the most likely result of rejecting the constitutional agreement would be: (i) the breakup of Canada; (ii) further negotiation on constitutional matters; (iii) everything stays as it is under the existing constitution. They then were asked if they thought that rejection would make it: (i) more likely, or (ii) less likely, that Quebec will separate from the rest of Canada, or (iii) if they thought rejection would not have any effect.

7. The results of a question-wording experiment in the 1988 Canadian National Election Study (CNES) are consistent with this hypothesis. The experiment shows that respondents who were asked if they supported the Canada-U.S. free trade agreement were less supportive if "the Mulroney government" rather than "Canada" was specified as the negotiator. These differences largely disappeared among respondents interviewed after the nationally televised, party-leaders debate when Liberal leader, John Turner, solidified the linkage between the FTA and the prime minister by accusing Mulroney of selling out the country to the United States on the issue. See Johnston et al. (1992: 151-52).

Note also that external evidence suggests that public feelings about the PCs affected attitudes towards the Accord rather than vice versa. Between July and November 1992, the PCs' vote intention share in monthly Gallup polls varied by only 1 per cent—dropping from 22 per cent in July to 21 per cent in August and September and returning to 22 per cent in October and November.

8. For other multivariate analyses of factors affecting voting in the referendum, see Johnston et al. (1996); LeDuc and Pammett (1995).

9. The confirmatory factor analysis that forms the basis for constructing these variables is described in Clarke and Kornberg (1994: 945-46).

10. Regarding the confirmatory factor analysis that guides the construction of these variables, see Clarke and Kornberg (1994: 948-49).

11. The measure of PC government support is the average score (on 100-point thermometer scales) for the federal PC party and its leader, Prime Minister Mulroney. The correlation (r) between the two thermometer scores is +.72.

12. Attitudes towards the FTA were scored: favour = 2; opposed = 0; uncertain or "don't know" = 1.

13. Confirmatory factor analyses of the 1992 data and those gathered in several earlier national surveys (see Chapter Three) show that Canadians structure their economic evaluations in terms of three factors: (a) sociotropic (retrospective and contemporaneous evaluations of the state of the national economy and government's responsibility for them); (b) egocentric (retrospective and contemporaneous evaluations of one's personal economic condition and government's responsibility for them); and (c) prospective (evaluations of future national and personal economic conditions and government's responsibility for them). In all cases, the model's fit is excellent—e.g., in 1992, χ^2_{25} = 7.15, p = .21. The construction of the six economic evaluation variables in the three-factor model is described in Chapter Three, note 6.

14. Party identification is measured as a series of dummy (0-1) variables; non-identifiers (20 per cent of the sample) are the reference category. For the party identification question sequence, see Chapter Two, note 1.

15. Support for national regime institutions is measured as the average score on 100-point thermometer scales for parliament, the federal civil service, and the federal judiciary. National community support is measured as the thermometer score for Canada. Note that confirmatory factor analyses of the 1992 and earlier survey data show that Canadians distinguish among their feelings about political authorities, regime institutions, and the national community (see Chapter Three, note 12, and Kornberg and Clarke, 1992: ch. 4). For the 1992 data, for example, a four-factor model has an excellent fit (χ^2_{27} = 4.70, p = .696). An alternative two-factor model, which ignores the authorities-regime distinction, has a markedly worse fit (χ^2_{210} = 281.64, p = .000). To provide a summary measure of support for regime institutions, we include feelings about the judiciary with those for parliament and civil service.

16. Region/ethnicity is a series of 0-1 dummy variables, with Ontario treated as the reference category. The other socio-demographic variables are: (i) age in years; (ii) gender: men = 0, women = 1; (iii) level of formal education: elementary school or less = 1, some secondary or completed secondary or technical school = 2; university = 3; (iv) annual family income: eight categories ranging from $10,000 or less = 1 to $80,000 or more = 8.

17. Ontario and the Atlantic provinces are considered together because the coefficient for the latter was insignificant in the probit analysis of referendum voting (see Table 4.4).

18. The results of a 1993 national survey of Reform Party members are suggestive in this regard. When asked to cite the most important issue in the 1993 federal election, nearly two-thirds (65 per cent) of the Reformers mentioned an economic issue, and nearly half of them (48 per cent) mentioned the deficit or debt. No other type of issue was mentioned by as many as 10 per cent of the party members. An overwhelming percentage (96 per cent) of Reformers also said that concern with economic issues was a very important reason why they joined the party. See Chapter Seven, Table 7.4.

F I V E

Doing Politics Differently

The 1993 federal election was dramatic and consequential. The near-destruction of two members of Canada's long-lived "two-party-plus" national party system (Epstein, 1964; see also Carty, 1992) in that election and the resounding successes enjoyed by two new ones radically transformed the political choices confronting Canadians. In this chapter, we will consider factors that prompted millions of voters to abandon the Progressive Conservative and New Democratic parties, and enabled one new party, the Bloc Québécois, to elect a majority of Quebec MPs and become the official opposition party in Parliament. We also will investigate how another new party, Reform, was able to become a major political force in the West and thereby assume for itself the mantle of representing the interests of that region—a mantle the Conservatives had worn for almost 40 years.

To help us comprehend the old parties' failures and the new parties' successes, we will map the evolution of Canadians' attitudes towards and support for the federal parties, as well as their evaluations of how well the national parties perform the functions generally ascribed to political parties in mature democracies. These data on public orientations towards the parties provide the context for an analysis of voting behaviour in the 1993 election. Scenarios based on this analysis show that the devastating defeat suffered by the Conservatives was more strongly related to their inability to convince voters that they could revive a recession-ridden economy than the failure of their new leader to strike a responsive chord with the electorate. Economic issues also contributed significantly to the successes enjoyed by Reform and the BQ. However, the new parties were not simply convenient sticks for beating a government that voters had tried and convicted of mismanaging the country's economy. Rather, the attractiveness of Reform and the BQ also reflected their perceived abilities to give voice to resurgent regional discontents in the West and Quebec, respectively, and, in the case of the Bloc, to champion the cause of Quebec sovereignty. In the conclusion, we argue that the 1993 election was critical because it significantly, and perhaps permanently, changed the composition and operation of the national party system.

THE PUBLIC AND THE POLITICAL PARTIES: DISAFFECTION AND DEALIGNMENT

On election day, the Conservatives were routed in every region of the country. Even the most zealous Tory "spin doctors" could not deny that their party had been nearly annihilated, losing 167 of the 169 seats it had won in 1988. The PC vote share plummeted from 43 per cent to 16 per cent. The NDP suffered a disaster of comparable magnitude—its seat and vote totals fell from 43 to 7 and from 20 per cent to 7 per cent, respectively. In sharp contrast, the new parties fared extremely well. Reform garnered 19 per cent of the vote and elected 52 MPs. The BQ gained 14 per cent of the vote, all within Quebec, and returned 54 MPs. As the largest minority party in Parliament, the Bloc—a party avowedly dedicated to the destruction of Canada in its current form—ironically assumed the role of "Her Majesty's Loyal Opposition."

These profound shocks to the national party system did not occur in a vacuum. Rather, there is abundant historical evidence that Canadians long have been unhappy with the performance of the federal and provincial parties and the larger political system in which they operate. In Chapter One, we have argued that these negative feelings are at least in part a product of the poor "fit" between the country's economic and social realities, on the one hand, and its governmental institutions and processes, on the other (see also Kornberg and Clarke, 1992: ch. 1). We have observed that a highly skewed distribution of population, very substantial differences in the value and character of the resources and industrial development of the several provinces, a national economy tightly integrated with and dependent upon that of a much larger and richer adjacent neighbour and, in particular, a political system combining a decentralized federal structure with Westminster-style parliamentary government have combined to produce periods of deep discontent. This has been particularly true in Quebec and the West. Therefore, it is not especially surprising that among the best-known early major studies of Canadian political parties are analyses of the rise and development of protest parties in those two regions.[1]

However, it was not until 1965 that John Meisel and associates[2] undertook the first systematic national study of the role of "parties in the electorate" in determining voting behaviour and the outcome of a Canadian federal election. This path-breaking study and a subsequent one conducted in 1968 introduced measures of the concept of party identification, new methods for ascertaining the public's feelings about key political objects and, perhaps most important, a systematic empirical basis for analyzing relationships among parties, elections, and the larger political process. The 1965 and 1968 studies, in turn, inspired a variety of large-scale quantitative investigations by a generation of Canadian social scientists, including national studies of voting behaviour in the 1974, 1979, 1980, 1984, 1988, 1993, and 1997 federal elections (e.g., Clarke et al., 1979, 1996; Johnston et al., 1992). Taken together, these several studies have sketched a portrait of a polity with an exceedingly complex party system in which, for example: the number and identities of contesting parties, and patterns of inter-party competition between and among them, can vary sharply from province to province; within-province competition at one level of government can be very different from competition at the other; periodic tendencies towards one-party dominance are apparent at both levels of government in various provinces; inter-party competition can be intense, despite the fact that many voters see almost no ideological or class differences among parties; voters' perceptions of parties are complex, being structured in terms of "left-right," "government-opposition," "major-minor," and "national-regional" dimensions; and party identification, as well as voting behaviour and the outcome of national and provincial elections, are strongly affected by highly volatile short-term forces.[3]

Although the several national election studies, taken one by one, have enriched our knowledge of Canadians' orientations towards

123

A Polity on the Edge

Table 5.1   Evaluations of the Performance of
Political Parties, 1991 and 1993 National Surveys

	1991		1993	
Statements about Political Parties	*Agree*	*Disagree*	*Agree*	*Disagree*
A. Do not tell people about really important problems	**77**	23	**70**	30
B. Look after everyone's interests	36	**64**	38	**62**
C. Big difference between party and performance	**96**	4	**94**	6
D. Encourage people to become active in politics	38	**62**	40	**60**
E. Do not give voters real policy choices	**71**	29	**62**	38
F. Help groups reach consensus	37	**63**	34	**66**
G. More interested in winning elections than governing	**87**	13	**82**	18
H. Help people to have say in politics	52	**48**	51	**49**
I. Divide, do not unify country	**67**	33	**56**	44
J. Bicker rather than solve problems	**94**	6	**93**	7
K. Recruit well-qualified candidates for Parliament	•	•	49	51
L. Do not listen to views of ordinary people	•	•	**72**	28

• Question not asked in 1991.
Note: Horizontal percentages; boldface numbers indicate negative evaluations.

political parties, they seldom have been employed to analyse the long-term dynamics of these orientations, or to address related questions concerning the evolution of the national party system and its relation to the larger political order.[4] Here, we employ them for just such purposes. Used in conjunction with other national surveys we have conducted over the past two decades, the election surveys provide the time-series data needed to assess changes in support for specific parties, as well as the evolution of affective and evaluative orientations towards Canadian political parties in general. Regarding the latter, in a series of national surveys carried out in the 1990s we have employed a series of "agree-disagree" statements to map public evaluations of the performance of the federal political parties. Respondents were asked to judge the performance of the parties in carrying out the kinds of policy-representational, interest-articulating, interest-aggregating and governing tasks typically ascribed to them in mature democracies. Answers to these questions elicited in our 1991 and 1993 studies are displayed in Table 5.1.

As is evident, large and in some cases overwhelming majorities stated that the parties do not tell people about really important issues facing the country; that there are big differences between parties' campaign promises and what they actually do if elected; that parties are more interested in winning elections than in governing effectively; that parties spend too much time bickering rather than addressing important problems; and that they do not listen to the views of ordinary people. The parties also were castigated for ignoring the general interest in favour of the interests of those who voted for them; for dividing rather than unifying the country; for not encouraging people to become active in politics; for not helping people voice their opinions; and for failing to recruit well-qualified candidates to run for public office. Parties received their highest marks for performing representational functions and facilitating citizen participation in the political process—for encouraging people to become politically active; for aggregating group policy preferences; and for enabling people to exert influence they would not have as individuals. However, as Table 5.1 shows, even in these instances only minorities of our survey respondents evaluated parties positively. More generally, negative judgements about party performance were the norm throughout the country and among all groups of party identifiers, not just those supporting the new parties (Bloc Québécois and Reform) that were challenging the existing party system. Indeed, on average, two-thirds of the judgements Canadians made about the parties in the 1991 and 1993 surveys were negative.

We next ascertained whether there was an organizing structure to people's evaluations of party performance. Although research on mass belief systems conducted over the past three decades (e.g., Converse, 1964; Zaller, 1992) cautions against assuming that public thinking about political parties mirrors the kind of abstract and nuanced conceptions of parties prevalent in scholarly writings about them, it is plausible that people's evaluations are not random or inchoate. Rather, they are organized, albeit loosely, in terms of one or more general underlying factors or evaluative dimensions. Empirically, confirmatory factor analyses (CFA) (e.g., Bollen, 1989) of the 1991 and 1993 survey data revealed that party performance evaluations reflected two such factors which can be labelled "governing-elections" and "participation-representation."[5] The two factors were positively, but not strongly, related (the inter-factor correlations are .28 in 1991 and .42 in 1993), and the correlations (factor loadings) between responses to the questions about the performance of the parties and the general factors were statistically significant but quite variable in magnitude. Taken together, these findings indicate that public evaluations of party performance are not ad hoc, unstructured, reactions untutored by knowledge of the functions ascribed to parties in contemporary mature democracies. Rather, these evaluations are loosely, but recognizably, organized in terms of two dimensions that define major classes of activities parties perform in such polities.

The results of the preceding analyses were used to construct summary scores on the "governing-elections" and "participation-representation" factors. Examining the distributions of these scores emphasizes the point that, circa the early 1990s, negative judgements about the performance of the national political parties were common among all major socio-demographic groups. Residents of Quebec and the West—regions of the country where unhappiness with the federal party system has been especially pronounced at various times in Canadian history—were joined by many of their fellow citizens in Ontario and the Atlantic provinces in giving the national parties a resounding "thumbs down" on both the governing-elections and participation-representation dimensions. In every region, negative evaluations on both dimensions were common among persons in all age, educational, gender, and income groups. Nor did partisanship sharply differentiate people's judgements on the two dimensions. Identifiers with all of the parties—not only Bloc Québécois and Reform partisans—were displeased with the parties' performances. Dissatisfaction with the parties transcended all of the major social and political divisions in the population.

One interpretation of these data is that the deep discontent Canadians expressed about political parties in the early 1990s was an exaggerated and temporary "period effect." Specifically, the negativism people were expressing at this time was the product of grievances generated by the ailing economy combined with fear and frustration engendered by a seemingly unresolvable constitutional impasse that threatened to tear the country apart. Although this

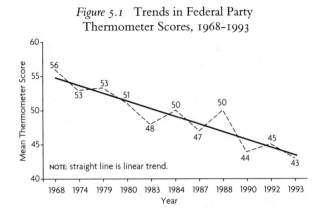

Figure 5.1 Trends in Federal Party
Thermometer Scores, 1968-1993

interpretation might seem plausible to a casual observer—after all, the economy *was* in bad shape, and the constitutional crisis *was* a highly salient fact of political life—it is important to bear in mind that unhappiness with party performance and disaffection from the national party system are recurrent themes in Canadian political history. Indeed, some observers would contend that unflattering judgments about party performance always have been the norm and are basically representative of prevailing tendencies in a political culture where parties long have been convenient targets of public wrath.

Longitudinal data on Canadians' affective orientations towards the Liberal, Conservative, and New Democratic federal parties derived from national surveys of the electorate conducted since 1968 provide an opportunity to investigate this conjecture. The data in Figure 5.1 are derived from responses to questions where respondents were asked to rate the political parties on 100-point "feeling" thermometer scales. One sees that average feelings about the three national parties have moved over time from lukewarm (50 is explicitly designated as the neutral point on the scale) to decidedly negative. The progression of scores is not steadily downward, but there is a strong negative trend, with the three-party average declining from a tepid 56 in 1968 to a dismal 43 in 1993. Thus, although the time series data needed to depict public sentiments about the political parties throughout Canadian history are unavailable, it is clearly the case that feelings about the parties have not been static over the past three decades. Rather, the negativism of the early 1990s represents the continuation of a trend that has been operative at least since the late 1960s, during which Canadians lack of enthusiasm for their national parties gradually turned into outright hostility. Negative attitudes towards the parties did not suddenly develop in the 1990s as a consequence of the vexing economic and constitutional difficulties bedeviling the country. Although these difficulties undoubtedly deepened the negativism, the dynamics of public discontent with the parties have a significant long-term component, a subject to which we will return in Chapter Seven.

IDENTIFICATION WITH THE FEDERAL PARTIES

Time series data on party identification provide additional evidence about the evolution of public attitudes towards the federal political parties. As noted in Chapter Two, the concept of party identification has long been a subject of controversy among Canadian political scientists. These debates were initiated by John Meisel (1975; see also Jenson, 1976) who interpreted the survey data gathered in the 1965 and 1968 national election studies as indicating that many Canadians had weak and unstable psychological attachments to political parties. These findings and the very strong cross-sectional correlations between party identification and electoral choice suggested that partisanship, like the vote itself, is strongly affected by short-term forces operating in the political arena at particular points in time. Subsequent research using cross-sectional and panel data gathered between 1974 and 1980 supported these conclusions by showing that many Canadians lacked durable partisan allegiances. Many voters identified only weakly with one of the federal parties, sizable minorities changed their party identifications between successive elections, and upwards of one person in four identified with different parties in federal and provincial politics.[6] Nor were voters with different federal and provincial party identifications found only in provinces such as Quebec and British Columbia where federal and provincial party systems are very different. Rather, they were present in all parts of the country.

Subsequent national surveys show that the patterns of partisanship documented in the 1970s were perpetuated in the 1980s and 1990s.[7] Thus, panel surveys conducted in the 1980s consistently showed

Five :: Doing Politics Differently

Figure 5.2 Stability of Federal Party Identification,
National Inter-Election Panels, 1974-1993

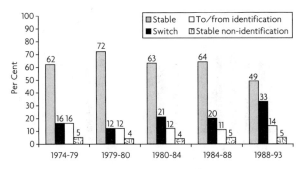

levels of partisan instability similar to those in the 1970s. Between 1984 and 1988, for example, 31 per cent either switched their federal party identifications or moved to or from being non-identifiers (see Figure 5.2). The comparable figures for the 1980-83, 1983-84, and 1988-90 panels were 30 per cent, 31 per cent, and 34 per cent, respectively. Indeed, there also was appreciable movement in partisanship over extremely short time intervals; 12 per cent changed parties and another 11 per cent moved to or from a party between the 1988 pre- and post-election surveys. Between 1988 and 1990, the percentage switching parties (22 per cent) was the highest for any two-wave panel conducted to that point in time, regardless of the duration of the interval between successive interviews. As Figure 5.2 illustrates, this was a harbinger of things to come—between the 1988 and 1993 federal elections, fully 33 per cent of those participating in the 1988-93 national panel survey switched their (federal) party identifications, and an additional 14 per cent switched from being a party identifier to being a non-identifier or vice versa. These numbers suggest that nearly one-half of the electorate changed their federal party identifications between the 1988 and 1993 elections. And, as we will demonstrate in Chapter Seven, these figures are not simply artifacts of "error" generated in the conduct of surveys or of the data that they produce.

Previous research using the panel components of the national election studies also has established that inconsistency in party identification[8] at the federal and provincial levels of government at a given point in time has significant effects on the subsequent strength and stability of identification at both levels (Clarke and Stewart,

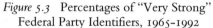

Figure 5.3 Percentages of "Very Strong"
Federal Party Identifiers, 1965-1992

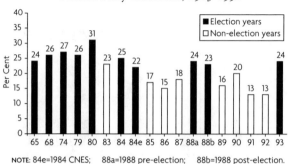

NOTE: 84e=1984 CNES;   88a=1988 pre-election;   88b=1988 post-election.

1987; Stewart and Clarke, 1997). As noted above, such inconsistency long has been a prominent feature of party identification in Canada. In 1974, for example, 64 per cent identified with the same party at both levels of government, but 30 per cent either identified with different federal and provincial parties or identified with a federal party but not a provincial one, or vice versa. As with partisan instability, the percentages of inconsistent partisans increased in the late 1980s and early 1990s. In 1993, 21 per cent identified with different federal and provincial parties, and an additional 10 per cent identified with a party at only one level of government.

Movements over time in the intensity of party identification also are apparent. In five national election studies carried out between 1965 and 1980, on average 27 per cent claimed that they were "very strong" identifiers, and in 14 surveys conducted between 1981 and 1993, an average of 20 per cent have done so (see Figure 5.3). Election mobilization effects are evident as well, with the percentage of very strong identifiers generally being higher in election-year surveys. Studies carried out in the interim between elections differ somewhat, however. In 1983, 23 per cent were very strong identifiers, but the figures for all subsequent non-election surveys are lower, falling to 13 per cent in 1991 and 1992. Similarly, the percentages of very strong identifiers in all but one (1965) of the 1965-80 election-year surveys were higher than those for five such surveys conducted in the 1981-93 period.

Taken together, these data document an erosion over time in the strength of federal party identification. We can investigate this possibility more rigorously using a trend analysis. For this purpose,

Five :: Doing Politics Differently

Figure 5.4 Percentages of Federal
Party Non-Identifiers, 1965-1993

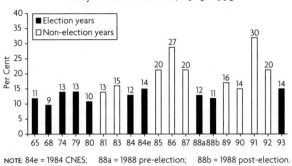

NOTE: 84e = 1984 CNES;   88a = 1988 pre-election;   88b = 1988 post-election.

we use data for the 1979-93 period, and regress the percentage of very strong identifiers on a constant, a linear trend term, and a dummy variable for election years.[9] This analysis reveals that, controlling for possible partisan mobilization effects generated by election campaigns, the percentage of very strong identifiers decreased by about two-thirds of a per cent (.66 per cent) each year between 1979 and 1993. This may not seem like a large effect, but cumulatively it can account for a 9-10 per cent decrease in the percentage of very strong identifiers over this time period. In addition, a significant, positive, election-year coefficient indicates that the percentage of very strong identifiers increased by approximately 6.6 per cent in election years.

The incidence of non-identification constitutes a second measure of the strength of partisanship across the electorate as a whole. Differences in the percentage of non-identifiers in the several election-year surveys are relatively small, with the minimum being 9 per cent in 1968 and the maximum 14 per cent in 1984 (CNES survey) and 1993 (Figure 5.4). Non-election year percentages tend to be larger (average = 19.4 per cent), with the incidence of non-identifiers being especially pronounced in 1986 (27 per cent) and 1991 (30 per cent). As with the analysis of very strong identifiers, we can determine whether the percentage of non-identifiers decreased over the 1979-93 period. Regressing the percentage of non-identifiers on a constant, a linear trend, and a dummy variable for election years shows that the trend variable has a positive (+.35), but statistically insignificant ($p > .05$) coefficient. This indicates that there was no systematic increase in the percentage of non-identifiers between

Figure 5.5   Federal Party Identification, 1965-1993

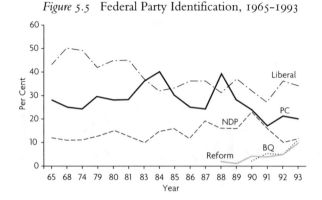

1979 and 1993. However, as anticipated, the elections matter, with the percentage of non-identifiers being nearly 7 per cent smaller in election years. Thus, at least through 1993, there is evidence that elections and campaign activities preceding them continued to mobilize partisan sentiments in the electorate.

Finally, we consider the *direction* of federal party identification to determine if there are negative trends in public support for one or both of the two parties, the Liberals and Progressive Conservatives, that historically have dominated the federal party system. In fact, patterns of partisan attachment to the two old-line parties have been quite different over the past three decades (see Figure 5.5). Between 1965 and 1981, the Liberal share of party identifiers never fell below 42 per cent, and averaged 46 per cent. However, between 1983 and 1993, the Liberal percentage has never exceeded 40 per cent and averaged only 33 per cent. Regarding the Conservatives, before 1983 their share averaged 27 per cent and varied in a narrow band (24-29 per cent). Then, between 1983 and 1993, it oscillated wildly, rising sharply in the two years in which the party won national elections (to 40 per cent in 1984 and to 39 per cent in 1988), and falling precipitously both in the period between these two contests, and in the aftermath of the latter. In 1991, the PC and the Liberal percentages fell to 17 per cent and 27 per cent, respectively. By 1993, the Liberal share of federal party identifiers had rebounded to 34 per cent. The Conservatives were far less fortunate—at the time of the 1993 election, only 20 per cent thought of themselves as Tory identifiers in federal politics.

Five :: Doing Politics Differently

As for other federal parties, since 1965 identification with the New Democratic Party generally has varied within a fairly narrow range (10-16 per cent). However, the party has enjoyed two sharp increases, with its percentage of identifiers swelling to 19 per cent in 1987, and then to 23 per cent shortly after its dramatic victory in the September 1990 Ontario provincial election. Neither gain was sustained, however. In both cases, the NDP share of federal party identifiers fell to 16 per cent a year later. The new Reform and the Bloc Québécois parties also enjoyed impressive growth spurts. These parties, neither of which existed prior to the late 1980s, claimed the combined support of 9 per cent of the electorate (Reform, 4 per cent; Bloc Québécois, 5 per cent) in 1991. By the time of the 1993 federal election, this figure had swelled to 21 per cent (Reform, 10 per cent; Bloc Québécois 11 per cent).

Quebec and the Prairies

As noted above, Quebec and the Prairies are the two regions where unhappiness with the federal party system has been most pronounced. Changes in Quebecers' partisan attachments played a major role in the overall erosion of Liberal strength in the 1980s. As late as 1981, nearly two-thirds of the Quebec electorate were federal Liberals (data not shown). Since then, the Liberal share has dropped sharply, such that by 1991—a year after the birth of the Bloc Québécois—only 22 per cent identified with the Liberals. In 1993, the Liberal share had increased—but not substantially—to 29 per cent. The erosion of Liberal identification in Quebec has not been accompanied by stable growth in support for the Conservatives or other federal parties. Although the number of PC identifiers surged in 1984 and 1988 (to 29 per cent and 37 per cent, respectively), in other years it has been consistently below 25 per cent. By 1991, the size of the PC cohort of identifiers had shrunk to 11 per cent. Two years later, the latter figure remained unchanged. The big news was the growth of support for dissident Bloc Québécois. In 1991, a year after the birth of the new party, 18 per cent of Quebecers claimed to be Bloc identifiers. By 1992, that figure had swelled to fully 42 per cent. Also noteworthy is the large number of Quebecers who do not identify with any federal party. Survey evidence indicates that the percentage of non-identifiers in Quebec has consistently exceeded that for any other province. Moreover, the incidence of non-identification in the province increased greatly after the early 1980s, such that in 1991 fully 43 per cent of Quebecers did not identify with any federal party, compared to 24 per cent in the rest of Canada. By 1993, the former percentage had eroded considerably (to 17 per cent), as large numbers of Quebecers rallied to the BQ.

Over the three decades leading up to the 1993 election, patterns of federal party identification in the Prairies were very different from those in Quebec. Perpetuating a story begun in the late 1950s, the Conservatives dominated for most of the period, and levels of non-identification closely approximated those for other parts of the country, other than Quebec. However, PC partisanship eroded considerably, if irregularly, after 1984. After the birth of the new Reform Party in the late 1980s, the number of Conservative identifiers went into freefall—dropping from 49 per cent in 1988 to 33 per cent in 1989, to 30 per cent in 1990 and to 26 per cent in 1991. When the 1993 election was held, only one Prairie voter in four was a PC identifier. Liberal support in the region also diminished in the late 1980s and early 1990s, with most of the decrease (from 23 per cent to 15 per cent) occurring in 1990-1991. Other parties gained strength, with Reform surging from 2 per cent in 1988 to 16 per cent in 1990, and then decreasing to 13 per cent in 1991. The New Democratic Party cohort increased from 15 per cent to 21 per cent. In 1993, partisanship in the Prairies was fragmented, with the percentages of Liberal, Reform, and NDP identifiers standing at 27 per cent, 25 per cent, and 13 per cent, respectively.

Viewed globally, the data on federal party identification over the past three decades portray an electorate that has experienced a "dealignment of degree." There was a downward trend in the percentage of strong identifiers and, while there was no consistent movement in the percentage of non-identifiers, the size of this group has varied widely and abruptly since the early 1980s. By 1993, only slightly over *one Canadian in 10* expressed a "very strong" identification with one of the federal parties, and nearly *one in three* did not identify with any of them. The erosion of federal partisanship was especially pronounced in Quebec where the electorate in 1993 was much more likely than other Canadians to reject *all* of the national parties. Partisan change had a directional component as well, with the Liberals suffering long-term losses in Quebec, the province that for decades was their major stronghold in federal politics. However, neither the Conservatives nor the NDP were able to make large, permanent gains at the Liberals expense in Quebec or elsewhere. Thus, by the time that the 1993 election was held, the context of electoral choice was conducive not only to the defeat of the governing Tories, but also to a more general revamping of the national party system.

THE TORIES (AND NDP) TROUNCED: THE 1993 FEDERAL ELECTION

Issues

Canada's economic distress made it a virtual certainty that the economy would dominate the issue agenda in the 1993 election. But the relative emphasis specific economic issues would receive was difficult to predict. Persistently high unemployment and the protracted recession were conspicuous problems, but the growing deficit had prompted widespread concern as well. The deficit, in turn, raised questions about the country's continuing ability to pay for highly popular social programs. Then, too, specific economic policies championed by Prime Minister Mulroney and his Tory colleagues, especially the free trade agreement and the goods and services tax (GST), seemed likely to play a role. In the event, the Liberals emphasized unemployment and the need to reinvigorate the staggering economy. However, they did not simply call for "jobs! jobs! jobs!" as the then opposition PCs had done in the last (1984) federal election held in the wake of serious recession. Instead, they adopted a strategy closely resembling that of the Democrats in the 1992 U.S. presidential election campaign. Like Bill Clinton, Liberal leader Jean Chrétien combined a cry of "it's the economy, stupid!" with an invitation to the electorate to "read my plan." His plan was outlined in a "Red Book"[10] that he carried with him on the campaign trail to demonstrate that he had the solution to joblessness and other economic ills vexing the electorate.

The economy also was central to the issue agenda pursued by the other old-line opposition party, the NDP. However, the NDP's credibility on economic issues, traditionally not its strong point, had been further eroded by its performance in Ontario, where it had become the government in September 1990, and appeared poised to realize its dream of national power (Whitehorn, 1994: 48). Unhappily for the party faithful, their dramatic victory in Ontario coincided with the onset of the recession. In trying to deal with the economic downturn, the Ontario NDP government led by Premier Bob Rae alienated a substantial proportion of both their traditional working-class supporters and the electorate more generally[11] by trying to be as conservative as the Conservatives on fiscal issues, while simultaneously pursuing what many voters considered a radical social policy agenda.

Regarding the two new parties, Reform attempted to attract disaffected voters in the West and elsewhere with its package of representational and direct democracy reforms. Also, consistent with its ideological proclivities, the party stressed deficit reduction and fiscal responsibility, and advocated cutbacks in expensive welfare programs that were portrayed as burdening hard-pressed taxpayers. As for the Bloc Québécois, it knew that it could attract hard-core *indépendantistes* without stressing the sovereignty issue. Nonetheless, the presence of an anti-system party in a national election seemed paradoxical, even in Quebec. Therefore, the party tried to broaden its support by appealing to frustrated pro-Canada Quebecers who might want to send Ottawa a message about their unhappiness with an unsatisfactory economic and political status quo.

The Conservatives, of course, faced a very difficult situation in establishing a credible issue agenda since they had been the government for nine years and many voters held them responsible for the country's economic woes and constitutional stalemate. If the PCs were to retain power, they somehow had to shift the blame and convince voters that they could manage the nation's affairs effectively. They tried to accomplish both goals with a leader-centred strategy premised on the assumption that the resignation of their massively unpopular leader, Brian Mulroney, would serve as a lightning rod for public discontent. His replacement, Kim Campbell, and her team were portrayed as a new generation of leaders, whose style and substance of governance differed from those of the old

Table 5.2 Most Important Issue and Party Closest, 1993 Federal Election

Issue	Most Important Issue*	Party Closest†						
		Lib.	PC	NDP	Ref.	BQ	Other	None
Deficit	21	20	24	3	**30**	6	1	6
Unemployment	34	**57**	6	7	9	6	1	14
Economy generally	23	**43**	13	3	15	9	1	16
Taxes	11	**41**	11	0	21	0	0	27
Free Trade Agreement	2	**39**	0	28	17	0	7	9
GST	•	**60**	3	0	10	0	0	27
Total Economic	*81*							
Health Care	2	**33**	2	26	21	0	7	12
Other social programs	1	33	12	**34**	6	0	2	12
Leadership	3	**51**	1	5	15	7	0	21
Change Government	2	**37**	2	12	18	4	4	24
Government accountability	3	**27**	11	6	**27**	3	9	17
National unity, Quebec independence	3	15	12	3	13	**43**	3	11
Other issues	9	**33**	7	12	21	7	5	14
None, don't know	7	—	—	—	—	—	—	—
Party closest (all issues)		**42**	12	7	18	8	2	11

* Multiple mentions, percentage of respondents mentioning issue.
† Horizontal percentages.   • less than .5 per cent
Note: Boldface numbers indicate party preferred by
majority or plurality of electorate on each issue.

"Mulroney crowd." However, once the election campaign began, it was far from clear what the new Tory chieftain proposed to do about the economic difficulties being stressed by her opponents and, when asked about the specifics of her policy agenda, Campbell stumbled. As the campaign progressed, the party's policy focus remained poorly defined, with deficit reduction eventually emerging as its primary theme.

Our 1993 national election survey data show that the contending parties emphasis on the economy was strongly reflected in the electorate's issue concerns. Fully 81 per cent of the respondents cited an economic issue as "most important,"[12] with no non-economic issue being mentioned by as many as 10 per cent (Table 5.2). Within the economic category, unemployment dominated—34 per cent mentioned joblessness, 21 per cent referred to the deficit, 11 per cent to taxes and 23 per cent to the economy generally. Although all the parties had emphasized the economy, the Liberals were clear winners on the issues. Overall, 42 per cent said the Liberals were closest to them on the issue they identified as the most important and, among persons selecting unemployment, fully 57 per cent chose the Liberals. No other party was seen as closest by as many as one-fifth of those interviewed. The Conservative issue rout was virtually total; overall, only 12 per cent preferred them on the issues. The PCs did best among people concerned about the deficit. However, even among this group, they were endorsed by merely 24 per cent, only 4 per cent more than favoured the Liberals on the issue and 6 per cent less than favoured Reform. The NDP fared poorly, too; it was seen as closest by a small plurality (34 per cent) of persons concerned with miscellaneous "other" social programs, but this group constituted a minuscule 1 per cent of the electorate.

Leaders

As noted in Chapter Three, Canadian parties' electioneering strategies typically emphasize the party leaders, with each party portraying its leader as having the "right stuff" to grapple with the issues that they have defined as pressing problems confronting the country. In 1993, all three old-line parties had new leaders. Before the campaign began, Jean Chrétien, a long-time cabinet minister in Liberal governments of the Trudeau era, was labelled a relic of the past by his opponents, who derided him as "yesterday's man." Given her gender and brief parliamentary tenure, this label certainly could not be applied to NDP leader Audrey McLaughlin. The new PC leader and recently installed Prime Minister, Kim Campbell, also was a "fresh face" and, as indicated above, PC strategists attempted to exploit this quality. In their attempt to deflect the electorate's wrath from their party, they advised Conservative candidates not to mention their party affiliation, but rather to represent themselves as members of the new Campbell team that would "do politics differently."

The strategy failed. Although the Conservatives moved up in the polls after Mulroney announced his impending departure in February

Five :: Doing Politics Differently

Table 5.3 Party Leader Images, 1988-1993 National Surveys

Party and Leader Affect Ratings*	1988	1990	1992 †	1992 ‡	1993 †	1993 ‡
Liberal	51	48	52		57	
Turner	44	—	—		—	
Chrétien	—	45	48		56	
PC	54	35	40		35	
Mulroney	50	28	33		24	
Campbell	—	—	—		39	
NDP	46	50	44		38	
Broadbent	54	—	—		—	
McLaughlin	—	49	44		43	
Reform	—	45	35	38	39	43
Manning	—	47	36	39	42	46
Bloc québécois[b]	—	—	—		28	59
Bouchard	—	—	—		35	56

Leader Character and Competence Ratings**		1988	1990	1992	1993 †	1993 ‡
Liberal						
Turner	Character	5.3	—	—	—	
	Competence	4.8	—	—	—	
Chrétien	Character	—	—	—	6.6	
	Competence	—	—	—	6.3	
PC						
Mulroney	Character	5.5	—	—	—	
	Competence	5.7	—	—	—	
Campbell	Character	—	—	—	5.6	
	Competence	—	—	—	4.2	
NDP						
Broadbent	Character	6.4	—	—	—	
	Competence	5.8	—	—	—	
McLaughlin	Character	—	—	—	6.5	
	Competence	—	—	—	5.1	
Reform[a]						
Manning	Character	—	—	—	5.6	5.8
	Competence	—	—	—	5.4	5.4
Bloc québécois[b]						
Bouchard	Character	—	—	—	4.9	6.7
	Competence	—	—	—	5.1	6.7

* Mean score on 100-point thermometer scale; ** Mean score on 10-point scale.
† Canada; ‡ Quebec only for Bouchard and BQ; Ontario, Prairies and British Columbia only for Manning and Reform.

1993, the selection of Campbell four months later provided only a small additional boost. Moreover, during the campaign Campbell was unable to establish an image as either an attractive or able leader—indeed, her average score on a 100-point thermometer scale was a dismal 39, the lowest of any leader other than BQ chieftain, Lucien Bouchard, whose nationwide rating (28) was far below his Quebec one (56) (see Table 5.3). Similarly, Campbell's scores on 10-point character and competence scales[13] were only 5.6 and 4.2, respectively. The latter score was the lowest for any leader in 1993, and lower than that accorded her predecessor, Mulroney, in 1988 (Table 5.3).

Campbell was not alone in her failure to strike a responsive chord with the voters. As in 1988, none of the party leaders was particularly well received in 1993. However, there were significant differences in public reactions to the Liberal leader, Jean Chrétien, and his counterparts. Chrétien's thermometer score (56) was fully 17 points higher than Campbell's, 14 points higher than Reform leader Preston Manning's, and 13 points greater than that for NDP leader Audrey McLaughlin (Table 5.3). Also, although Chrétien's character and competence ratings were hardly stellar (6.6 and 6.3, respectively), they still were higher than those of his rivals. Unlike his predecessor, John Turner, whose ratings had been lower than those of all other leaders in 1988, in 1993 Chrétien succeeded in establishing at least a *relatively* favourable public image.

Modelling the Vote

There is abundant evidence that party preferences on salient campaign issues and party leader images have significant effects on electoral choice. As in our analysis of voting behaviour in the 1988 federal election (see Chapter Two), thermometer scores were employed to summarize voters' feelings about the party leaders. Party-issue preferences were measured as the party closest on the most important election issue, with this variable weighted by the significance accorded the issue in the vote decision.[14] The 1993 vote models also included measures of federal and provincial party identifications. As observed above, sizable minorities of Canadians identify with different parties in federal and provincial politics, and party identifications at both levels of government can affect electoral choice at a particular level. Since earlier research has demonstrated that partisan attachments are influenced by voters' party preferences on the issues and their feelings about the party leaders (e.g., Archer, 1987), we employed 1990-93 panel data, measuring federal and provincial party identifications in the 1990 wave of interviewing.[15] The use of 1990 party identification measures thereby provided controls for long- and short-term forces acting earlier in time. In this regard, recall that by the autumn of 1990 public support for the governing PCs had been seriously eroded by the economic difficulties and constitutional crisis confronting the country.

Since the 1993 election was one in which two new parties were threatening to overturn the existing system, we included several additional variables to assess considerations that may have affected how voters reacted to the new parties. Two of these variables were factor scores that summarize party performance evaluations on the "governing-elections" and "participation-representation" dimensions that structure such evaluations. We hypothesized that people who negatively evaluated the existing party system along these dimensions would be more likely than those who made positive judgements to vote for one of the new parties. Given its manifest importance as a motivating force for BQ support, another variable measured attitudes towards Quebec independence.[16] Also, because the Liberals emerged during the campaign as the only party having a realistic chance of capturing a majority of seats, we included a "wasted vote" variable identifying voters who stated that they opted for an alternative party because their preferred one was seen to have no chance of winning.[17] It was anticipated that the Liberals would benefit from such perceptions; other parties, with the exception of the BQ whose *indépendantiste* platform made it a "unique option" for Quebec voters, would suffer from them. Finally, although voters' socio-demographic characteristics typically have weak relationships with electoral choice in Canada (see, e.g., Clarke and Stewart, 1992), the options presented by the two new parties may have magnified the influence of these characteristics. Thus, the models included measures of age, annual family income, gender, level of formal education, and region of residence.[18]

Since the dependent variables were dichotomies (e.g., vote PC, vote for other party), probit was chosen for estimation purposes.

Table 5.4   Probit Analyses of Voting in the 1993 Federal Election

	Vote				
	Liberal	PC	NDP	Reform[†]	BQ[‡]
Predictor Variables	*b*	*b*	*b*	*b*	*b*
Constant	-2.81◆	0.06	0.50	-0.74	-1.12
Region					
Atlantic	-0.28	0.20	0.81✚	-0.48	•
Quebec	-0.13	-0.60✚	-0.96	•	•
Prairies	-0.61◆	0.22	0.47	0.31	•
British Columbia	-0.33	-0.61▲	1.17◆	0.05	•
Age	0.01	0.01	-0.02▲	-0.00	-0.02
Education	0.01	-0.00	-0.02	-0.16▲	0.08
Gender	0.32✚	-0.16	-0.40▲	-0.14	0.20
Income	0.14◆	-0.06▲	-0.14✚	-0.09▲	0.07
Federal party identification, 1990	0.18◆	0.18◆	0.16✚	0.13▲	•
Provincial party identification, 1990	0.23◆	0.02	0.21✚	•	•
Party leader affect					
Chrétien	0.03◆	-0.01✚	-0.01▲	-0.01	-0.02▲
Campbell	-0.01	0.02◆	0.00	-0.01	-0.01
McLaughlin	0.00	-0.00	0.02◆	-0.01✚	-0.03▲
Manning	-0.01✚	-0.01	-0.01	0.04◆	0.01
Bouchard	-0.01✚	-0.01	-0.00	0.01▲	0.06◆
Party closest, most important issue	0.40◆	0.49◆	0.42◆	0.33◆	0.54◆
Quebec independence	-0.16▲	-0.19▲	-0.21	0.08	0.74✚
Wasted vote perceptions	1.34◆	-0.56✚	-1.31◆	-0.41▲	0.19
Evaluations of political parties					
Participation-representation	0.09	0.19▲	-0.01	-0.15▲	-0.18
Governing-elections	0.07	-0.00	0.03	-0.10	-0.06
McKelvey R^2 =	.82	.64	.73	.79	.93
% correctly classified =	88.2	92.4	96.1	91.1	95.6
Proportional reduction in error (λ) =	.71	.47	.58	.66	.91

◆ $p \leq .001$;   ✚ $p \leq .01$;   ▲ $p \leq .05$; one-tailed test.
† Quebec excluded; ‡ Quebec only; • variables not included in the analysis.

Five :: Doing Politics Differently

Overall, the models performed well. In every case, they correctly classified the behaviour of very large percentages of voters (range: 88.2–95.6 per cent), and the proportional improvements in correct classifications over what could be achieved without knowledge of the predictor variables were substantial (.47 to .91) (Table 5.4). The explanatory power of the models also was impressive, with estimated R^2 values varying from .64 to .93.

Many of the predictor variables behaved as hypothesized. Controlling for federal and provincial party identifications and several other variables, party preferences on the most important election issue had significant positive effects in all five analyses, as did feelings about the party leader whose party's vote is being analysed (Table 5.4). In several of the analyses, feelings about leaders of other parties had negative effects. Partisan attachments also had predictable influences; federal party identification consistently exerted significant effects, and provincial party identification did so in two of the three analyses (Liberal and NDP voting) where the measure is available.[19] Other variables were influential as well. As hypothesized, "wasted vote" perceptions positively affected Liberal voting and negatively affected PC, NDP, and Reform voting. Also as hypothesized, BQ voting was impervious to these effects, a finding consistent with the Bloc's singular appeal to separatist forces in Quebec and its status as a party having no chance of, or interest in, forming a national government. The party's *indépendantiste* appeal was evident in that favourable attitudes towards Quebec independence had the expected positive impact on BQ voting and negative ones on voting for the other three parties (Liberals, PC, NDP) that campaigned in the province. As for general evaluations of party performance, the participation-representation factor achieved significance in two cases—negative evaluations on the participation-representation dimension enhanced the likelihood of voting for Reform, and diminished the likelihood of voting PC. Finally, socio-demographic characteristics had significant effects but, similar to the results of analyses of voting behaviour in previous Canadian federal elections, their collective impact was quite modest.[20]

A Polity on the Edge

Party Leaders versus Economic Issues

After the Conservatives unprecedented debacle, Tory activists and media pundits were quick to blame their new leader for the rout. According to this account, Campbell's personality and style made her very unpopular, and this, together with her inexperience and clumsy performance on the campaign trail, precipitated the party's electoral disaster. The argument has *prima facie* plausibility; as noted, previous studies have demonstrated strong, if variable, leader effects on voting behaviour in a number of Canadian federal elections (e.g., Clarke et al., 1979, 1996). For example, in 1984 and 1988 negative images of Liberal leader John Turner were widespread and did much to dissuade voters from casting a Liberal ballot. Similarly, in an earlier era, Liberal leader Pierre Trudeau generated strong reactions (both positive and negative) in the minds of the electorate, and these reactions had important effects on voting behaviour More generally, the argument for a strong "Campbell effect" in 1993 is important because, if true, it suggests that the governing party's fate was largely determined by idiosyncratic factors associated with an ill-considered choice of a particular leader rather than by the deep-seated economic and constitutional difficulties that had bedevilled the governing PCs during virtually the entire period after their 1988 election victory.

Could a more warmly received new PC leader have offset the party's lack of issue appeal? We addressed this question by using the estimated coefficients in the multivariate model of PC voting to construct three scenarios in which Campbell's feeling thermometer score was increased from its actual level (39 points). In the first scenario, it was set at 50 points, the score attained by her predecessor, Brian Mulroney, in the previous (1988) federal election. In the second, it was raised to 56 points, the same as her Liberal rival, Jean Chrétien. In the third, it was boosted to the highest rating recorded by *any* party leader for which national survey data are available—the 68 points achieved by Liberal leader Pierre Trudeau in the "Trudeaumania" election of 1968. These alternative assumptions about Campbell's popularity were considered in conjunction with five increasingly pro-Conservative assumptions about party-issue preferences.[21] The probability that a voter would cast a PC ballot was computed for each of the resulting combinations of leader feelings

Five :: Doing Politics Differently

Table 5.5 Probabilities of Voting Conservative
in 1993 by Alternative Assumptions about Leader
Popularity and Party Preferences on Most Important Issue

| | Actual Popularity 39 | Assumptions about Leader Popularity If Campbell had been as popular as: | | |
		Mulroney in 1988 50	Chrétien in 1993 56	Trudeau in 1968 68
Assumptions about party-issue preference				
A. Actual party-issue preference in 1993	11	15	17	23
B. Favour other party and issue not very important	16	21	24	31
C. Neutral among parties or no important issue	31	37	41	49
D. Favour PCs and issue not very important	49	57	63	68
E. Favour PCs and issue very important	83	87	89	93

Note: Numbers in table are probabilities of voting Conservative in 1993,
given alternative assumptions about leader popularity and party-issue preferences.

and party-issue preferences. For these calculations, it was assumed that the voter resides in Ontario and is in other respects "average" (i.e., other variables were set at their mean values).

The scenarios reveal that enhanced leader popularity, by itself, would have done little to help the Conservatives. For example, given the actual distribution of party-issue preferences, if Campbell had been as well liked as her Liberal rival, Chrétien, the PC vote probability would have increased from only 11 per cent to 17 per cent (Table 5.5). Even if she had been as enthusiastically received as Trudeau had been a quarter-century earlier, the probability of voting for her party would still have been only 23 per cent. In sharp contrast, issues mattered a great deal in 1993. Regardless of feelings about their leader, favourable linkages between the PCs and the issue voters designated as most important produced large increases in the likelihood of a PC vote. For example, given Campbell's actual thermometer score (39), the probability of voting Conservative climbed from 11 per cent among persons with the average party-issue preference score to 83 per cent among those who preferred the

Tories on an issue deemed very important to their vote. If Campbell had been as well liked as her Liberal counterpart, Chrétien, the comparable increase is from 17 per cent to fully 89 per cent. Of course, the principal problem for the Conservatives was that, unlike 1988 when 44 per cent had preferred them on the most important election issue, only 12 per cent did so in 1993.

In sum, negative evaluations of highly salient economic issues, not simply poor judgment or bad luck in choosing an unpopular and inexperienced new leader, paved the way for the Conservatives' disastrous performance in 1993. Although Campbell's initially favourable reception in the pre-campaign period (Woolstencroft, 1994: 14) seemed to indicate that the Tories' leader-centred strategy might yield handsome dividends, the dynamics of the campaign served to forge her identity as the leader of a governing party that was widely seen as having mismanaged the country's economy and as having few remedies for fixing it. Despite the attempt to hide her party label, the prominence accorded party leaders as spokespersons for their parties in Canadian elections meant that the identification of Campbell in the minds of voters as the *PC leader* was inevitable. Ironically, the Conservatives' decision to place particularly heavy emphasis on their new leader reinforced this linkage. Campbell's vaguely defined rhetoric about "doing politics differently" appeared vacuous, given the economic malaise gripping the country. That vacuity, combined with her widely publicized gaffes when responding to reporters' questions about such salient issues as reducing unemployment and protecting the social safety net, suggested that the new Tory leader and her party did not have policies to remedy these pressing problems. These perceptions solidified as the campaign progressed and, as they did, support for Campbell and her party plummeted to the abysmal levels recorded prior to her predecessor's retirement announcement several months earlier.

Choices in and for Quebec

In 1993, the forces affecting electoral choice in Quebec were both similar and different from those at work elsewhere in the country. The analysis of BQ voting presented above (see Table 5.4) reveals that the Bloc vote was affected by a variety of factors, including voters'

Figure 5.6 Percentages of Voters Correctly Classified
by Various Predictor Variables, Quebec, 1993

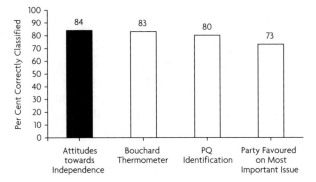

feelings about the party leaders, particularly Lucien Bouchard, and party preferences on salient election issues. Regarding the latter, the mix of *election* issues in Quebec was very similar to that elsewhere. Indeed, the percentage of persons mentioning an economic issue as "most important" was identical (81 per cent) to other areas of the country. Also, concerns about national unity, the constitution, and the threat to Canada posed by the BQ were only slightly more likely to be listed as important issues in Quebec (8 per cent) than elsewhere (2 per cent). However, it should not be inferred from these data that preferences about Quebec's future status inside or outside of the Canadian federation did not matter. On the contrary, pro-con attitudes concerning Quebec independence significantly influenced BQ voting over and above all other predictor variables in the vote model (Table 5.4). These effects were quite powerful. By itself, the independence variable was able to correctly classify fully 84 per cent of Quebecers as BQ/non-BQ voters (see Figure 5.6). Moreover, attitudes towards independence were strongly correlated with feelings about Bloc leader Lucien Bouchard, preferences for the BQ on the issue deemed most important in the election, as well as identification with the Parti Québécois in provincial politics. In turn, as Figure 5.6 illustrates, these variables were strong predictors of BQ voting. Electoral support for or opposition to the BQ thus was a product of a tightly integrated set of political orientations, among the most powerful of which were voters' attitudes towards Quebec's future relationship with the Canadian political community.

CONCLUSION: PARTISAN DEALIGNMENT, ELECTORAL CHOICE, AND PARTY-SYSTEM CHANGE

The disasters suffered by two old-line parties in the 1993 federal election forcefully demonstrate the volatility of Canadian voting behaviour. Substantial partisan dealignment means that rapid, thoroughgoing changes in the national and provincial party systems are ongoing possibilities. In this regard, the questions asked by political insiders and political scientists alike in the immediate aftermath of the 1993 election were whether the changes in the national party system occasioned by that contest were temporary, and whether the *status quo ante* would be restored. The questions continue to be debated. There are a number of reasons why we think that a return to the old system is unlikely. First, although partisan flexibility long has been a hallmark of public political psychology in Canada, individual partisan instability between the 1988 and 1993 elections reached the highest levels ever recorded. Indeed, only 49 per cent of people in our 1988-93 national panel survey identified with the same party they had five years earlier and fully one-third identified with another one (Figure 5.2). Second, we now have the benefit of hindsight—as will be discussed in Chapter Eight, the results of the 1997 federal election indicate that neither Reform nor the BQ is a one-election phenomenon. Third, the 1997 result re-emphasizes what was apparent in 1993, namely, that the new parties benefit greatly from having regionally concentrated bases of support. Although, as we will observe in our discussion of new political parties and their varied problems, a strong regional identification is hardly an unmitigated plus for a party like Reform that wishes to be recognized as a *national* party. However, in the short term, the combination of regionally concentrated voting strength and a single-member plurality electoral system has enabled both new parties to win large numbers of seats and thereby become major players in national politics. The BQ and Reform have been successful in part because they have been able to tap springs of generalized regional disaffection with the three old-line parties and Canadian political system more generally. These springs are likely to continue to flow in the foreseeable future and, hence, to present continued electoral opportunities for the new parties.

Five :: Doing Politics Differently

These considerations prompt us to suggest that the 1993 election can be characterized as a type of "critical" election. Unlike the classic critical elections described by V.O. Key (1955) where enduring shifts in the aggregate balance of party strength are accompanied by individual-level partisan realignment, the 1993 election was one where widespread partisan *dealignment* facilitated the destabilization of an existing party system. It worked powerfully to erode support for two of the parties by giving full play to a conjunction of long-standing regional and ethno-linguistic discontents, widespread unhappiness with the performance of the old-line parties, and protracted economic difficulties. *Pace* Key, the possibility that the 1993 election heralded a significant alteration in Canada's national party system does not require that the electorate currently is composed of persons with strong and stable party identifications aligned with politically relevant social cleavages. Rather, by electing large numbers of MPs to Parliament and simultaneously marginalizing two of the three old parties, the new parties fractured the long-standing "two-party-plus" system by legitimizing themselves as credible options in two historically disaffected regions where demands for more adequate representation in national politics have been loud and persistent. The new parties' continuing presence could make a genuine multi-party system an ongoing reality. Whether such a party system is long overdue and whether it is "good" or "bad" for Canada's effective governance are matters we will consider in the concluding chapter.

NOTES

1. See Irving (1959); Lipset (1968); Macpherson (1953); Pinard (1971); Quinn (1963); Stein (1973); Young (1969); Zakuta (1964).

2. The principal investigators for the 1965 study were Philip Converse, John Meisel, Maurice Pinard, Peter Regenstreif, and Mildred Schwartz. Meisel was the principal investigator for the 1968 study.

3. See, *inter alia*, Clarke et al. (1979, 1996); Clarke and Stewart (1987); Kornberg, Mishler, and Smith (1975); Lambert et al. (1987); LeDuc et al. (1984); Meisel (1975); Pammett (1987); Stewart and Clarke (1997).

4. An exception is the series of essays by Meisel (1975: ch. 5; 1991: chs. 15, 18) who argued that although Canada's parties remain important political institutions, the national party system is in a state of decay, and the parties are increasingly unable to perform major functions ascribed to them

by students of democratic government. According to Meisel (1991: 235), these functions are: "(1) the structuring of the vote; (2) the integration and mobilization of the mass public; (3) the recruitment of political leaders; (4) organize a government; (5) the formation of public policy; and (6) the aggregation of interests."

5. The goodness-of-fit statistic for the 1991 analysis is $\chi^2_{29} = 39.98$, p = .084. For 1993 the statistic is $\chi^2_{44} = 41.44$, p = .582.

6. See, e.g., Clarke et al. (1979: ch. 5; 1996: ch. 3); Clarke and Stewart (1987); LeDuc et al. (1984); MacDermid (1989); Stevenson (1987); Stewart and Clarke (1997).

7. Since the party identification questions were changed in the 1988 and 1993 CNES, we do not employ data generated by these questions.

8. The term "inconsistency" simply denotes that people do not identify with the same federal and provincial parties. As Blake (1982) has noted, such inconsistent partisan attachments may have a rational basis.

9. The variable is scored 1 for election years, and 0 for non-election years.

10. The "Red Book" was entitled *Creating Opportunity: The Liberal Plan for Canada*. The Liberals' economic plan and their campaign strategy are described by Clarkson (1994: 33-6).

11. When asked to rate their provincial government on a 100-point thermometer scale, the mean score for Ontario respondents in the 1993 post-election survey was a dismal 36 points, 11 points below the national average. The means for the other regions were: Atlantic provinces = 61, Quebec = 57, Prairie provinces = 55, British Columbia = 42. Similarly, the national NDP's thermometer score was lower in Ontario (36) than in any other region.

12. The question is: "In your opinion, what was the *most* important issue in the election?" (emphasis in original). Some respondents mentioned more than one issue, and a total of five issues were recorded.

13. The questions are: "Let's talk again about the national party leaders—using a scale from 1 to 10 with 1 being *very bad* and 10 being *very good*, how would you rate Kim Campbell's *overall performance* as prime minister? And how would you rate Kim Campbell's *honesty and ethics*?" (emphasis in original). Similar questions were asked about each of the four opposition party leaders.

14. The scoring of the issue variable depends on which party's vote is being analysed. For example, in the PC case, voters selecting the PCs as closest on the most important election issue are scored 1, those selecting another party, -1, and those selecting no party or saying there was no important issue, 0. These scores are weighted by multiplying them by a variable assessing the perceived importance of the issue in the vote decision. The latter variable is scored: "very important" = 3; "fairly important" = 2; "not very important," "no important issue," or "don't know" = 1. The resulting index varies from +3 to -3.

15. The construction of the federal and provincial party identification variables depends on which party's vote is being analysed. For example, in the PC vote analysis, the measures of federal and provincial party identification are scored: very strong PC = +3, fairly strong PC = +2, weak or leaning PC = +1, non-identifier = 0, weak or leaning other party = -1, fairly strong other party = -2, very strong other party = -3.

16. The question is: "Some people think that Quebec might separate from the rest of Canada and become an independent country. Are you in favour of Quebec separating or opposed to it?" Responses are scored: "in favour," +1; "opposed," -1; "don't know," 0.

17. Respondents were asked: "When you were making up your mind to vote, did you *really prefer another party*, but decide against it because you thought it had *no chance of winning*?" (emphasis in original). Positive responses (13 per cent) are scored 1; negative responses (87 per cent) are scored 0. Note that we are not arguing that voting behaviour affected by "wasted vote" considerations conforms to the (stringent) requirements for strategic voting in rational choice theory; see Johnston et al. (1992: 198).

18. Age is measured in years; annual family income has nine categories ranging from $10,000 or less = 1, to $80,000 or more = 9; gender is women = 1, men = 0; formal education is elementary or less = 1, some secondary = 2, completed secondary or technical, community college = 3, some university = 4, completed university (B.A., B.Sc., or more) = 5. Region is a set of four dummy variables with Ontario as the reference category.

19. Reform and the BQ do not compete in provincial politics and thus measures of provincial party identification are not available for these parties.

20. Probit analyses using socio-demographic variables as the only predictors illustrate the weakness of these variables for explaining electoral choice. In these analyses, the McKelvey R^2 statistics average .19 and range from .05 (PC) to .34 (NDP).

21. Values for the party-issue preference variable are: (a) -1.5, the actual average PC score on the party-issue preference variable; (b) -1, a voter favoured another party on the most important issue, but it was not very important for the vote; (c) 0, a voter did not believe any issue was important; (d) +1, a voter preferred the PC on the most important issue, but that issue was not very important to the vote; (e) +3, a voter favoured the PC on the most important issue and it was deemed very important to the vote.

SIX

To the Brink

The future of Canada was "on the line" on the evening of October 30, 1995. When the ballots in the Quebec sovereignty referendum were counted, the electorate had "chosen Canada"—but just barely. As we observed at the beginning of this book, for the second time in less than two decades Quebecers had rejected a separatist Parti Québécois government's sovereignty-association proposal. But, unlike 1980 when such a proposal had been defeated by a solid three-to-two count, in 1995 the "*nons*" exceeded the "*ouis*" by only 52,000 votes (50.6 per cent vs. 49.4 per cent). More than any other event in recent history, the extraordinarily narrow margin of victory for the federalist forces in the 1995 sovereignty referendum dramatized that Quebecers support for Canada's national political regime and community remained highly problematic as the twentieth century drew to a close. This chapter analyses factors that influenced voting behaviour in the referendum and the impact on the event on public opinion in Quebec and the rest of the country.

The significance of a study of the 1995 sovereignty referendum transcends the Canadian case. The extent to which institutional devices such as referendums help to resolve or, possibly, exacerbate pressing problems confronting contemporary democracies is an important topic. As noted in Chapter Four, referendums are being used with increasing frequency to decide fundamental political questions in democracies, new and old alike. Referendums are interventions in the political life of a democracy that can influence public and élite beliefs, attitudes, and opinions, and reshape political discourse and behaviour. The 1995 referendum not only had the ability to influence all of these things, it also had the potential to reconfigure the structure of a national political system and the community of which it is a part.

We begin this chapter by articulating theoretical perspectives that help us to explain voting behaviour in an event such as Quebec's 1995 sovereignty referendum. After providing an overview of the referendum campaign and the contextual forces at work as Quebecers cast their ballots, we present data on political beliefs, attitudes, and opinions that may have influenced voters' referendum choices. Multivariate statistical techniques are employed to analyse how these various factors affected voting behaviour. The results of these analyses are used to construct scenarios to gauge the strength of factors that could have altered voting behaviour and the referendum outcome. Then, public reactions in Quebec and the rest of Canada to that outcome are assessed, and we consider what the 1995 sovereignty referendum tells us about the utility of such procedures for resolving fundamental political issues confronting Canada and other democratic political systems.

POLITICAL SUPPORT IN CANADA AND OTHER DEMOCRACIES

Recall that in Chapter One we argued that political support may be usefully conceptualized as an affective orientation (a feeling of like or dislike) towards political objects and processes. The affect can be positive, neutral, or negative, and the objects of support can range from the concrete and well-defined to the highly abstract and amorphous. Democratic theory distinguishes among support for political authorities, regimes, and communities (e.g., Easton, 1965; Mayo, 1960). Research has demonstrated that these distinctions resonate in the public mind; Canadians distinguish support for authorities from support for regime and community, and support at the three levels varies in intensity and stability (Kornberg and Clarke, 1992: ch. 4). It is highest and most stable for the national political community, lower and less stable for major regime institutions, such as Parliament, the civil service, and the judiciary, and lowest and most volatile for top-level political authorities. In Canada, support at all three levels is dynamic and interrelated, the dominant flow being upward: from authorities, to regime, to community.

Six :: To the Brink

What are the sources of political support? We contend that, although often viewed as competing and incompatible theoretical alternatives, the political culture and political economy perspectives both are required to provide a satisfactory explanation of citizen political support (Kornberg and Clarke, 1992: ch. 1; see also Clarke, Dutt, and Kornberg, 1993). Specifically, support has its origins in people's political socialization experiences broadly defined, as well as their instrumental judgements about the impact the political system and its various components has on them and others. In turn, both of these two sources of political support have two principal components. These components are individual and socio-political group identities and democratic norms and values in the case of socialization experiences, and evaluations of the effective and equitable/fair operation of government in the case of performance judgements. Effectiveness and equity/fairness evaluations are not made in the abstract, divorced from other elements of political psychology, but rather are grounded in fundamental political cultural beliefs and values that are products of socialization. Some of these beliefs and values may be widely shared by members of a political community. However, others may vary across important population subgroups, such as those defined by region, ethnicity, language, and social class. These latter beliefs and values help to generate and reinforce politically relevant societal cleavages, and contribute to inter-group conflicts that can have significant consequences for the integrity of political systems.

Widespread citizen support is crucial for the maintenance of democracies because their system-legitimatizing ideologies expressly circumscribe the frequency and severity of the coercive measures that governments may employ to secure public compliance with their authoritative edicts. This is not to say that the use of coercive measures is unknown in democracies (e.g., Schwartz, 1983). Such measures may be invoked not only to enforce the discharge of routine obligations of citizenship, such as the payment of taxes, but also to ensure the provision of valued personal services, such as serving in the armed forces in wartime. Normally, however, democratic governments depend largely on voluntary compliance rather than upon coercion to secure even the latter kinds of services. Consequently, a democracy is necessarily at serious risk when a significant number of citizens, especially if they are regionally concentrated, decide for whatever reasons that they no longer want to support an existing political system.

In present-day mature democracies, rival political orders based on the principles of communism, fascism, or traditional authoritarianism have lost their appeal. Democracy and political legitimacy have become virtually synonymous. Thus, the risk to the continued existence of a democratic polity increases substantially when a dissident group can plausibly argue that an alternative political regime and community will be *more democratic* than a current one. Institutional configurations are relevant as well. Although designed to accommodate diversity and defuse conflict, a decentralized federal system such as Canada's provides the institutional basis for political disintegration, and control of a sub-national (state, provincial) government provides separatist groups with important opportunities to further their objectives (e.g., McRoberts, 1988; Russell, 1992; Schwartz, 1974). In the Canadian case, when the separatist Parti Québécois recaptured power in the September 1994 Quebec provincial election, Premier Jacques Parizeau and his Péquiste colleagues quickly proceeded to implement a plan for a referendum on Quebec sovereignty. According to the PQ's analysis, victory in such a contest would both legitimize their efforts to make Quebec an independent state and catalyse the process by which that goal could be achieved.

It bears emphasis that a referendum is not held in a political vacuum. Rather, powerful contextual forces are at work. When a governing party frames the referendum question and then campaigns vigorously to secure its adoption, while one or more opposition parties work equally strenuously to defeat the proposal, a referendum inevitably takes on many of the characteristics of a national or sub-national *election*. Like an election, a referendum's outcome can be significantly influenced by public reactions to the politicians and parties supporting and opposing the referendum's passage (see Brulé, 1992; Clarke and Kornberg, 1994; Franklin, Marsh, and McLaren, 1994; Pettersen, Jenssen, and Listhaug, 1996; Pierce, Valen, and Listhaug, 1993; van der Eijk and Franklin, 1996: ch. 21). In the 1995 Quebec case, Bloc Québécois leader Lucien Bouchard was more effective and more warmly received than his Parti Québécois ally, Premier Jacques Parizeau. The prospects of a "oui" majority were markedly enhanced when Bouchard took an active role in the campaign and then assumed leadership of the sovereignty forces. Similarly, it is conceivable that the referendum's outcome might have been very different if the federalist forces had been led by someone other than Prime Minister Chrétien. The prime minister was disliked and distrusted by many Quebecers because they believed he had reneged on the federal government's promise during the 1980 sovereignty referendum to give Quebec a "renewed federalism" in exchange for a vote to stay in Canada. Recognizing his unpopularity, Chrétien and his advisers adopted a strategy of "strict silence" that ultimately gave way to veiled and then naked threats when it became clear that a "oui" majority was a distinct possibility. These strategic choices did much to establish the campaign context in which voters made their choices.

Other factors, some of which are seemingly only tangentially related to the decision at hand, also can have important effects on voting behaviour in referendums. In 1995 Canada was emerging from a serious, prolonged recession. As we have shown in previous chapters, judgements about the economy and the federal government's handling of it had turned markedly negative during the early 1990s, and positive assessments remained in short supply afterwards.[1] As the referendum campaign began, the slow and painful economic recovery encouraged voters to discount the claims of Prime Minister Chrétien and Finance Minister Paul Martin Jr. that Quebec's continued membership in the Canadian political community made economic good sense. The ability of Chrétien, Martin, and their colleagues to convince voters that staying in Canada was worthwhile was hindered further by their decision to make major cutbacks in several popular social programs, after explicitly promising during the 1993 federal election that they would mend the country's frayed social safety net (Clarkson, 1994). Instrumental arguments that Canada merited Quebecers' continued support thus were much less compelling *circa* 1995 than they had been at the time of the first sovereignty referendum 15 years earlier.

CHOICES IN CONTEXT

In Chapter One, we observed that historically French Canadian nationalism has been driven by two goals: independence and

A Polity on the Edge

economic security (Cook, 1995: 106-07). These goals are potentially in conflict, and attempts to achieve them have been characterized by caution and ambiguity. A primary example is the first (May 20, 1980) sovereignty-association referendum in which the Parti Québécois tried to convince Quebecers that they could have both political independence *and* an economic association with the rest of Canada (ROC). By attempting to frame the choice Quebecers faced in this way, the Parti Québécois was adhering to an *étapiste* (step-by-step) strategy designed to ally the fears of Quebec voters and dispel doubts concerning the wisdom of the *souveraineté* option (McRoberts, 1988: ch. 9). Fifteen years later, the PQ again adopted a "you can have your cake and eat it too" approach. As in 1980, the question posed to the electorate was crafted so that it did not specify what the province's future relationship with Canada would be should Quebec achieve sovereignty. The ambiguity of the question was enhanced by making heroic assumptions concerning voters' knowledge of the enabling legislation that had been passed in the Quebec National Assembly preparatory to the referendum.[2] If nothing else, the text of the question: "Do you agree that Quebec should become sovereign, after having made a formal offer to Canada for a new Economic and Political Partnership, within the scope of the Bill respecting the Future of Quebec and of the agreement signed on June 12, 1995?" indicated that a provincial government could be as creatively ambiguous in crafting a proposal requiring a very concrete response as a federal one had been three years earlier.

However, it can be argued that the wording of the referendum question was ultimately inconsequential for a sizable segment of the electorate. For voters in this group, *any* sovereignty referendum was viewed as posing a choice between future membership in one of two alternative political communities—Canada *or* Quebec. The referendum thus involved a choice between competing political identities. One's perception of oneself as Canadian or Québécois was what mattered. Viewed in this light, the decision was an easy one for that minority of Francophone Quebecers who were passionately in favour of sovereignty because they believed that the full development of their identity as Québécois required that Quebec become an independent state. Similarly, the choice was not problematic for the overwhelming majority of non-Francophones.

Six :: To the Brink

They viewed themselves as *Canadians* first and foremost, and to remain so, Quebec had to remain an integral part of Canada.

But, there were many other voters. A substantial number of Francophones and a smaller number of Anglophones would find the decision to vote *"oui"* or *"non"* most difficult. For some of these people, this was because they loved Canada and Quebec equally well. For others, it was because the decision was an affair of the "mind" not the "heart," and their ballots would be cast on the basis of forecasts concerning their relative individual and collective well-being in a united Canada or a sovereign Quebec. When making these forecasts, Quebecers were operating in a context in which information about the economic, cultural, and political consequences of a *"oui"* or *"non"* vote was necessarily incomplete. As was intended, the wording of the referendum question was ambiguous enough for a person intending to vote *"oui"* to assume that a deal could be struck that would enable a sovereign Quebec to maintain its ties with Canada. Other than disparaging traditional "profitable federalism" arguments that it made economic good sense for Quebec to remain part of Canada, PQ leaders and their allies were careful not to discourage voters from believing that they might be able to have their own country and still enjoy the benefits of being a part of Canada.

As the campaign progressed, proponents and opponents of the proposal tried to fill the information gap with messages that were threatening, reassuring, or both. As noted above, the initially low levels of support for sovereignty in public opinion polls encouraged Prime Minister Jean Chrétien and other federal government officials to adopt a "strict silence" strategy. However, support for sovereignty began to increase in the late summer when leaders of the principal pro-sovereignty groups united behind the Bloc Québécois' Lucien Bouchard (Figure 6.1). Some analysts joined federalist spin doctors in discounting polls showing support for sovereignty was surging. The claim was advanced that many of those who stated that they "didn't know" or refused to say how they would vote were, in fact, hidden federalists. But, even if one assumed that two-thirds of the "don't knows" and "refusals" in the polls would vote "no," there was clearly a strong upward trend in the percentage of sovereignty supporters (Figure 6.2). In early September, declared support for sovereignty reached the mid-40 per cent range, and the possibility

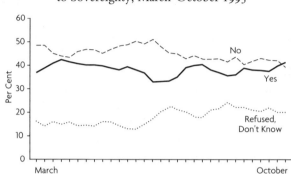

Figure 6.1   Support for and Opposition
to Sovereignty, March–October 1995

that a majority of Quebecers actually would vote *"oui"* could no longer be dismissed.

Ottawa reacted to the ominous trends in the polls by pushing the panic button. Federal government officials issued an increasingly aggressive series of warnings concerning the dire consequences of a *"oui"* vote. In a parliamentary speech in late September, Prime Minister Chrétien joined the chorus by warning Quebec that he would not allow Canada to be shattered by a narrow *"oui"* majority on an ambiguous question. This was followed by a "no more Mr. Nice Guy" speech by Finance Minister Martin who proclaimed that Canada would not enter into any economic partnership with a sovereign Quebec. Martin stated that Quebecers would be treated as "foreigners" if they opted for sovereignty. The finance minister emphasized his point by adding that once they had left Canada, Quebecers would be no different than Costa Ricans as far as Ottawa was concerned. Other federal government spokespersons let it be known that the economic and political costs of a *"oui"* vote would be heavy indeed. Quebec would have to pay its share of the national debt, and Quebecers would no longer enjoy the benefits of Canada's generous social programs. They also would lose their Canadian passports and the protection of Canada's armed forces, forfeit their right to participate in national politics and federal elections. It was even possible that the federal government would dismember Quebec and force it to surrender a large portion of its vast northern territory to the province's strongly pro-Canada Aboriginal population.

In the closing days of the campaign, when it became apparent that threats had not stemmed the pro-sovereignty tide, Chrétien

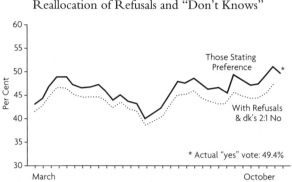

Figure 6.2 Support for Sovereignty with and without
Reallocation of Refusals and "Don't Knows"

went on national television and begged Quebecers not to destroy
Canada by taking what would be an irrevocable step. During the
last weekend before the vote the prime minister's appeal was echoed
by Canadians across the country. Thousands of people poured into
Montreal to stage a massive rally to demonstrate their affection
and respect for Quebecers and their heartfelt desire for Quebec
to remain a part of Canada. Reacting to the significance of the
issue about to be decided and the unrelenting barrage of claims
and counterclaims to which they were subjected, an overwhelming
majority (93.5 per cent) of the electorate went to the polls to decide
the future of Quebec and Canada.

THE DETERMINANTS OF REFERENDUM VOTING

Pre- and post-referendum surveys of the Quebec electorate were
conducted to generate data on factors that affected voting in
the referendum (see Appendix). Survey respondents were asked a
wide variety of questions pertinent to the theoretical perspectives
articulated above. One set of questions focused on satisfaction
with the operation of democracy in Canada and beliefs concerning
whether a sovereign Quebec would be more or less democratic than
a united Canada. One hundred-point thermometer scales were used
to measure support for Canada, Quebec, the federal and provincial
governments, and political leaders and parties. Other questions
ascertained whether people thought of themselves as Canadians
first, as Quebecers first, or whether they identified equally with

both communities. Respondents also were asked to evaluate the effectiveness of the federal government in several policy areas, to judge the equity/fairness of the operation of Canada's political system and society, and to agree or disagree with statements concerning some of the principal positive and negative consequences that were expected to flow from either the passage or defeat of the referendum question. Another battery of agree/disagree statements focused on positive and negative consequences that might ensue if Quebec actually became a sovereign state. Since the reactions of people in all parts of the country to the sovereignty referendum and its outcome would be important for Canada's future, we also conducted pre- and post-referendum surveys among representative samples of non-Quebecers. By posing the same questions to Quebecers and persons in the rest of Canada, we are able to compare the beliefs, attitudes, and opinions of the two groups in the pre- and post-referendum periods.

Pas Comme Les Autres

The data on community identifications and support simply and forcefully demonstrate why Quebec separatism threatens the integrity of the Canadian polity. As Figure 6.3 shows, *circa* 1995 there were massive differences between Quebecers and other Canadians in their community self-identifications. When asked if they generally thought of themselves as Canadians or as Quebecers, Albertans, Ontarians, and so forth, overwhelming majorities in all regions other than Quebec chose "Canadian," and only very small minorities chose a provincial identity. However, in Quebec, only 31 per cent stated "Canadian," whereas a majority (53 per cent) said "Quebecer." As Figure 6.3 also shows, this response pattern is a result of the identifications of Quebec Francophones; nearly three-fifths of this group chose "Quebecer," whereas only one-quarter chose "Canadian." Francophones' tendency to identify with Quebec rather than Canada is strongly correlated with age; among those under 25, fully 75 per cent identified themselves as Quebecers and only 15 per cent as Canadians, whereas among those 66 and older, the comparable percentages are 32 per cent and 44 per cent, respectively (data not shown). In sharp contrast, a strong

Six :: To the Brink

Figure 6.3 Identification with Canada or Province
by Region, 1995 Pre-Referendum Survey

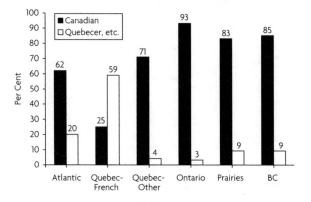

pro-Canada bias is evident in the identities of non-Francophone
Quebecers of all ages. Overall, 71 per cent of non-Francophones
considered themselves to be Canadians and only 4 per cent, to
be Quebecers.

Feeling thermometer data echo these patterns. When asked to
rate their feelings about "Canada in general" on a 100-point like-
dislike scale, average scores among respondents in every region
except Quebec were very high, ranging from a low of 80 for Prairie
residents to a high of 85 among Ontarians. However, the average
in Quebec was much lower (62) and, again, there were very large
differences between Francophones and other Quebecers and by age
cohort within the former group. Among Francophones, the average
thermometer score for Canada was only 57 points and it varied from
a low of 51 among the 18-24 age group to a high of 66 among those
the two oldest age brackets (57-65, and 66 and over). However,
among non-Francophones, the overall mean was fully 80 points, and
no age group had an average score less than 78.

These patterns are not unique to our 1995 data. Rather,
as Figure 6.4 documents, differences in feelings about Canada
between Quebec Francophones, on the one hand, and Quebec
non-Francophones and persons in the rest of Canada, on the other,
have been a persistent feature of the public mind at least since the
mid-1970s.[3] Among all three groups feelings of warmth towards
Canada have fluctuated over time, being higher in (federal) election
years than in non-election ones. However, they declined markedly

163

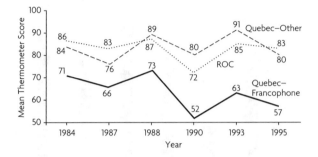

Figure 6.4 Average Thermometer Scores for Canada in
Quebec and the Rest of Canada, 1984-1995 National Surveys

among Francophones at the time of the failure of the Meech
Lake Constitutional Accord in 1990, with regression analyses (not
shown) indicating that, controlling election-year effects, the Meech
Lake debacle was associated with a sizable (9.4 point), permanent
decrease in affect for Canada among Francophones. Although the
Accord's demise did not permanently influence the feelings of
non-Francophones, average levels of support for Canada were
considerably lower among both groups (by 12 and 14 points,
respectively) in 1995 than at the time of the first sovereignty
referendum in 1980.

Francophone and non-Francophone Quebecers also differed in
their feelings about national political institutions such as Parliament,
the civil service, and judiciary. Although Canadians outside of
Quebec have great affection for their country, surveys conducted
over the past two decades document that their feelings about key
institutions of the national political regime are markedly more
reserved (Kornberg and Clarke, 1992: chs. 4, 5). This also is true in
Quebec. Nonetheless, the 1995 surveys revealed that Francophones
had lower levels of affect for the national political regime than
did other Quebecers who, in turn, resembled Canadians living
elsewhere in the country (data not shown). In addition, the two
groups of Quebecers differed in their evaluations of the effectiveness
of the federal government in several important policy areas, and in
their judgements of the overall equity/fairness of Canada's political
system and society. Although both groups tended to be very
critical, Francophones were more negatively disposed than were
other Quebecers. Again, the two groups differed in their summary

Six :: To the Brink

Table 6.1   Average Thermometer Scores for
Federal Political Institutions and Federal and Provincial
Parties and Politicians, 1995 Pre-Referendum Survey

	All Quebecers	Francophone Quebecers	Non-Francophone Quebecers	Rest of Canada
Federal Political Institutions				
Parliament	44	42	57	54
Civil Service	45	43	55	50
Judiciary	53	52	57	51
Federal Politicians				
Jean Chrétien	43	39	68	66
Lucien Bouchard	58	64	27	23
Quebec Provincial Politicians				
Daniel Johnson	43	40	61	•
Jacques Parizeau	44	48	19	•
Mario Dumont	52	56	31	•
Federal Parties				
Liberal Party	48	45	65	60
Bloc Québécois	55	60	26	18
Quebec Provincial Parties				
Parti Québécois	52	57	26	•
Liberal Party	48	45	61	•
Action Démocratique du Québec	48	52	30	•

• question not asked in rest of Canada

appraisals of Canada's performance as a democracy—only 13 per cent of Francophones, as compared to 31 per cent of non-Francophones stated that they were "very satisfied," whereas 25 per cent of the former but 17 per cent of the latter said that they were either "not very" or "not at all" satisfied with "the way democracy works in Canada."

Massive differences between Francophones and other Quebecers were evident at the political authorities level. Considering federal authorities, Table 6.1 indicates that the average scores accorded Prime Minister Chrétien and the governing federal Liberal Party were only 39 and 45 points, respectively, by Francophones, but fully 68 and 65 points, respectively, by non-Francophones. The

A Polity on the Edge

Table 6.2 Assessments of the Consequences of
Alternative Referendum Outcomes, Francophone and
Non-Francophone Quebecers, 1995 Pre-Referendum Survey

	Agree (%)		Disagree (%)	
	Francophone	Other	Francophone	Other
If the referendum proposal passes				
1. The federal goverment will accept Quebec's decision and negotiate an agreement that will lead to a politically sovereign Quebec.	65	31	26	54
2. Businesses will leave Quebec and a lot of people will lose their jobs.	29	86	67	11
3. Aboriginal Peoples, like the Cree and Inuit, will try to take control of a large part of Quebec.	33	71	58	21
4. The federal government will enter into an economic partnership with a politically sovereign Quebec.	71	30	21	60
5. The value of the Canadian dollar will decline sharply.	44	85	48	13
6. Nothing will be settled because the federal government won't accept Quebec's decision.	33	47	60	40
7. The language and culture of Anglophone Quebecers will eventually disappear.	10	38	86	57

pattern was reversed for provincial authorities—the average scores for Premier Jacques Parizeau and the Parti Québécois were 48 and 57 by Francophones, but merely 19 and 26 by non-Francophones. Differences of similar magnitudes existed for the Bloc Québécois and the provincial Liberal parties and their leaders. Francophones were much more positive about the BQ than the Liberals, whereas non-Francophones were much more warmly disposed towards the latter party than the former one.

Table 6.2 continued

	Agree (%)		Disagree (%)	
	Francophone	Other	Francophone	Other
If the referendum proposal is defeated, a "non" vote...				
1. will strengthen the Quebec economy.	28	56	66	34
2. will end uncertainty about the constitution.	26	22	67	69
3. will mean that Québécois language and culture will eventually disappear.	27	4	69	96
4. will mean that Quebec will lose its bargaining power to get a new constitutional deal with the rest of Canada.	39	16	55	81
5. will protect the jobs and economic opportunities of Quebecers.	37	73	59	15
6. will mean that Quebec will lose a lot of political influence in the federal system.	42	14	54	86
7. will mean the Québécois nation will be humiliated in the eyes of the world.	27	9	70	87

Note: "Don't know" responses used to calculate percentages, but not shown in table.

Assessing Alternative Referendum Outcomes

The survey data clearly indicate that Quebecers were deeply divided on a range of fundamental political orientations that may have significantly influenced their voting behaviour in the sovereignty referendum. However important, these orientations were not the only forces at work as voters prepared to go to the polls. Some of these forces reflect uncertainty concerning what would happen if the referendum proposal passed or failed. This uncertainty was heightened during the referendum campaign as federalist and separatist spokespersons painted starkly different pictures of the future of Quebec should its electorate endorse the PQ's independence option. To ascertain voters' assessments of the possible positive and negative consequences of *"oui"* and *"non"* outcomes, we asked survey respondents if they "agreed" or "disagreed" with two batteries of statements about what might occur should the referendum pass or be defeated. Because passage of the referendum did not necessarily mean that Quebec would become sovereign, a second battery of agree-disagree statements were used to ascertain voters' views about what would happen if sovereignty became a reality.

If the Referendum Had Passed?

Responses to these questions revealed that Francophones were much more likely than non-Francophones to reject the idea that a *"oui"* vote would have deleterious political and economic consequences. For example, 65 per cent of Francophones but only 31 per cent of non-Francophones believed that the federal government would accept a *"oui"* verdict and proceed to negotiate sovereignty, and fully 75 per cent of the former group but only 30 per cent of the latter one thought that the federal government would be willing to enter into an economic agreement as part of a sovereignty deal (Table 6.2). Similarly, minorities of Francophones, but large majorities on non-Francophones thought that a *"oui"* vote would cause businesses to flee Quebec, that Aboriginal peoples would try to seize large sections of the province, and that the value of the dollar would decline sharply. Forecast consequences of a *"non"* vote were very different among the two groups. Non-Francophones were much more likely than Francophones to believe that rejection of the referendum proposal would strengthen Quebec's economy and protect jobs. Non-Francophones also were much less apt to think that a *"non"* vote would cause Quebec to lose it bargaining power to get a new constitutional deal, or lose its power in the federal system.

If Quebec Became Sovereign?

With the exception of identically large majorities (74 per cent) believing that the federal government would make a sovereign

Six :: To the Brink

Table 6.3 Assessments of the Consequences
of Sovereignty for Quebec, Francophone and
Non-Francophone Quebecers, 1995 Pre-Referendum Survey

	Agree (%)		Disagree (%)	
	Francophone	*Other*	*Francophone*	*Other*
1. Quebecers will lose their access to Canada's important social programs, like health care and unemployment insurance.	30	76	62	13
2. For the first time Quebec will take its rightful place in the community of nations.	69	24	26	66
3. The federal government will make a sovereign Quebec pay a big share of Canada's national debt.	74	74	22	17
4. Culture and the arts will flourish in a sovereign Quebec.	68	29	25	58
5. There will be more jobs and economic opportunities for all Quebecers.	36	8	56	90
6. Québécois will finally become "*Maître chéz nous.*"	69	47	28	51
7. Minorities will lose their protection under the constitutional Charter of Rights and Freedoms.	18	55	76	32
8. Canada will refuse to let Quebec join NAFTA, the North American Free Trade Agreement.	31	43	59	48
9. The Canadian Armed Forces will no longer protect Quebec.	49	66	41	24
10. Quebec will continue to elect members to the House of Commons.	23	12	67	80
11. Quebecers will lose their rights to Canadian citizenship and a Canadian passport.	51	80	41	14
12. Quebec will continue to use the Canadian dollar.	63	27	27	60

Note: "Don't know" responses used to calculate
percentages, but not shown in table.

Quebec pay its share of the national debt, substantial differences between the two groups also were apparent in their responses to the battery of questions about the consequences of sovereignty. Francophones were consistently, and by large margins in several instances, prone to "accentuate the positive" and to "discount the negative." On the positive side, large majorities of Francophones (upwards of 70 per cent) but decided minorities of non-Francophones (less than 30 per cent) agreed that sovereignty would enable Quebec to take its rightful place in the community of nations, that culture and the arts would flourish in a sovereign Quebec, and that a sovereign Quebec could continue to use the Canadian dollar (see Table 6.3). On the negative side, Francophones were much less likely than non-Francophones to worry that minorities would lose constitutional protection in a sovereign Quebec, that Quebecers would lose access to social programs, that Quebecers would lose their Canadian passports and citizenship, or that Canada would refuse to let an independent Quebec join NAFTA. Many of those in the Francophone majority thus believed that a *"oui"* vote, sovereignty, and eventual independence would have desirable cultural, economic, and political consequences. For such people, "the bloom was definitely off the rose" of profitable federalism.

Attitudes towards Constitutional Options

Consistent with the above interpretation, widespread dissatisfaction with existing federal arrangements is evident in responses to a battery of statements soliciting attitudes towards constitutional options for Quebec. Table 6.4 shows that fully two-thirds of Francophones viewed the constitutional status quo unfavourably, and overwhelming majorities endorsed changes involving either the devolution of power to all provinces or an asymmetric federalism that accorded some form of "special status" to Quebec. Moreover, fully seven in ten favoured sovereignty for Quebec if it involved continuing economic and political association with the rest of Canada, and a majority, albeit a small one (53 per cent), favoured outright independence. Although these latter two options were rejected by huge majorities of non-Francophones, the size of the Francophone majority was such that 63 per cent of the entire electorate endorsed

Table 6.4   Attitudes towards Various
Constitutional Options, 1995 Pre-Referendum Survey

Constitutional Options	very favourable	somewhat favourable	somewhat unfavourable	very unfavourable
Status Quo				
Francophones	12	22	25	42
Non-Francophones	31	34	22	14
All Quebecers	14	24	25	37
More Power, All Provinces				
Francophones	45	45	8	3
Non-Francophones	28	48	10	15
All Quebecers	42	45	8	5
Special Status for Quebec				
Francophones	44	35	11	10
Non-Francophones	13	25	27	36
All Quebecers	39	34	14	14
Sovereignty With Association				
Francophones	44	27	11	18
Non-Francophones	11	11	16	62
All Quebecers	39	24	12	25
Full Independence				
Francophones	33	20	14	33
Non-Francophones	3	4	6	87
All Quebecers	28	18	13	42

Note: Horizontal percentages

sovereignty with association, and a near majority (46 per cent) were favourably disposed to full independence. It is noteworthy that these attitudes contrast sharply to those expressed in a survey conducted at the time of the 1980 sovereignty referendum. At that time, 47 per cent favoured sovereignty and only 25 per cent endorsed independence (Pammett et al., 1983). Clearly, many Francophone Quebecers had shed their inhibitions about the consequences of leaving Canada when they cast their ballots in the 1995 referendum. In the next section, we examine the constellation of forces affecting their decisions on that day.

Analysing the Vote

When specifying a model of referendum voting, we hypothesized that support for the national political community and regime, and identification with Canada or Quebec as a political community would weigh heavily in people's decisions.[4] Further, consonant with our theoretical perspective that political support has its origins in political socialization experiences, on the one hand, and instrumental judgments about the impact of the political system, on the other, we included several socio-demographic variables to proxy the former and two summary variables to index the latter. Socio-demographic variables include language (Francophone, non-Francophone), age group, education, gender, and income.[5] Summary evaluative variables tap judgements about the federal government's effectiveness in several policy areas and the equitable/fair performance of Canada's political system and society.[6] Two variables measuring perceptions of the democratic character of Canada and a sovereign Quebec also are included in our model of the vote. These variables are satisfaction with the operation of democracy in Canada and judgements whether a sovereign Quebec would be more democratic than a united Canada.[7] Five other variables in the model summarized perceived "upside" and "downside" consequences of the referendum proposal passing or failing and Quebec becoming sovereign.[8] Finally, because referendums, even ones on issues that go to the heart of a country's continued survival, can assume characteristics of "normal" elections, we included measures of voters' feelings about the federal and provincial party leaders of the "*oui*" and "*non*" forces.[9] Since the dependent variable is a dichotomy (voted "*non*" = 0, voted "*oui*" = 1), binary probit analysis is used for estimation purposes. The analysis is conducted using the pre-post referendum panel data, with all variables except the vote being measured in the pre-referendum survey.

Consistent with expectations, a large majority of the predictor variables in the model are statistically significant and properly signed (see Table 6.5). As anticipated, low levels of support for the national political community, identification with Quebec rather than Canada, membership in the Francophone language community, and being in a younger age cohort all were positively associated with a "*oui*" vote. Negative evaluations of Canada as a democracy, and the belief that an independent Quebec would be more democratic than a united Canada also were positively related to a *"oui"* vote. Assessments of the possible costs and benefits of a *"oui"* versus a *"non"* vote and the possibility of sovereignty were significant as well—Quebecers who discounted the risks of sovereignty were more like to vote *"oui"*. So, too, were persons who had a high regard for Bouchard and Parizeau, the leaders of the sovereignty forces. In contrast, positive feelings about the champions of a united Canada, Chrétien and Johnson, enhanced the likelihood of a *"non"* vote. Although negative evaluations of federal government performance in various policy areas prompted a *"oui"* vote, neither support for major institutions of the national political regime (the federal Parliament, civil service, judiciary) nor judgements about the fair and equitable operation of the national political system and Canadian society had significant direct effects on the vote. That they did not, one might argue, is profoundly ironic since for more than 60 years Canadian political élites—national and provincial—have allocated enormous time, energy, and public resources to fine-tuning the institutional and procedural machinery of the political system with the aim of building support for the national political community (see, e.g., Russell, 1992).

Since an overwhelming majority of non-Francophones cast a *"non"* ballot, while Francophones were divided in their referendum choices, we replicated the probit analyses for persons in the latter group. The results echo those just reported—among Francophones, a *"oui"* vote was positively associated with factors such as community-level feelings and identifications, judgements about the democratic character of Canada and a sovereign Quebec, and assessments of the possible risks of a *"oui"* vote (see Table 6.5). Once again, however, controlling for all of these factors, authorities-level feelings mattered; people who were positively disposed towards the leaders of the sovereignty campaign and negatively disposed to their federalist adversaries tended to vote "yes." Viewed more generally, the explanatory power of the full and Francophone-only models is impressive—for both analyses, the estimated R^2 is .94, and fully 96 per cent of the votes are correctly classified.

Table 6.5   Probit Analysis of Voting in
the 1995 Quebec Sovereignty Referendum

Predictor Variables	All Quebecers			Francophones Only		
	b	*s.e.*	*t*	*b*	*s.e.*	*t*
Age cohort:						
18-24	1.52	.56	2.71◆	1.59	.57	2.78◆
25-33	1.03	.51	2.04✚	0.94	.51	1.82✚
34-47	0.64	.50	1.28	0.74	.52	1.42▲
48-56	1.18	.57	2.09✚	1.26	.58	2.18✚
57-65	0.09	.59	0.15	0.08	.59	0.13
Education	0.21	.14	1.56▲	0.23	.14	1.66✚
Gender	− 0.08	.27	− 0.31	− 0.25	.28	− 0.88
Language (French vs. Other)	1.11	.53	2.10✚	•	•	•
Annual family income	− 0.05	.06	− 0.80	− 0.07	.06	− 1.17
Canadian-Quebecer identity	− 0.18	.10	− 1.83✚	− 0.18	.10	− 1.79✚
National community support	− 0.03	.01	− 3.07◆	− 0.03	.01	− 2.79◆
Federal govt. performance	− 0.11	.05	− 2.18✚	− 0.11	.05	− 2.14✚
Equity/fairness	− 0.06	.08	− 0.71	− 0.05	.08	− 0.55
National regime support	− 0.01	.01	− 0.43	− 0.01	.01	− 0.80
Democratic performance	− 0.39	.22	− 1.75✚	− 0.37	.23	− 1.59▲
Quebec vs. Canada democracy	0.62	.26	2.38◆	0.64	.27	2.37◆
Positive consequences of *"oui"*						
vote and sovereignty	0.78	.19	4.05◆	0.75	.20	3.84◆
Negative consequences of *"oui"*						
vote and sovereignty: (1)	− 0.39	.18	− 2.16✚	− 0.37	.18	− 2.04✚
(2)	− 0.45	.16	− 2.85◆	− 0.48	.16	− 3.00◆
Positive consequences						
of *"non"* vote	− 0.59	.17	− 3.56◆	− 0.61	.17	− 3.62◆
Negative consequences						
of *"non"* vote	0.38	.17	2.18✚	0.48	.18	2.65◆
Party leaders:						
Chrétien and Johnson	− 0.03	.01	− 2.71◆	− 0.03	.01	− 2.87◆
Bouchard and Parizeau	0.04	.01	4.25◆	0.04	.01	4.30◆
Constant	0.66	1.18	0.56	2.03	1.12	1.81✚
McKelvey R^2 =	.95			.94		
% correctly classified =	96.3			96.2		
Proportional reduction in error (λ) =	.91			.89		

◆ $p \leq .01$;   ✚ $p \leq .05$;   ▲ $p \leq .10$; one-tailed test.
• variable not included in analysis

Party Leader Affect, Risks of Sovereignty, and Referendum Voting

We contend that the political context within which a referendum occurs can be very consequential, regardless of the nature of the proposal being considered. One aspect of that context concerns voters' images of the politicians who are the principal advocates for and against the proposal. Results of the multivariate analyses are consistent with this claim; net of all other considerations, feelings about the party leaders who directed the federalist and sovereignty campaigns significantly influenced the probability of voting *"oui."* But, how strong were these party leader effects? To answer this question we constructed scenarios in which we varied the values of the leader variables while setting other variables in the model at their mean values. Since a very large majority of non-Francophones voted *"non,"* while Francophones were divided, we focused our attention on forces affecting the behaviour of the latter group.

These scenarios indicate that, *ceteris paribus*, voters' feelings about party leaders significantly affected the probability of casting a *"oui"* ballot. For example, initially an "average" Québécois has a .66 probability of voting *"oui."* However, if separatist leader, Premier Jacques Parizeau, whose thermometer rating was a very mediocre 48 points, had been as well liked as his predecessor, René Lévesque, had been in 1980 (61 points), the probability of a *"oui"* vote climbs to .75. Given the extremely close division of the ballots, this increase would have been sufficient to change the referendum result. In contrast, if feelings about Parizeau are held constant, but feelings about the even more unpopular Jean Chrétien (39 points) are raised to a level enjoyed by former Prime Minister Pierre Trudeau, in 1980 (68 points), the probability of a *"oui"* vote falls to only .48. In such a case, the referendum proposal would have been defeated by a much wider margin. The importance of feelings about the party leaders also is suggested by a scenario involving Bloc Québécois leader Lucien Bouchard. If Bouchard, who was well liked by Francophones (64 points), had been as unpopular as his separatist colleague, Parizeau, the probability of a *"oui"* vote would have fallen by 12 points (from .66 to .54) and, once again, the margin of defeat of the sovereignty forces would have been greater. A more general analysis in which the probability of a *"oui"* vote is calculated for all possible combinations of party leader thermometer

Figure 6.5   Probabilities of a "Yes" Vote: Two Scenarios

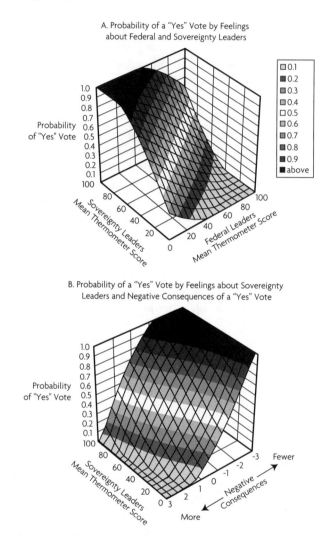

A. Probability of a "Yes" Vote by Feelings
about Federal and Sovereignty Leaders

B. Probability of a "Yes" Vote by Feelings about Sovereignty
Leaders and Negative Consequences of a "Yes" Vote

scores also suggests that public feelings about the leaders mattered. The probability surface depicted in Figure 6.5A has a pronounced "northwest to southeast" tilt, thereby indicating that feelings about both federalist and sovereignty leaders significantly affected the likelihood of voting "*oui*."

These assessments of the influence of feelings about party leaders assume all other factors are held constant. However, other significant factors also are contextually conditioned and, hence, we are interested in observing how variations in them influenced leader effects. Judgements about the positive/negative consequences of a *"oui"* or *"non"* vote and sovereignty are particularly important. Recall that voters were making their decisions in a context in which Canada was slowly emerging from a long and painful recession and a newly elected Liberal federal government headed by Prime Minister Chrétien had made deep cuts in highly popular social programs. Above, we have argued that this political-economic environment had considerable potential to diminish the force of "profitable federalism" arguments concerning the desirability of Quebec's continuing membership in the Canadian federation. In turn, changed views of the instrumental value of federalism would alter Quebecers risk assessments of the consequences of voting *"oui"* or *"non."*

Our scenarios indicate that, in fact, risk assessments were powerful determinants of the vote. Consider a situation in which voters had become more positive about the consequences that would occur if the referendum passed, and more negative about the consequences that would ensue if it failed. Increasing the two variables that measure these assessments by one-half a standard deviation and then by one full standard deviation increases the probabilities of a *"oui"* vote from .66 to .85 and to .95, respectively. If voters perceived greater dangers if the referendum passed and sovereignty followed, and fewer negatives if the referendum failed, the effects were substantial as well. In this latter scenario, a one-half standard deviation decrease in the variables measuring these assessments reduces the probability of a *"oui"* vote from .66 to .40, and a one standard deviation decrease reduces it to only .17.

However, as powerful as risk assessments are, they do not obviate the effects of feelings about the contending party leaders. A scenario in which the thermometer scores for the sovereignty leaders are manipulated in combination with negative assessments of the referendum passing illustrates this point. The probability surface depicted in Figure 6.5B shows that when voters made either very many or very few negative assessments (i.e., the assessment variables are set at more than *two* standard deviations above or below their means), feelings about leaders matter little. In such situations, voters are overwhelmingly likely to cast *"non"* or *"oui"* ballots, respectively. But, leader effects become increasingly significant when risk assessments are more balanced. For example, for voters whose scores on the variables measuring negative consequences of the referendum passing and positive consequences of it failing are raised by one-half a standard deviation, the probability of a *"oui"* vote falls from .66 to .40. However, if feelings about PQ leader Jacques Parizeau (48 points) rise to the level of feelings about René Lévesque in 1980 (61 points), the probability climbs to .50. Such an increase would have been enough to alter the outcome and, quite possibly, the country's future.

RETHINKING CANADA? THE IMPACT OF THE REFERENDUM

Since the results of the vote revealed that the country was teetering on the edge of a "political abyss," one might hypothesize that the referendum catalysed significant changes in the political beliefs, attitudes, and opinions of Quebecers and other Canadians. The hypothesis is plausible, but it is not supported by the data. As Table 6.6 shows, among Francophone and other Quebecers attitudes towards both sovereignty with continuing political and economic ties to Canada and full independence were virtually the same after the referendum as they were before it. In fact, among the former group, sovereignty with association was slightly more popular in the post-referendum survey (67 per cent vs. 63 per cent), and favourable attitudes towards full independence were virtually unchanged (45 per cent vs. 46 per cent). In the rest of Canada (ROC) opposition to both of these options was massive both before and after the referendum.

Attitudes towards other constitutional options also were quite stable. Although the referendum dramatized the possibility of "losing Quebec," a large majority (70 per cent) of Canadians in other provinces continued to endorse the constitutional status quo, and only a small minority (19 per cent) approved of an asymmetric constitutional solution that would give special status to Quebec. Even an amorphous, symbolic asymmetry embodied in recognition of Quebec as a "distinct society" was endorsed by only a minority (47 per cent) of those in the ROC. Indeed, the only type of constitutional change to receive majority support outside of Quebec was a general devolution of power to all provinces, and even this

Table 6.6   Percentages of Quebecers and Other Canadians Favouring*
Various Constitutional Options, 1995 Pre- and Post-Referendum Surveys

	Pre-Referendum	*Post-Referendum*
A. Quebecers		
Status Quo		
Francophones	34	17
Non-Francophones	65	45
All Quebecers	38	19
More Power, All Provinces		
Francophones	90	89
Non-Francophones	76	76
All Quebecers	87	87
Special Status for Quebec		
Francophones	79	79
Non-Francophones	38	51
All Quebecers	73	74
Sovereignty with Association		
Francophones	71	75
Non-Francophones	22	22
All Quebecers	63	67
Full Independence		
Francophones	53	53
Non-Francophones	7	6
All Quebecers	46	45
Recognize Quebec as Distinct Society		
Francophones	•	86
Non-Francophones	•	69
All Quebecers	•	84
B. Canadians in Other Provinces		
Status Quo	79	70
More Power All Provinces	55	59
Special Status for Quebec	16	19
Sovereignty With Association	12	13
Full Independence	34	26
Recognize Quebec as Distinct Society	•	47

*   Percentages include those "very" and "somewhat" favourable;
•   Question not asked in pre-referendum survey

option gained only 4 per cent in approval (from 55 per cent to 59 per cent) across the pre- and post-referendum surveys. If there was a lesson to be learned from the referendum about the necessity of constitutional change to preserve the country, people in English-speaking Canada did not grasp it. "No special deals for Quebec" remained the watchword of public attitudes in the ROC.

In Quebec, the referendum's effects on public attitudes towards constitutional alternatives were manifested primarily in an increased propensity to reject the status quo. The percentages of Francophones and non-Francophones endorsing this option decreased from 34 per cent to 17 per cent and from 65 per cent to 45 per cent, respectively. Special status for Quebec increased in popularity (from 38 per cent to 51 per cent) among non-Francophones, while remaining overwhelmingly popular (at 79 per cent) among Francophones. Large majorities of both groups also endorsed more power for all provinces, and many non-Francophones (69 per cent) joined an overwhelming majority of Francophones (86 per cent) in calling for recognition of Quebec as a distinct society. In sharp contrast, sovereignty association and independence continued to divide the electorate very deeply. Fully 75 per cent of Francophones, but only 22 per cent of non-Francophones favoured sovereignty for Quebec with continued association with Canada, and 53 per cent of the former group but only 6 per cent of the latter one favoured full independence.

In Quebec and elsewhere the referendum also had little impact on public support for Canada, major institutions of the national political regime, and federal and provincial political authorities. There is no evidence in the ROC of any rally effect whereby people increased their political support for the national political community, regime, and authorities because of the threat to the integrity of the country posed by the referendum and the strength of the sovereignty forces demonstrated in the balloting. Thus, the mean thermometer scores for Canada, the federal parliament, and Prime Minister Chrétien in the pre- and post-referendum ROC panel surveys were 84, 53, and 66 versus 84, 56, and 66, respectively. Similarly, the average thermometer score accorded Quebec by ROC respondents in the post-referendum survey was a lukewarm 56 points, only 3 points above that recorded in the pre-referendum survey.

In Quebec, the only noteworthy change concerned feelings about Lucien Bouchard. Consistent with the idea that Bouchard demonstrated a personal appeal in the referendum campaign that transcended his advocacy of the sovereignty option, his thermometer scores increased by nearly 10 points among non-Francophones and Francophones voting *"non,"* while remaining extremely high among Francophones voting *"oui."* More important, however, there is no indication of sizable pre-post referendum change in feelings of any of these groups towards the national political community, regime, and authorities. After the referendum Quebec remained what it was before the balloting—a province deeply divided in a country deeply divided.

CONCLUSION: REFERENDUMS AND THE POLITICS OF COMMUNITY CHOICE

After the sovereignty referendum ballots were counted, the leaders of the federalist and sovereignty forces offered very different interpretations of the process and the result. In Prime Minister Chrétien's view "[t]he people have spoken, and it is time to accept that verdict." In sharp contrast, Quebec Premier Parizeau concluded that "the battle for the country is not over. And it will not be until we have won" (Wilson-Smith, 1995). In making these statements, both Chrétien and Parizeau strongly contradicted the spirit of positions they had taken before they knew the result of the referendum. Recall that Chrétien had explicitly stated that he would *not* accept a narrow *"oui"* majority as legitimating efforts by the Quebec government to negotiate sovereignty. However, *post factum*, a narrow *"non"* majority was very different—according to the prime minister, it was sufficient warrant to declare a decisive, democratically based victory for the federalists. If Chrétien's political logic seemed to involve a blatantly biased view of the referendum decision-making process, so did that of his pro-sovereignty adversary. After all, Premier Parizeau was the principal proponent of the referendum, and he had steadfastly maintained that a *"oui"* vote would provide a public mandate for his government to negotiate Quebec's independence. But, one might ask, if a *"oui"* majority—however slim—in a referendum constituted public endorsement of the premier's cherished sovereignty project, why did a *"non"* vote not signify its rejection of that project? The subtext of the premier's post-referendum declaration was clear—the legitimacy of the referendum process hinged on the result it produced.

The contradictions between Chrétien's and Parizeau's pre- and post-referendum rhetoric vividly illustrate the limits of referendums as devices for deciding community-level disputes, when conflicts are structured by deep and reinforcing socio-political cleavages. In situations where contending groups have fundamentally different views of the composition of a desired political community, referendums are more likely to demonstrate divisions than to create consensus. The 1995 Quebec sovereignty referendum dramatized the depth of the former and failed utterly to forge the latter. As shown above, there virtually was no convergence whatsoever in the constitutional positions of Francophone Quebecers, non-Francophone Quebecers, and other Canadians in the aftermath of the referendum. Indeed, the referendum and reactions to its outcome may have actually widened the chasm between federalists and souverainistes. When a bitterly disappointed Jacques Parizeau commented that a *"oui"* majority had been frustrated by a combination of "money and the ethnic vote," he heightened tensions between Francophones and other Quebecers, while undercutting the claims of souverainistes that the democratic *bona fides* of their movement were superior to those of the federalists. Rather than being open and inclusive, the *"maître chéz nous"* democracy advocated by the sovereignty forces suddenly appeared closed and ethnocentric. For their part, federalist élites did little to alleviate the fears they deliberately generated among voters during the referendum campaign. In the months after the referendum, there were continuing media reports of a so-called "Plan B" whereby the federal government would take draconian measures to keep Quebec from becoming independent should a future sovereignty referendum yield a *"oui"* majority.

Some would claim that such a majority is not only possible, it is inevitable. After all, the 1995 proposal failed by only a faction of one per cent, and the age gradient in public identification with and support for the national political community is such that the most strongly pro-Canada voters are found in the oldest age cohort. As these persons pass from the electoral stage, they will be replaced by younger voters, most of whom favour sovereignty. We will explore such "demographics of sovereignty" scenarios in greater detail in Chapter Nine, but their bottom line is very pessimistic for pro-Canada advocates—a "*oui*" majority is inevitable in the long run. The possibility of a "*oui*" majority in a future referendum also is suggested by the fact that a quarter of those in our post-referendum survey who reported voting "*non*" acknowledged that at some point during the campaign they had considered voting "*oui*." If even a small fraction of them had actually done so, the referendum proposal would have passed.

On the other hand, the survey data also indicate that precisely the same proportion (25 per cent) of those reporting voting "*oui*" said that they had considered voting "*non*." Further, fully 35 per cent of the "*oui*" voters also stated that their primary reason for doing so was to "send a message" to the federal government and, presumably, the rest of Canada. Rather than trying to break up the Canadian political system, they were trying to use the opportunity provided by the referendum to change it. These data caution that the inevitability of Quebec's departure after *any* future sovereignty referendum may be too easy an assumption. Much depends on when a referendum is held and the context in which in which the balloting occurs. As will be discussed in Chapter Nine, the large age-related differences in support for sovereignty suggest that, *ceteris paribus*, the possibility of a "*oui*" majority is increasing from year to year. However, as we have shown in this chapter, the *ceteris paribus* assumption is a strong one—at any particular point in time, referendum voting is driven by a mix of long- and short-term forces.

Regarding the latter, recall that, net of all other factors, public assessments of the risks associated with a "*oui*" or a "*non*" vote and eventual sovereignty strongly influenced voters' decisions. Evaluations of governmental performance and voters' feelings about and images of the politicians who were leading the federalist and sovereignty forces also exerted significant effects. Such risk assessments, government performance evaluations, and party leader orientations are subject to the influence of various contextual factors including the state of the national and provincial economies, and the dynamics of the referendum campaign. Despite the fundamental questions being addressed, referendums assume some of the characteristics of federal or provincial elections, and short-term forces can be very important. The concatenation of several of these short-term forces favoured a "*oui*" vote in 1995. Whether they would do so in a future referendum is unknown. But in the long run, this may not matter because demographic forces may produce an electorate in which short-term pro-Canada forces of any reasonably conceivable magnitude cannot offset long-term pro-sovereignty trends produced by processes of demographic replacement. In Chapter Nine we will consider the possible evolution of such a pro-sovereignty electorate.

Viewed more generally, it should be kept in mind that referendums are departures, albeit temporary ones, from the process of representative government that is the hallmark of mature democracies such as Canada. Proponents of the greater use of referendums in such political systems argue that by having the people rather than the politicians decide, referendums can resolve otherwise intractable issues. However, it bears re-emphasis that the Canadian experience strongly suggests that the issue-resolution capacities of referendums should not be overestimated. Although some observers claimed that the resounding "no" vote in the 1992 national referendum on constitutional reform ended "the era of mega constitutional politics" (Russell, 1993), the 1995 Quebec sovereignty referendum dramatically demonstrated the continuing reality of the country's crisis of integration. Nor did the decision of Quebecers, twice within 15 years, to vote "*non*" on sovereignty end the debate on the future of Quebec and Canada. In the wake of the 1995 referendum, the Quebec electorate remained closely divided on the sovereignty issue, and the question continued to occupy the hearts and minds and to absorb the creative energy of Quebecers and other Canadians alike.

NOTES

1. For example, in the pre-referendum survey, 66 per cent of Quebecers judged the national economy was doing "not very well," and 55 per cent believed that the federal government was doing a "poor" or "very poor" job in managing it. Nor were Quebecers optimistic about the future; only 14 per cent anticipated that the economy would get better over the next year or so, and only 23 per cent thought that their personal financial situation would improve.

2. Although a copy of the bill was sent to all households, how many voters actually read it is unknown. The contents of the bill are described in Young (1998: 276-78).

3. The 1974, 1979, and 1980 data are from the Canadian National Election surveys; the 1983-93 data are from the Political Support in Canada surveys.

4. National community support was measured as a respondent's feelings "in general about Canada" as recorded on a 100-point thermometer scale. National regime support was the respondent's mean thermometer score for feelings about the parliament in Ottawa, the civil service in Ottawa, and the judiciary. To measure identification with Canada or province, respondents were asked: "Do you generally think of yourself as a Canadian, a Quebecer, or what?" with the order of the terms "Canadian" and "Quebecer" being rotated in random half-samples. Respondents were then asked: "How strongly [Canadian/Quebecer] do you feel, very strongly, fairly strongly, or not very strongly?" Responses to the two questions were combined to yield a scale running from very strong Canadian (+2) to very strong Quebecer (-2).

5. The socio-demographic variables are: (i) age—five age cohorts corresponding to important periods in post-World War II Quebec political history are constructed. The age categories (in years) are: 18-24, 25-33, 34-47, 48-56, 57-65, 66 and older; (ii) annual family income—an 11-category variable ranging from under $10,000 per year (scored 1) to over $100,000 per year (scored 11). Missing data were recoded to the median category (5); (iii) education—elementary school or less (scored 1), some secondary (scored 2), completed secondary and/or community college (scored 3), some college or university (scored 4), completed college or university (B.A., B.Sc. or more) (scored 5); (iv) gender—men were coded 1; women, 2; (v) language—using responses to a question about language usually spoken at home, Francophones were scored 1, and Anglophones and others, 0.

6. To measure evaluations of federal government performance, respondents were asked to indicate "how well the federal government is doing" in 10 policy areas. Responses were scored "very well = 2, "fairly well" = 1, "not very well" or "don't know" = 0, and summed to produce a federal government performance index ranging from 0 to 20. Equity-fairness judgements were measured using an additive index (range: 0-8) based on responses to eight "agree-disagree" statements concerning the operation of Canada's political and social systems. Responses indicating the respondent believed the systems were operating equitably/fairly were scored 1, and other responses were scored 0.

7. Answers to the question regarding the performance of Canada as a democracy were scored: "very satisfied" = 4, "fairly satisfied" = 3, "not very satisfied" = 2, "not at all satisfied" = 1. "Don't knows" were recoded to the median ("fairly satisfied") category. Regarding democracy in Quebec, respondents were asked if a sovereign Quebec would be more or less democratic than a Quebec that is part of Canada. "More democratic" responses are scored +1, "less democratic" responses, -1, and "no difference," "it depends" and "don't know" ones, 0.

8. An exploratory factor analysis (varimax rotation) yielded five factors that collectively explained 51.5 per cent of the variance in the 26 items on the perceived consequences of "*oui*" and "*non*" majorities in the referendum and Quebec sovereignty (see Tables 2 and 3). Factor one structured positive consequences of a "*oui*" majority and sovereignty; factor two, negative consequences of a "*oui*" majority and sovereignty; factor three, negative consequences of a "*non*" majority; factor four, positive consequences of a "*non*" majority; factor five, a second factor capturing negative consequences of a "*oui*" majority and sovereignty.

9. The correlation (r) between the two federalist leaders thermometer scores is quite strong (.73), as is that between the two sovereignty leaders thermometer scores (.76). To avoid possible collinearity problems, we construct summary federalist and sovereignty leader scores as the averages of the scores for the individual federalist and sovereignty leaders.

SEVEN

Tried and Found Wanting

New political parties do not "just happen." Perhaps most basically they can be thought of as organizational vehicles responding to groups of people by aggregating and articulating issues and concerns that those groups do not believe are being addressed adequately or even expressed by an existing party system or the larger political system (see, e.g., Aldrich, 1995). In the Canadian case, new parties historically have arisen in times of serious economic and social distress. Thus, as was previously noted, the prolonged hardships of the Depression-ridden 1930s gave birth to the Co-operative Commonwealth Federation (CCF) (later the New Democratic Party) and Social Credit. More generally, new Canadian parties have entered the political arena as expressions of the dissatisfaction of particular ethno-linguistic and regional groups with the representation of their varying interests by existing parties and governmental institutions. Important examples include the United Farmers and Progressives in the 1920s, the Union Nationale in the 1930s, the Parti Québécois in the late 1960s, Reform in the late 1980s, and the Bloc Québécois in the early 1990s.[1]

Although mass discontent provides the catalyst for new parties, they are created by the actions of political élites. The latter are likely to form new parties under the impetus of the same social, economic, and political conditions that fuel citizen discontent. In some cases, these élites have not been associated with existing parties; in others, they have left them. In any event, they share the belief that they cannot (or no longer can) exercise influence or perhaps even "get a hearing" for their views in either their own or other existing parties. These beliefs may reflect the fact that they have been losers in intra-party power struggles over specific policies or broader ideological concerns. For example, in Canada, the Parti Québécois was founded in 1968 by René Lévesque, a former cabinet member in a Liberal provincial government in Quebec, who despaired over that party's ability to satisfy the aspirations of Québécois nationalists (Bothwell, 1998: 122-23). In an earlier era, a number of the founders of the CCF and Social Credit were former members of the Progressive Party, who believed the existing parties could not effectively represent the economic interests of what was then a primarily agrarian West (Morton, 1950).

In this chapter we will consider factors facilitating the emergence of the Reform and Bloc Québécois parties, with emphasis on the former, since its ultimate goal is to form the government of Canada rather than—as is the Bloc's goal—to leave Canada. This will set the stage for the analysis of the most recent (1997) federal election in the next chapter. In 1997 the Bloc again captured more seats and votes in Quebec than any other party, although Reform supplanted it as the official parliamentary opposition to the governing Liberals. The continuing electoral strength of Reform and the Bloc in 1997 ratified the changes in the federal party system that had occurred in 1993, and thereby indicated that the old "two-party-plus" system was now a genuine multi-party one.

FACTORS FACILITATING THE EMERGENCE OF NEW PARTIES

As observed in earlier chapters, for a long time *"plus ça change"* seemed to be a reasonably accurate characterization of the macro dynamics of the federal party system. As the parties prepared for the 1993 national election only the Liberals and Conservatives had ever won a majority of seats in Parliament, and no new party had seriously challenged the Grit-Tory duopoly since the Depression spawned the CCF and Social Credit as western-based vehicles of political protest. Although Social Credit enjoyed a brief surge of support in Quebec in the early 1960s (Pinard, 1971; Stein, 1973), and the popularity of the CCF's successor, the NDP, revived in the early 1970s and again in the late 1980s (Whitehorn, 1994), circa 1990 the national party system was basically little different from what it had been decades earlier. Appearances to the contrary, this status

Seven :: Tried and Found Wanting

Table 7.1   Evaluations of the Performance
of Political Parties, 1995 and 1997 National Surveys

	1995		1997	
Evaluations: Parties...	*Agree*	*Disagree*	*Agree*	*Disagree*
A. Don't address real problems	**63**	36	**76**	24
B. Look after everyone's interests	39	**60**	39	**61**
C. Difference between say and do	**92**	8	**93**	7
D. Encourage political participation	31	**67**	36	**63**
E. Don't offer real choices	**60**	39	**61**	38
F. Help groups reach agreement	31	**67**	36	**62**
G. Interested in elections, not governing	**78**	21	**78**	21
H. Give people a say in politics	54	**43**	52	**47**
I. Divide, don't unify country	**53**	45	**59**	40
J. Bicker too much	**89**	10	**90**	9
K. Choose well-qualified candidates	42	**57**	44	**54**
L. Don't listen to ordinary people	**67**	32	**73**	26
M. Care about votes, not opinions	**59**	40	**68**	31
Negative Responses: Mean	8.55		8.85	
standard deviation	2.99		2.75	

Note: Boldface numbers indicate negative responses;
"don't know" responses included in calculations.

quo was not immutable. In the 1993 federal election, two new
parties, the Bloc Québécois and Reform, captured scores of seats
in Quebec and the West, respectively, and became major actors on
the national political stage. The successes of the BQ and Reform
were accompanied by the near destruction of two of the old-line
parties, the PCs and NDP.

Data presented in Chapter Five showed that at least since the
late 1960s Canadians have expressed precious little enthusiasm
for the Liberals, Progressive Conservatives, or New Democrats.
Also, national surveys conducted over the 1968-93 period reveal a
negative trend in public sentiments about the parties (see Figure 5.1).
The negativism has continued in recent years. Although the mean
thermometer score (on a 100-point scale) for the three old-line
parties rose slightly (from 43 to 45) between 1993 and 1995, by 1997
it had decreased again (to 43 points). Moreover, as was the case
in 1991 and 1993, the 1995 and 1997 national surveys reveal that
large majorities of Canadians continued to believe, *inter alia* that:

Figure 7.1 Negative Evaluations of Canadian
Political Parties, 1993, 1995, 1997

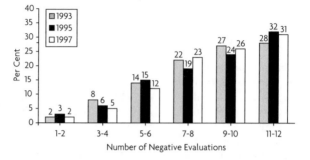

Number of Negative Evaluations

the parties do not address real problems; there is a big difference
between what parties say and what parties do; parties do not offer
the voters real choices; parties are interested in winning elections
rather than in governing; parties bicker too much; and parties care
only about people's votes, not their opinions (Table 7.1). Majorities
also disagreed with the propositions that parties look after everyone's
interests and encourage political participation.

The consistency of the negative tone of public judgements
about the parties in successive surveys is striking. Indeed, there is
remarkable stability in responses to the 13 evaluative statements,
with the average number of negative judgements[2] ranging from 8.55
in 1993 and 1995 to 8.85 in 1997. Nor do these summary figures
mask the presence of a sizable cadre of party enthusiasts. Across the
country as a whole, the percentage of people making four or fewer
negative evaluations in 1993, 1995, and 1997 surveys was only 10
per cent in 1993, 9 per cent in 1995, and 7 per cent in 1997. Clear
majorities—55 per cent in 1993, 56 per cent in 1995, and 57 per
cent in 1997—offered nine or more negative assessments (see Figure
7.1). And the negativism was not confined to particular areas of
the country; as Figure 7.2 illustrates, widespread unhappiness with
party performance was not restricted to those regions (Quebec, the
Prairies, British Columbia) that strongly supported the Bloc and
Reform in 1993 and 1997. Disapproving evaluations have been the
norm in all parts of the country throughout the 1990s.

The negative tenor of Canadians' affective and evaluative orientations towards the political parties is consonant with the relatively
fleeting character of partisan attachments at both the federal and

Figure 7.2   Average Number of Negative Party
Evaluations by Region, 1993, 1995, 1997 National Surveys

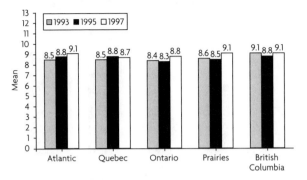

provincial levels. As shown in Chapter Five (see Figure 5.2), several
national panel surveys conducted since the 1970s consistently have
indicated that large numbers of Canadians do not have stable party
identifications. Instability in party identification is important because
it provides the psychological basis for changes in voting behaviour.
The latter, in turn, are necessary if new parties are to challenge the
political status quo successfully. As Converse and Dupeux (1966; see
also Budge, Crewe, and Farlie, 1976; Dalton, Flanagan, and Beck,
1984) argued, based on their analyses of partisanship in the United
States and France, the effects of a widespread absence of durable
party identifications can be far reaching, because instability in the
party system may lead to instability in the larger political order.

A reasonable conjecture is that the instability of party identification in Canada is related to the negative reactions many people
express when asked about the parties. Discontent with party
performance is a motor of partisan change. Data displayed in Figure
7.3 address this hypothesis. This figure shows the relationship
between party performance evaluations measured in 1993 and the
percentage of respondents in our 1993-95 national panel whose
federal party identifications were directionally unstable. Among
those making three or fewer negative party evaluations, 27 per
cent either switched their party identifications or moved between
identification and non-identification. The comparable figures among
those with four to six, seven to nine, and 10 or more negative
evaluations are 33 per cent, 36 per cent and fully 40 per cent
respectively. In short, the more negative evaluations people make at

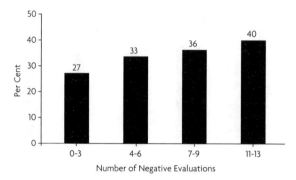

Figure 7.3 Percentages of Unstable Federal
Party Identifiers by Negative Evaluations of
Party Performance, 1993-1995 National Panel

time t₁, the more likely they are to change their party identifications between time t₁ and time t₂.

Partisan Instability (Briefly) Reconsidered

The widespread instability in party identification in Canada is consistent with the massive swings in party support and the changes in the national party system that have occurred in the 1990s. But, is party identification in Canada *really* unstable—can we believe what the data gathered in national panel surveys (i.e., surveys where the same people are interviewed at two or more points in time) conducted over the past quarter-century are telling us? In a challenging paper published in 1997, Schickler and Green argued that, in fact, we cannot. Specifically, they claimed that once random measurement errors in answers to the survey questions are taken into account, the instability of party identification evident in panel surveys in Canada (as well as Germany, Great Britain, and the United States) largely disappears. In the Canadian case, Schickler and Green contend that instability in party identification is evident only in a 1992-93 national panel.[3] According to their account, prior to the early 1990s Canada was a country where the vast majority of voters were stable party identifiers.

Schickler and Green certainly are correct to emphasize the need to take measurement error into account in assessing the stability of party identification or other political orientations. Also, their

Seven :: Tried and Found Wanting

Figure 7.4 Movers and Stayers, Mixed Markov Latent
Class Models of the Stability of Federal Party Identification

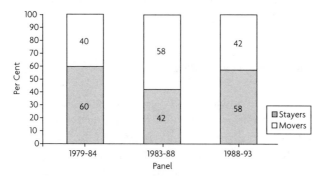

finding that party identifications were unstable in the early 1990s
is consistent with the rise of Reform and the Bloc Québécois and
the recent changes in the national party system that the successes of
these two new parties precipitated. However, we contend that
the Canadian electorate long has contained sizable percentages
of both flexible and durable partisans. *Pace* Schickler and Green,
partisan instability is nothing new in Canada. Substantial numbers
of unstable ("mover") and stable ("stayer") identifiers long have
been the norm. Recent advances in statistical modelling, specifically
the development of a technique called mixed Markov latent class
(MMLC) analysis (see Clarke and McCutcheon, 1998), enable us to test
this hypothesis while taking into account the problem of measurement
error in survey responses stressed by Green and Schickler.

Applying the MMLC technique to the four-wave 1988-93 national
panel data[4] indicates that a mover-stayer model has a very good fit
with the data. Moreover, the percentage of unstable party identifiers
(movers) is very substantial—42 per cent (see Figure 7.4). An
alternative model specifying that everyone is a stayer, i.e., that the
apparent presence of unstable identifiers in the panel data is merely a
consequence of random error in responses to the party identification
questions, fits the data very poorly.[5] The superiority of the mover-
stayer model also is apparent in MMLC analyses of four-wave panel
data gathered in the 1970s and 1980s. Again, the analyses indicate
that the percentages of unstable party identifiers in these earlier
surveys were decidedly nontrivial. Indeed, 40 per cent of the
respondents in the 1979-84 panel and fully 58 per cent of those in
1983-88 one were in the mover chains (Figure 7.4). There is strong

evidence, then, that partisan instability is a longstanding feature of Canadian political psychology—one that clearly antedates the recent upheaval in the national party system.

Other Facilitating Conditions

In addition to the instability of voters' psychological attachments, several other conditions facilitated the emergence of Reform and the Bloc Québécois. As noted previously, the historic grievances in both the West and Quebec with the quality of their parliamentary representation were exacerbated by the economic recession of the early 1990s, the fallout over the free trade agreement and the GST, and, of course, the acrimony generated by the failed Meech Lake Accord and the 1992 national referendum on constitutional reform (see, e.g., Bothwell, 1998: chs. 10-11). Leadership also played an important part. In Canada, the tendency in contemporary democracies for political parties to be personified by their leaders has been magnified by a "brokerage" style of electioneering (see, e.g., Clarke et al., 1996: ch. 1). In the cases of Reform and the Bloc, Preston Manning and Lucien Bouchard, respectively, played crucial roles in bringing their parties into being.

Although neither leader had highly visible *national* profiles when their parties were founded, they were salient figures in the West and Quebec, respectively. Bouchard had enjoyed considerable visibility as a cabinet minister in the Mulroney government and as a personal friend of the prime minister. Their friendship notwithstanding, Bouchard resigned his cabinet post in May, 1990. The issue was changes in the Meech Lake Accord, which Bouchard had believed was a "done deal" (Bothwell, 1998: 206). A group of five MPs, two of whom were Liberals, joined with Bouchard and two other former Conservatives to fight for Quebec sovereignty, assuming the role of "messengers" from Quebec to English-speaking Canada. After the Accord failed to secure ratification in June 1990, Bouchard and his new "Bloc" decided to enter a candidate (Gilles Duceppe) in an August 1990 federal by-election in Quebec, although Bouchard continued to insist that they were not forming a new political party. Despite this disclaimer, Duceppe won the by-election and became the first MP to be elected to the federal Parliament under the Bloc's banner. Several months later, in the spring of 1991, Bouchard and the other parliamentary members of the group finally decided to become an official political party. A party manifesto dedicated to the achievement of a sovereign Quebec was written, and the business of recruiting members and candidates for Parliament began.

A year later the BQ created associations in 73 of the 75 Quebec ridings. Lacking funds, the new party turned to its provincial counterpart, the Parti Québécois, for financial and organizational support. The latter's efforts had helped defeat the October 1992 national referendum on constitutional reform by a 57-43 margin in the province. According to Cornellier (1995: 67), the "no" side's victory by such a substantial edge was the spark that energized Bouchard and his new party. By February 1993 the BQ had recruited 40,000 members and by June of that year the party's membership rolls had doubled to 80,000. With the money raised through membership dues, and the assistance of the PQ, the BQ was able to recruit a full slate of candidates for the October 1993 election. The Bloc elected 54 MPs and, as the second largest party in Parliament, was entitled to claim the title of "official opposition." During the period between the 1993 election and until Bouchard fell seriously ill, the party was very much a party dominated by him. Well-liked, trusted, and respected, Bouchard was loathe to delegate any authority to even his closest party colleagues. Indeed, writing in 1995, Cornellier (1995: 156) argued that, quite simply, "the Bloc is Bouchard."

The strategy laid down by Bouchard during this period continued to be operative even after he gave up the party's leadership to become leader of the Parti Québécois and Premier of Quebec in January 1996. It recognizes that the social and economic policy proclivities of the party's members are very diverse—spanning the traditional ideological spectrum from democratic socialists on the left to "small-c" conservatives on the right. Thus, unlike the other parliamentary parties, the Bloc has been careful to avoid taking an official position on every issue. Since the party's *raison d'être* is Quebec sovereignty and its guiding principle is to work for the interests of Quebec while furthering that goal, when those interests are not directly involved no position is necessary. In this regard, the BQ's strategy resembles that adopted by Parti Québécois founder René Lévesque in the late 1960s (McRoberts, 1988: ch. 7). Since Quebec sovereignty is what matters, it has provided an operational definition of what constitutes "synthesis of all valid perspectives" for the Bloc. Additional ideological litmus tests would be counterproductive.

Reform Leader Preston Manning lacks the charisma and oratorical powers of Lucien Bouchard. However, as Thomas Flanagan (1995) makes clear, his philosophical conservatism, strong political will, organizational skills, family name (he is the son of long-time Alberta Premier Ernest Manning) and especially, his formidable intellect, make him an attractive leader to former Social Credit and Conservative partisans and many other Westerners as well. In sum, the concatenation of a number of factors helps explain the emergence of the Bloc and Reform parties and the substantial public support they enjoyed in the 1993 and 1997 federal elections. The ability of the BQ and Reform to maintain most (in the case of the BQ) or all (in the case of Reform) of their strength through two elections is quite remarkable. Most new parties in Canada and other democracies that have experienced a favourable initial responses have been unable to sustain it.

A number of factors tend to inhibit the success of new parties. First, the adverse economic conditions that stimulate widespread discontent with existing parties do not last forever. When good times return, an important motor of disaffection is removed. Moreover, governing parties are not passive in the face of economic distress and the unhappiness it generates. They try in various ways, some successful, some less so, to combat an economic slump by implementing policies that are intended to ameliorate the malaise. Equally important, governing parties employ teams of pollsters, spin doctors and media gurus who work assiduously to influence public opinion. These individuals not only try to create the impression that a governing party's economic policies are effective, but also that the party and its leader are concerned—that they "feel our pain." A governing party's enormous publicity advantage as "the Government" helps it foster a favourable climate of opinion that constrains and diminishes the impact of the economic criticisms of opposition parties—new and old alike.

New parties are almost always at a severe disadvantage in the publicity game because, in varying degrees, they lack the financial and other resources needed to mount a sustained attack on existing parties. Moreover, if the new parties lack representation in parliament, they cannot take advantage of the free publicity provided by televised coverage of parliamentary debates and question period, media reports of the activities of parliamentary parties and individual MPs, and the franking privilege and travel allowances which MPs in existing parties use to advertise themselves and their party to their constituents (see, e.g., Cain, Ferejohn, and Fiorina, 1987; Clarke and Kornberg, 1992). Also, the media, whose attention new parties desperately need in order to gain salience in the public mind, tend to "move on" quickly to what are seen as more newsworthy stories after the formation of a new party is announced. After a short period, new parties are no longer news.

The Bloc and Reform parties were less affected by a number of these factors than many new parties have been in other democracies or, for that matter, than have been new parties in Canada's past. Both the Bloc and Reform were able to use the membership dues paid by their new supporters to help finance their initial organizational and electoral activities. And, as noted above, in gearing up for the 1993 election, the Bloc also profited from substantial financial and organizational assistance provided by the Parti Québécois. In addition, early on both parties won by-elections and thereby gained footholds in Parliament. And, in a very real sense, the Bloc was in Parliament even before it won a by-election or formally announced itself as a party because its founders (Bouchard and the other defectors from the Progressive Conservative and Liberal caucuses) were already MPs. Moreover, the media could not ignore Manning and Reform because the party was obviously benefiting from the serious meltdown of federal PC support in the West. In addition, the ideological appeals of a PC party led by Brian Mulroney and Kim Campbell did not resonate as strongly with "small-c" conservative true believers in the West as did those of a Reform party led by Preston Manning, the son of a man many remembered as "Mr. Western conservatism." Similarly, the media could not ignore the Bloc after it joined forces with the PQ to bring about the defeat in Quebec of the 1992 referendum on constitutional reform by a very solid 57 per cent to 43 per cent margin. Bouchard acknowledged that the 1992 referendum defeat was a kind of political lifeline—"it was the 1992 referendum that got us moving again" (Cornellier, 1995: 67).

As noted, existing parties are not passive in the face of threats posed by a new party. Rather, the former react to the conditions that have stimulated the latter's emergence and, in some cases, adopt as their own, the policy proposals that have made the new party attractive. Even if this is difficult for a governing party to do, one or more opposition parties may be well positioned ideologically to undercut the policy appeal of a new party. In Canada, a prominent historical example of such policy appropriation was the Liberal Party's adoption of Progressive and CCF policies, including the CCF's pioneering public health-care program (Young, 1969; Zakuta, 1964).

The strategy does not always work. As we will see in Chapter Eight, in the 1997 federal election the Conservatives and their new leader, Jean Charest, tried to appeal to so-called "soft nationalists" in the Quebec electorate. Ultimately, however, a federalist party such as the Conservatives could go only so far in playing the nationalist card. Moreover, by trying to carve out a middle ground on the issue of Quebec's future relationship with the rest of Canada, they risked being trumped by both the Liberals and the BQ. In the acrimonious aftermath of the 1995 referendum, the issue continued to polarize the electorate between federalists on the one side and sovereignists one the other. Thus, as the campaign drew to a close, the dynamics of party competition were such that Charest and the Tories found themselves the victims of a classic "third-party squeeze." They were ground between the forces of federalism represented by the governing Liberals and the forces of sovereignty represented by the BQ.

Nor were either Reform or the Bloc really threatened by the kinds of "election traps" new parties usually face. Normally, general elections—especially the first one or two—are critically important for the success of a new party. To establish its *bona fides* as a serious political option, a new party must quickly capture *both* a significant share of the popular vote *and* a sizable share of seats in a legislature (Miller et al., 1990). This difficulty was less of a problem for both new parties because Canada's single-member plurality electoral system meant that their geographically concentrated bases of support would enable them to translate votes into seats very effectively. Also, the costs of competing in a national election were reduced for the BQ and Reform because Canadian election campaigns are relatively short, and their regional bases of support made it obvious where they should concentrate their limited resources for maximum effect. However, another dimension of the election trap is the barrier to new party support created by the "wasted vote" psychology. The theme of "they can't win" is one the Liberals and Conservatives have constantly invoked in the past against the New Democrats, Social Credit, and other third-party challengers. The "wasted vote" problem is a potential "Catch 22" that can prevent new and other minor parties from ever being able to validate a claim to having the "capacity to govern."

Related to the latter problem are what may be termed the "policy differentiation" and "cleavage" traps. That is, new parties may be strongly tempted to differentiate themselves from existing ones by articulating clearly defined positions on highly salient issues, or by portraying themselves as spokespersons for particular social groups defined by criteria such as region, ethnicity, or social class. Taking such positions or adopting such advocacy roles may motivate people who never have participated in politics to join new parties and inspire identifiers with existing parties to abandon them for the new one(s). More generally it may demonstrate to a sceptical electorate that a new party is, in fact, "different," "means business," and is not just another "me too" party.

However, there are dangers associated with these strategies. As Downs (1957) argued in his classic analysis of party competition and electoral choice, the problem with the policy-differentiation and position-taking strategy is it risks alienating and dividing major social and economic groups whose support is needed if the party is to enjoy national success. The problem with targeting groups in a particular geographic area is that it risks creating or reinforcing an image of being a regional party, lacking any general desire to win national elections so as to implement policies and programs benefiting citizens across the country as a whole. In the case of the BQ, since it made no secret of its *raison d'être*—indeed, it proudly represented itself as the voice in federal politics of Québécois nationalists advocating a politically independent Quebec—neither the policy differentiation nor the cleavage traps constituted dangers. However, for Reform, wanting from its very beginning to be a major player in national politics and led by a man clearly relishing the prospect of some day becoming prime minister, these traps are interrelated and constitute serious long-term threats. To have a realistic chance of winning a federal election, Reform will need to be seen as a party that advocates policies that will benefit Canadians in every region, not just Westerners.

New parties encounter organizational problems as well. If they fail to make real inroads in their first few election forays, they face a loss of morale, interest, and efficiency among the party's members and activists. Disappointed "pragmatists" interested in quick electoral success and, possibly, political careers for themselves, will be tempted to exit the party, leaving it largely to "purists," for whom party activity is primarily a means of "sending a message" expressing fiercely held ideological positions. In any voluntary organization purists are both valued and needed for organizational maintenance purposes. They stick with their organization when the going gets tough and provide the financial and human resources needed to survive hard times. But, in the case of a political party such as Reform that has ambitions for national power, the dominance of purists may push the party into policy differentiation traps that limit its appeal to a large and diverse electorate. Again, this is less of a problem for the BQ because, as we observed above, Reform is about governing Canada, the Bloc is about leaving it.

A NEW PARTY'S MEMBERS AND ACTIVISTS: THE CASE OF REFORM

Our consideration of the problems and prospects faced by new parties led us to undertake a study of members, activists, and constituency level officials in the Reform Party. This study enables us to address questions that long have been of interest to students of political parties in Canada and elsewhere. Who joins political parties, especially new ones? Why do they join? What prompts some members to become actively involved in their party organization? When answering these questions in the context of research on Reform, we can employ techniques of survey research and multivariate statistical analysis that were not available when important new parties such as the Progressives, CCF, and Social Credit were formed in the 1920s and 1930s. The possibility that local party organizational electoral activity can have significant effects on a party's vote share (e.g., Whiteley et al., 1994) suggested that an analysis of factors prompting Reform party members to become active in their local party organizations would be important. More generally, an investigation of public support for Reform, if it were carried out at the time of the 1993 national election, might provide us with the opportunity of studying a new party precisely at the time when its future and that of the existing party system were very much on the line. There was the possibility of being "present at the destruction" of an old party system and "present at the creation" of a new one. These considerations prompted us to conduct two coordinated surveys. One was a telephone survey of a representative national sample of 1,469 persons eligible to vote in the 1993 federal election. Another was a mail questionnaire sent to a stratified (by province) random sample of 4,000 Reform Party members.[6]

Reformers: Who They Are, What They Believe, What They Do

SOCIO-DEMOGRAPHICS   A comparison of Reform Party members with Reform identifiers and voters for Reform and old-line (Conservative, Liberal, NDP) parties in 1993 indicates that the first three of these groups were very similar in that a large majority were men (70 per cent) who resided in the four provinces west of Ontario (68 per cent) (see Table 7.2). However, Reform members tended to be somewhat better educated than Reform voters, and they were marginally more likely to have professional or managerial occupations and to enjoy higher incomes. The biggest difference was age—Reform members were much older than Reform identifiers and Reform voters. The average age of party members was 57, compared to 42 and 47 for Reform identifiers and voters, respectively. Over two-fifths of the Reform party members indicated that they were retired.

MOTIVES FOR JOINING   Since it seemed likely that a new party like Reform would attract persons who were particularly unhappy with the established parties, respondents in the party member and election surveys were asked if they agreed or disagreed with a series of statements concerning the performance of the national parties. Earlier, we have discussed how people participating in the latter survey answered these statements. Here, we compare answers offered by Reform members, Reform voters, and voters for the old-line parties. Table 7.3 shows that the response patterns for the three groups were strikingly consistent. In every case, Reform members had the largest percentages of negative responses, followed

Table 7.2   The Demographics of Reform
Party Support, 1993 National Surveys (%)

| | Reform Party | | | Other* |
	Members	Identifiers	Voters	Voters
Age				
18-22 (new voters)	1	12	6	6
23-30 (Mulroney era)	4	16	10	9
31-46 (Trudeau era)	23	37	37	36
47-57 (Diefenbaker/Pearson era)	19	16	24	18
58 and over (pre-Diefenbaker era)	53	20	23	31
Mean age	57	42	47	48
Education				
Elementary or less	5	5	4	5
Some secondary	16	14	14	15
Completed secondary/comm. college	41	54	51	46
Some university	16	9	10	11
Completed university (B.A., B.Sc.)	22	18	22	23
Gender				
Man	70	60	62	45
Woman	30	40	38	55
Annual Family Income				
Under $20,000	14	10	9	13
$20,000-$39,999	32	32	24	30
$40,000-$59,999	27	34	34	27
$60,000-$79,999	14	11	12	14
$80,000 or more	14	14	21	15
Current/Former Occupation				
Professional	18	14	17	16
Managerial	19	18	16	12
Clerical, sales	14	16	22	23
Skilled, unskilled labour	32	31	27	28
Farmer	10	5	6	2
Homemaker	6	11	11	13
Student	1	6	2	6
Region				
Atlantic	2	2	3	12
Quebec	•	0	0	17
Ontario	31	37	35	45
Prairies: Manitoba	5	4	4	5
Saskatchewan	7	6	5	3
Alberta	28	30	27	6
British Columbia	28	22	26	12

* Old-line parties: i.e., Liberal, PC, NDP;   • less than 0.5%

Seven :: Tried and Found Wanting

Table 7.3 Evaluations of the Performance of Political Parties by Reform Members, Reform Voters and Old-line Party Voters, 1993 National Surveys

Statement	Reform Members Agree	Reform Members Disagree	Reform Voters Agree	Reform Voters Disagree	Old-line Party Voters Agree	Old-line Party Voters Disagree
A. Don't tell about important problems	**87**	11	**73**	26	**64**	34
B. Look after everone's interests	15	**82**	26	**72**	43	**52**
C. Big difference between words and deeds	**98**	1	**97**	2	**91**	7
D. Encourage political participation	21	**73**	35	**62**	39	**54**
E. Don't offer real choices	**71**	26	**61**	38	**55**	43
F. Help groups reach agreement	12	**79**	20	**72**	35	**56**
G. More interested in winning elections	**95**	3	**90**	9	**73**	24
H. Help to give people a say in politics	33	**61**	39	**56**	54	**40**
I. Do more to divide than unify country	**75**	19	**56**	35	**50**	45
J. Spend time bickering and quarrelling	**95**	3	**94**	6	**90**	9
K. Recruit well-qualified candidates	18	**76**	40	**55**	50	45
L. Don't listen to ordinary people	**91**	6	**81**	16	**64**	32

Number of Negative Evaluations:				
	Mean	9.8	8.7	7.3
	Median	10.0	9.0	8.0
	Mode	11.0	11.0	8.0
	standard deviation	2.1	2.3	2.6

Boldface indicates negative evaluation of party performance
Note: Horizontal percentages; percentages calculated using "don't know" and "no opinion" responses.

by Reform voters who, in turn, were followed by old-line party voters. However, these differences were matters of degree, not kind. That the established political parties had been "tried and found wanting" by many Canadians, not just Reform supporters, is reinforced by the summary statistics at the bottom of Table 7.3. On average, Reform members offered 9.8 negative judgements (of a possible 12) of the party system. Reform voters offered slightly fewer (8.7) and, although voters for other parties were not quite as critical, on average a clear majority of their assessments (7.3) were disapproving.

A battery of 16 statements was included in the party member survey to provide additional information on why people were motivated to join Reform. The statements had the following preface: "People have different reasons for becoming a member of the Reform Party. Please indicate *how important* the following are for you." Respondents

A Polity on the Edge

Table 7.4   Reasons for Becoming a Member
of the Reform Party, 1993 National Survey

Reason	Very Important*	Not Very Important	Most Important†
Fun and excitement of party membership	13	66	3
More equal provincial power, Triple E Senate	67	24	8
Friends or family are party members	22	49	1
Dissatisfaction with PCs, Mulroney	85	2	22
Individual freedom, less government	89	1	16
Want to run for public office some day	2	91	1
Special interests have too much power	86	1	9
People like me can exert influence in Reform	60	8	4
To help make business contacts	2	90	1
Concern with deficit, economic problems	96	•	31
To support a candidate I believe in	78	4	5
Better regional representation in Ottawa	75	6	7
Concern with social issues like drugs, crime	86	2	14
To support party leader, Preston Manning	66	8	7
Concern Quebec is too powerful	76	4	17
Concern with moral principles in government	96	1	29

* Horizontal percentages; "somewhat important" category not shown.
† multiple mentions coded; • less than 0.5%.

were then asked: "Please indicate which of the reasons above was *most important of all* when you *first* decided to *become* a member of the Reform Party." Overwhelming majorities indicated that they joined the party because of their issue concerns and dissatisfaction with the perceived failures of former Prime Minister Brian Mulroney and his Progressive Conservative government (see Table 7.4). Fully 96 per cent stated that they were concerned about the upward spiralling national deficit and the country's other economic problems; 86 per cent were worried about social pathologies such as juvenile crime and drug abuse; and 85 per cent were displeased with the prime minister and his party. Large majorities also indicated that they decided to join the party because they wanted the West to have a stronger voice in Ottawa, or because they believed that Quebec and various "special interests" were exercising undue influence. In addition, many stated that they joined because they were keen to reduce the scope of government, and to ensure that it operated according to high moral principles. Finally, majorities said that they joined because they liked Reform leader, Preston Manning, or a local Reform candidate.

Seven :: Tried and Found Wanting

Very few Reformers joined their new party in response to what students of political parties call "material" incentives (see, e.g., Eldersveld, 1964; Kornberg, Smith, and Clarke, 1979; Miller and Jennings, 1986; Whiteley et al., 1994). Table 7.4 shows that desires for personal advancement or financial gain were almost wholly absent; only 2 per cent indicated that making business contacts was a "very important" reason for joining, and only 1 per cent said this reason was "most important." Identically small numbers indicated that the possibility of making a bid for public office had prompted them to join. So-called "solidary" incentives also had relatively little appeal; most Reformers denied that the social aspect of party membership had encouraged them to join. Only 22 per cent and 13 per cent, respectively, said that having friends or family in the party, or the fun and excitement of party membership, were very important reasons for joining, and only 1 per cent and 3 per cent, respectively, said that these reasons were *most* important. In sum, an overwhelming majority of Reformers reported that they had joined the party in response to "purposive" incentives. Policy and (poor) governmental performance mattered a great deal more in their decisions to become a party member than did fame, fortune, family, or friends.

IDEOLOGICAL BELIEFS Consonant with their party's policy platform and more general public image, most Reform members' evaluations of government performance reveals a strong neo-conservative bent (see also Flanagan, 1995; Laycock 1994; Sigurdson, 1994). When asked to think *generally* about government and how it works, huge majorities agree that, *inter alia*, governments are too big and complex to operate efficiently, people expect too much from governments, governments invariably waste a lot of the taxpayers' money, governments make too many rules and regulations, private businesses are more efficient than governments, and government spending is excessive because of the influence of privileged interest groups (Table 7.5, Part I). Similarly, most Reformers disagreed with the propositions that governmental officials can be trusted, are smart, and governments would provide better services if tax rates were increased. Consistent with the responses, fully 73 per cent of the Reform members placed themselves on the right of centre on a summary seven-point, left-right ideological scale, and only

A Polity on the Edge

Table 7.5   Political Attitudes and Beliefs,
Reform Party Members, 1993 National Survey

I. Evaluations of Government Performance	Agree	Disagree*
A. Governments generally do good job providing services	47	47
B. Government too big and complex to operate efficiently	91	7
C. People expect more than any government can deliver	77	21
D. Can trust government officials to do what is right	19	77
E. Government provides better services if higher taxes	8	90
F. Governments always waste a lot of money	90	9
G. Governments blamed for problems not their fault	40	54
H. Most government officials are smart people	29	65
I. Governments don't work because too many regulations	80	14
J. Private businesses more efficient than governments	90	6
K. Governments spend too much because of special interests	96	2
L. Governments don't work because officials are dishonest	53	39
M. Deficits because people want more than will pay for	59	36
N. Problems facing government too difficult to solve	58	38

II. Distribution on Left-Right Ideological Continuum (%)

Left						Right	Mean Score
1	2	3	4	5	6	7	
1	1	4	22	30	31	12	5.2

III. Attitudes towards Direct Democracy Devices	Agree	Disagree*
A. National referendums take power from politicans and give it to the people	82	15
B. Referendums won't solve important issues	18	78
C. Canada should have a law so majority can recall MPs	93	4
D. Important questions decided by federal and provincial governments and not by referendums	20	73
E. If MPs disagree with constituents, they should do what constituents want	82	13
F. People should be able to petition to hold a referendum	92	5

* percentages calculated using "don't know" and
"no opinion responses" not shown in table.

6 per cent located themselves on the left side of the scale (Table 7.5, Part II).

Reformers' distrust of government and political élites more generally led overwhelming majorities to endorse referendums and other devices of direct democracy. Thus, 82 per cent agreed that referendums transfer power from the politicians to the people, the same percentage believed that citizens should be able to petition to hold a referendum, and 73 per cent disagreed that important questions should be decided by the federal and provincial governments rather than by referendums (Table 7.5, Part III). There also was virtual unanimity (92 per cent) that a majority of constituents should be able to their recall members of Parliament, and over four-fifths (82 per cent) insisted that members of Parliament should adhere to the wishes of the people when there is a conflict between those wishes and what the MP thinks is right. Overall, Reformers' responses underscore the extent of their disaffection with the existing political order. They do not limit their complaints to the activities of particular politicians or particular old-line parties, but rather bear a strong animus against governments and public officials *generally*. Consistent with the principles espoused by Social Credit and other earlier Canadian right-wing populist movements, Reformers believe power should reside with "people" not "politicians" (see, e.g., Irving, 1959; Macpherson, 1953; Pinard, 1971; Stein, 1973).

RECRUITMENT AND ACTIVITY PATTERNS   In keeping with Reform's recent arrival on the political stage (the party was founded in 1987), the vast majority (87 per cent) of party members in our 1993 survey stated that they had joined the party during the past four years, and over half (54 per cent) said they had been members for two years or less (see Table 7.6). Consistent with the idea that they were simultaneously very dissatisfied with the existing party system and other aspects of the established political order *and* strongly attracted to Reform's specific policies and more general ideological stance, 80 per cent of the Reform members indicated that they had joined the party on their own initiative rather than in response to an invitation to do so. This "push-pull" recruitment process clearly came at the expense of the Progressive Conservatives. Although not asked if they had been *members* of another party before joining Reform, nearly two-thirds (65 per cent) indicated that they previously had been Conservative party identifiers, whereas only 10 per cent, 5 per cent, and 8 per cent had been Liberal, NDP, or Social Credit identifiers, respectively.

Joining Reform is a form of "chequebook" or "credit card" political participation, requiring only that the joiner pay an annual fee of $10. As noted above, these dues provided Reform with a useful, albeit modest, financial base that would have been very difficult or impossible to assemble from corporations, unions, or other organized interest groups that were closely tied to existing parties and the political-economic establishment. Although money is undeniably important, parties, particularly new ones, require more from members than just their dollars. In this regard,

Table 7.6 Recruitment and Activity Profiles of Reform Party Members, 1993 National Survey

Mode of Recruitment:	%
volunteered	80
was asked to join	20

Length of Membership:	
less than one year	14
one to two years	40
three to four years	33
more than four years	13

Party Office-Holding:	
yes, hold office	5
no, but used to hold office	3
no, never held office	92

Party Activities:	
convince friends to vote Reform	58
contribute money to Reform	52
recruit new party members	47
attend meetings in riding	45
attend party assemblies	17
fund raising	14
canvassing	11
take people to polls	11
scrutineer, poll clerk	8
work in riding office	8
attend national party assembly	6

Mean number of activities	2.6

Reform enjoyed considerable success in getting its members to become *activists*, with a majority (52 per cent) saying that they worked for the party during the 1993 federal election campaign (see Figure 7.5). The tasks performed by Reformers were typical of activists in Canadian local party organizations (e.g., Kornberg, Smith and Clarke, 1979: chs 5,6). Although few Reformers stated they currently hold (5 per cent), or previously held (3 per cent), a party office or had ever attended a national party assembly (6 per cent), majorities or sizable minorities attended party meetings, tried to convince friends to vote Reform or join the party, and

Figure 7.5 Number of Hours of Party
Work Per Week, Reform Party Members, 1993

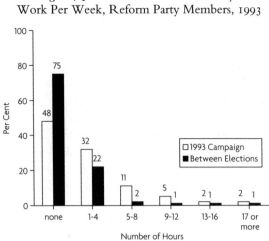

donated money to the cause (Table 7.6). Predictably, their activity
levels subsided in inter-election periods; 75 per cent said they were
inactive, and only 2 per cent worked more than four hours per week
in the interims between elections (Figure 7.5)

MODELLING INTRA-PARTY PARTICIPATION   As the data just reported
indicate, the extent of involvement by Reformers in their party
varied widely. Previous studies indicate that a variety of factors
influence levels of activity in voluntary organizations such as political
parties (see, e.g., Kornberg, Smith, and Clarke, 1972). Accordingly,
we specified a multivariate model of differential intra-party participation by Reformers. The dependent variable summarized scores on
three variables—number of hours worked in the 1993 campaign,
number of hours worked in periods between election campaigns,
and number of activities performed.[7] Guided by previous research
on activity in local party organizations, the model incorporated
several groups of predictor variables. One group includes motives
for becoming a member of Reform,[8] evaluations of national and
personal economic conditions,[9] an index measuring negative evaluations of the national party system,[10] summary measures of affect for
the old-line parties and Reform,[11] and a measure of satisfaction with
the practice of democracy in Canada.[12] Given Reform's distinctive
image as a neo-conservative protest movement, we hypothesized that

negative evaluations of national and personal economic conditions, negative assessments of the party system, low levels of affect for the old-line parties, high levels of affect for Reform, and dissatisfaction with Canadian democracy would be associated with enhanced activity in the party organization. Similarly, persons who joined the party because of concern about issues such as the quality of western representation, the increase in crime, and the breakdown in morality and family values would be more active than persons who joined to use the party as a vehicle for personal advancement or because friends or family were involved. Also, given Reform's neo-conservatism and its populist enthusiasm for direct democracy, it was hypothesized that party members further to the right on the ideological spectrum,[13] those who distrusted government and evaluated governmental performance negatively,[14] and those who endorsed referendums and other mechanisms of citizen control[15] would be motivated to be especially active in their party organizations.

Members' perceptions of Reform's electoral prospects at the national and local (riding) levels[16] constituted a second group of predictor variables. Assuming that perceived lost causes do not generate enthusiasm and viable ones do, we hypothesized that members who perceived Reform's national and local chances favourably were more likely to participate than members who thought that the party's electoral prospects were dim. Party office-holding and expectations[17] thereof constituted yet another set of predictors, and it was hypothesized that people who hold party offices or expect to in the future would be more active than others.

Several socio-demographic variables (age, education, gender, income, province of residence)[18] also were included. It was hypothesized that better educated individuals and persons with higher incomes would be more active than other party members. Although previous research often has reported that middle-aged persons are more politically active than those in younger and older age groups (e.g., Mishler and Clarke, 1990), many Reformers are older, retired persons. Since such individuals typically have more free time than those in the workforce, we expected that, among Reform party members, age would be positively related to party activity. Regarding gender, since our earlier studies of differential activity in Canadian party organizations indicates that women are at least as active as men (Kornberg, Smith, and Clarke, 1979: ch. 8), we

Seven :: Tried and Found Wanting

Table 7.7 Multiple Regression Analysis of Factors Affecting Levels of Party Activism among Reform Party Members, 1993 National Survey

Predictor Variables	b	Std. b	t
Demographics:			
Age	0.33	.10	4.87◆
Education	0.04	.06	3.06◆
Gender	− 0.02	− .01	− 0.42
Income	0.01	.01	0.53
Province:			
British Columbia	0.03	.01	0.68
Saskatchewan	0.16	.04	2.03▲
Manitoba	0.03	.01	0.36
Ontario	0.18	.08	3.51◆
Quebec & Atlantics	0.10	.01	0.73
Left-right ideological position	0.05	.05	2.80✚
Government evaluations:			
limited capacity	0.02	.02	1.27
trust	0.06	.06	2.92✚
inefficiency	− 0.01	− .01	− 0.65
waste	0.01	.01	0.39
Satisfaction with Canadian democracy	− 0.05	− .04	− 2.23▲
Citizen control:			
referendums	0.09	.09	4.91◆
MPs as delegates	0.04	.04	2.26▲
Dissatisfaction with party system	0.02	.04	1.90▲
Party affect:			
oldline parties	− 0.01	− .06	− 3.25◆
Reform	0.01	.10	5.11◆
Economic evaluations:			
personal	− 0.02	− .04	− 1.83▲
national	− 0.02	− .02	− 0.84
Reasons for joining:			
representation	0.07	.07	3.37◆
personal	0.01	.01	0.66
morality, values	− 0.03	− .03	− 1.77▲
individualism	− 0.00	− .00	− 0.15
Electoral prospects:			
national	0.06	.04	2.09▲
riding	0.11	.10	5.09◆
Party office-holder	0.64	.31	14.68◆
Expect to hold party office	0.39	.28	12.66◆
Constant	− 4.10	—	− 11.18◆
		$R^2 = .40$	

◆ p ≤ .001;   ✚ p ≤ .01;   ▲ p ≤ .05; one–tailed test.

did not anticipate that there would be gender differences in party activity. Lastly, given Reform's western origins and its relative strength in that region compared to other parts of Canada, province of residence was included to determine if there were organizational differences in various areas of the country that would affect intra-party participation rates.

A multiple regression analysis indicates that many predictor variables behaved as anticipated (see Table 7.7). Persons who joined Reform because they wanted to increase western representation in the federal government, those who were dissatisfied with the operation of democracy in Canada, and those who favoured referendums and other devices of direct democracy all were significantly more active than other party members. Reformers who were most negatively disposed toward the existing parties and evaluated their performance most harshly also tended to be more active, as were those further to the right on the ideological continuum.

However, these findings were not the whole story. Several other variables had significant and, in some cases, strong effects on intra-party participation. Members who were optimistic about the party's national and local electoral prospect were more heavily involved in their local organizations than were other members, as were those who held party offices or expected to do so. Concerns about economic conditions were relevant, too, and, as hypothesized, negative evaluations of one's personal economic circumstances spurred involvement. Regarding demographics, although gender and income were immaterial, older and better-educated persons were more active. Province of residence played a statistically significant, but minor role—Reformers living in Saskatchewan and Ontario tended to be more active than party members who reside in Alberta or other parts of the county.[19]

CONCLUSION: NOT FOR FAME OR FORTUNE

Reform and the Bloc Québécois were political success stories of the 1990s. Sizable numbers of Canadians voted for these new parties in the 1993 federal election and, as the second largest party in Parliament, the separatist BQ assumed what was, for it, the ironic title of "Her Majesty's Loyal Opposition." The new parties had a major impact on the national party system, and their successes were accompanied by the near destruction of two old-line parties, the Progressive Conservatives and NDP. Reform and the Bloc were not one-time wonders. Rather, both parties again made strong showings in the 1997 federal election. Although support for the BQ receded somewhat, it remained the largest single party in Quebec. Reform continued to be a major force in the West, and elected enough MPs to displace the BQ as the official opposition party in Parliament. The continuing electoral strength of Reform and the BQ and the continuing weakness of the PCS and NDP in 1997 indicated that Canada's national party system had been, perhaps permanently, reconfigured by the new parties. As the twentieth century drew to a close, Reform and the Bloc were serious political players on the Canadian political stage.

Support for political parties goes beyond voting for them. Some people become party members, and some members work actively for their parties during election campaigns and in the interims between these contests. The energy, time, and money people devote to a political party can be vital to its success or failure. This is especially true for new parties, such as the Bloc and Reform, that have at best limited access to the abundant financial resources fuelling the election campaigns of old-line parties. To gain insight into the factors that motivate people to become active supporters of a new party, we conducted a large survey of Reform party members at the time of the 1993 federal election.

Many Reform party members indicated that they had become campaign activists. Very large majorities of active and inactive members did not join Reform to secure financial advantage or to launch a political career. Rather, they were responding to purposive incentives—the party provides a vehicle for expressing displeasure with the old-line parties and the political establishment more generally, and an opportunity for advancing a neo-conservative policy agenda. Many party members were Westerners voicing long-standing discontents about their region's status in a political system where the institutional arrangements of a Westminster-model Parliament and a single-member plurality electoral system "stack the political deck" in favour of Ontario and Quebec. These persons were strongly attracted by Reform's proposals to increase the region's representation in the federal government.

A Polity on the Edge

Reform is not wholly a western phenomenon; substantial minorities of Reform voters and party members were Ontarians. Like their western counterparts, Ontario Reformers had lengthy "laundry lists" of economic, social, and political grievances. And like Westerners, a large majority of Ontario Reformers believed that all of the old-line parties and successive federal governments, Liberal and Conservative alike, have ignored them in favour of Quebec and an array of special interests. Reform's neo-conservative policies and promises to satisfy longstanding demands for representation, participation, and recognition resonated strongly with its party members in all parts of the country.[20]

The 1997 federal election demonstrated that the strong electoral performances of Reform and the Bloc in 1993 were not flukes. By maintaining their bases of support in the West and Quebec, respectively, the new parties again were able to translate votes into seats effectively. But their futures remain unclear. Obviously, the BQ's fate is tied to the evolution of Quebecers' attitudes towards the desirability of sovereignty versus continued membership in the Canadian political community. Reform is very different—it wishes to govern Canada, not to break it apart. Whether Reform can rally the cohort of voters in Ontario and the Atlantic provinces it needs to make a serious bid for national power is a question we consider in Chapter Eight, which analyses factors at work in the 1997 federal election. The intertwined futures of the BQ and PQ, Quebec and Canada are the subjects of Chapter Nine.

NOTES

1. There is a sizable literature on protest parties in Canada. See, e.g., Irving (1959); Lipset (1968); Macpherson (1953); Pinard (1971); Quinn (1963); Stein (1973); Young (1969); Zakuta (1964).
2. For statements A, C, E, G, I, J, L, and M in Table 7.1 "agree" responses are scored 1, and other responses are scored 0. For statements B, D, F, H, and K "disagree" responses are scored 1, and other responses are scored 0. The recoded responses are summed to yield the number of negative evaluations (range: 0-13) of the party system.
3. The data were gathered as part of the 1993 CNES. The 1992-93 panel is comprised of persons surveyed in connection with the 1992 referendum on the Charlottetown Accord and the 1993 federal election.

4. Multiple-wave panel data are required to estimate the parameters in mixed Markov latent class models. Estimation with less than four waves of data involves the imposition of a number of parameter equality constraints that may not be tenable.

5. The mover-stayer model also outperforms a MMLC model that specifies that everyone is a mover.

6. The party member sample was drawn from the party's official list of approximately 100,000 dues-paying members. The response rate was 64.4 per cent, with 2,574 (weighted N = 2,593) of 4,000 questionnaires being returned.

7. The three activity variables are organized in terms of a single factor that explains 72.2 per cent of their variance. The factor loadings ranges are: campaign activity (.74), inter-campaign activity (.70), number of activities (.73).

8. Responses to the 16 statements regarding reasons for joining Reform (see pp. 7-8 and Table 3) are scored: "most important" = 4, "very important" = 3, "somewhat important" = 2, "not very important" = 1. A principal components factor analysis yields four factors that explain 46.5 per cent of the item variance. Based on the factor loadings, we label these factors "representation," "personal," "morality, values," and "individualism," respectively.

9. The questions measuring evaluations of national economic conditions were: (a) "Thinking *generally* about how the Canadian economy is doing these days, would you say it is doing: (i) very well, (ii) fairly well, (iii) not very well;" (b) "Over the *past three or four years*, do you think the Canadian economy has: (i) gotten better, (ii) gotten worse, (iii) stayed about the same;" (c) "In handling the economy, would you say the *federal government* has done: (i) a very good job, (ii) a good job, (iii) a poor job, (iv) a very poor job." A principal components factor analysis of these three items yields one factor that explains 55.1 per cent of their variance, with factor loadings of .78, .72 and .73, respectively. The questions measuring evaluations of personal economic conditions were: (a) "Thinking about *your own* economic situation, how satisfied are you? (i) very satisfied, (ii) fairly satisfied, (iii) a little dissatisfied, (iv) very dissatisfied;" (b) "Do you think that government has a great deal, something or not much at all to do with this? (i) a great deal, (ii) something, (iii) not much, (iv) don't know." Answers to these two questions were combined to yield an index ranging from +4 (very satisfied and government bears a great deal of responsibility) to -4 (very dissatisfied and government bears a great deal of responsibility).

10. See note 2 above. Item M in Table 7.1 ("parties only care about votes, not opinions") was not asked in the party member survey.

11. Party affect is measured using 100-point thermometer scales. Affect for the old-line parties is measured as the average thermometer score for the Liberal, PC, and New Democratic parties.

12. The question is: "On the whole, are you very satisfied, fairly satisfied, not very satisfied, or not at all satisfied with the way *democracy* works in Canada?" Response categories are scored: "very satisfied" = 4, "fairly satisfied" = 3, "not very satisfied" = 2, "not at all satisfied" = 1.

13. The question is: "People often classify themselves as being on the 'left' or 'right' in politics. On a scale of 1 to 7 indicating left versus right, where would you place yourself?" The seven-point scale runs from 1 (left) to 7 (right).

14. Responses to 14 statements on evaluations of various aspects of government performance (see Table 7.5, Panel I) are coded: "agree" = 1, "disagree" = -1, "don't know" = 0, and subjected to a principal components factor analysis which explains 43.2 per cent of the item variance. Based on the strength of factor loadings for various items, the resulting four factors are labelled: (a) limited capacity, (b) trust, (c) inefficiency, and (d) waste.

15. Responses to statements A, C, E, and F in Table 7.5, Panel III are scored: "agree" = 1, "disagree" or "don't know" = 0, and responses to statements B and D are scored: "disagree" = 1, "agree" or "don't know" = 0. A principal components factor analysis yields two factors which explain 52.3 per cent of the item variance. The strength of factor loadings for various items indicates that the two factors tap attitudes towards referendums, and MPs as delegates, respectively.

16. Estimates of Reform's national electoral prospects are measured using the following question: "[I]f you had to guess, approximately how many seats in the House of Commons do you think Reform will win in the 1993 federal election?" Since it is plausible that the motivational force of anticipated Reform success in winning seats is subject to diminishing marginal returns, we compute the (natural) logarithm of the respondent's estimate of the number of seats Reform would win. The question used to measure estimates of Reform's local electoral prospects is: "What about your *local* riding—how would you rate Reform's chances?" Response categories are: "excellent chance to win" = 4, "good chance to win" = 3, "some chance to win" = 2, "not much chance to win," "don't know" = 1.

17. The party office holding question is: "Do you hold an office (e.g., riding president) in the party organization?" Responses are scored: currently hold office = 3, formerly held office = 2, never held office = 1. The expected party office holding question is: "Do you expect to hold an office in the party organization in the future?" Responses are scored: "yes, definitely" = 4, "probably" = 3, "maybe" = 2, "no" = 1.

18. Age is the (natural) logarithm of respondent's age in years; education is a six-category variable ranging from elementary school or less (scored 1) to completed university degree (scored 6); gender is scored: man = 0, woman = 1; annual family income is a five-category variable ranging from $20,000 or less (scored 1) to $80,000 or more (scored 6). For purposes of the regression analysis, province of residence is measured as a series

of 0-1 dummy variables for British Columbia, Saskatchewan, Manitoba, Ontario, and Quebec and the Atlantic provinces (combined). Alberta is the reference category.

19. A regression model of intra-party participation that includes the six province-of-residence dummy variables, but no other predictors, explains only 0.3 per cent of the variance.

20. Analyses reveal that the policy and ideological concerns of western Reformers are very similar to those of party members residing in other parts of the country. The only substantial difference is that Westerners emphasize the need to enhance their region's representation and influence in federal politics. Archer and Ellis (1994: 302-03, Table 7) report similarly small regional differences in their analysis of the beliefs and opinions of Reform national assembly delegates.

EIGHT

No Winners

The flexibility of Canadians' partisan attachments makes elections risky business for all political parties. In the 1990s the risks parties run when they go to the people increased as party identifications became weaker and less stable. We contend that these properties of partisanship have important consequences. At the individual level, they enable short-term forces associated with feelings about party leaders and attitudes towards currently salient issues to exert strong effects on electoral choice. At the aggregate level, the widespread absence of durable partisan allegiances, coupled with persistent dissatisfaction with parliamentary representation and party performance, facilitate rapid, large-scale changes in support for both particular parties and the party system as a whole. This is exactly what occurred in the 1993 federal election when the Progressive Conservative and New Democratic parties, two charter members of Canada's long-lived "two-party-plus" national party system (Epstein, 1964; Carty, 1992), were nearly annihilated. The disasters suffered by the PCs and New Democrats, coupled with the successes and regionally concentrated bases of support enjoyed by the two new parties, Reform and the Bloc Québécois, led us to consider whether both the country and its national party system were undergoing changes that might affect a realignment and, if so, what further changes might be in the offing. In the last chapter we focused on the emergence of Reform and asserted that the 1997 election would help determine whether it was merely a "flash" party (Converse and Dupeux, 1966), or whether it had the staying power needed to transform the current national party system into a multiparty one.

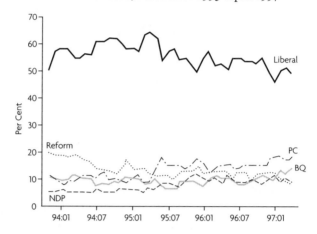

Figure 8.1 National Trends in Federal
Vote Intentions, November 1993-April 1997

Our analysis of the 1997 federal election begins with a brief review of the political and economic factors that shaped the context in which the election occurred. Then, we employ data from national surveys conducted during the election campaign to map the evolution of party support in various regions. Next, we consider partisan attachments, people's feelings about the party leaders, and perceptions of important election issues and the parties preferred on these issues. A multivariate model of forces affecting voting behaviour is used to determine how changes in feelings about party leaders, party-issue preferences, and partisan identifications could have changed the outcome of the election. The results of this analysis lends force to the conclusion that the 1997 election was one that "everyone lost." Canada's national parties, like the country itself, continue to face an uncertain future.

THE ROAD TO NOWHERE: THE 1997 CAMPAIGN

Prelude

For most of the three and one-half years between the 1993 and 1997 elections, Prime Minister Chrétien and the federal Liberal Party appeared to enjoy strong public support. As Figure 8.1

illustrates, national public opinion surveys consistently showed the Liberals holding a commanding lead. With well over 50 per cent of Canadians stating that they intended to vote Liberal, the party typically enjoyed three times as much support as its nearest rival. Thus, when the election writ was issued on April 27, 1997, the Liberals seemed poised to win a very comfortable majority. It was not to be. On the morning after the balloting several powerful cabinet ministers found themselves out of a job and, although the Liberals were still the government, their once solid majority in the House had evaporated, being reduced to merely four seats. Moreover, Chrétien and his party could not claim a *national* mandate to govern. Of the 155 seats they had won, fully 101 were in a single province—Ontario.

Data on regional distributions of voting intentions in monthly Canadian Facts surveys help illuminate what went wrong for Chrétien and his party. In the aftermath of the 1993 election, Liberal support exceeded that of the other parties in both Ontario and the Atlantic provinces, although the Conservatives appeared to be viable competitors in the latter region. In Quebec, the Liberals ran evenly with the Bloc Québécois after party founder Lucien Bouchard was succeeded by, first, Michel Gauthier and, then, Gilles Duceppe. In the West generally, and in British Columbia in particular, the Liberals seemed poised to make substantial gains. However, the appearance of Liberal strength west of the Ontario border was only that and, in fact, the party's support was quite fragile.[1]

In addition to, and intertwined with, these regional challenges, the Liberals faced economic difficulties. The country had gradually recovered from the serious recession of the early 1990s, but the outlook remained unclear. On the upside, the success of the Liberals' deficit-reduction program had exceeded the government's expectations and Finance Minister Paul Martin's pre-election budget in February 1997 forecast that the country would enjoy a surplus by the end of the century. On the downside, and contrary to what the Liberals had promised in their 1993 election platform (Clarkson, 1994), unemployment remained disturbingly high, with joblessness hovering around 10 per cent. Reflecting the mixed news, public opinion was sharply divided and, on the eve of the campaign, the nationwide percentage (36 per cent) of people who judged that the economy had worsened during the previous year equalled

Figure 8.2   Retrospective Judgements about the
Performance of the National Economy by Region

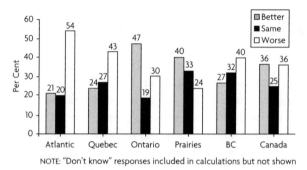

NOTE: "Don't know" responses included in calculations but not shown

the percentage who thought it had improved.[2] However, these
national figures masked sharp regional differences. As Figure 8.2
shows, majorities or pluralities in the Atlantic provinces, Quebec,
and British Columbia believed that the economy had deteriorated,
and only in Ontario and the Prairies did pluralities think it had
improved.

Why Are We Doing This?

The Liberals' underlying weaknesses were compounded by events
that occurred early in the campaign. The very decision to hold
the election was questioned, and when asked why he was going to
the people so early in his government's term, the prime minister
seemed unable to provide a satisfactory answer. Also, the timing of
the election call coincided with the flooding of the Red River that
drove thousands of Manitobans from their homes. Throughout the
country, there was an undercurrent of feeling that the government
should have focused its energies on combating the disaster rather
than holding an unneeded election, and some western commentators
complained that the election would never have been called if the
flood had occurred in central Canada. Adding to the Liberals' woes
was a public relations fiasco caused by Reform's leak of the Liberal
campaign platform (the 1997 " Red Book") and the prime minister's
uninspired performance in the party leader debates. Two weeks into
the campaign, the Liberals' initial 48 per cent national vote intention
share had fallen by 12 points (see Figure 8.3A). Other parties gained,

Eight :: No Winners

Figure 8.3   The Dynamics of Vote Intentions
during the 1997 Federal Election Campaign

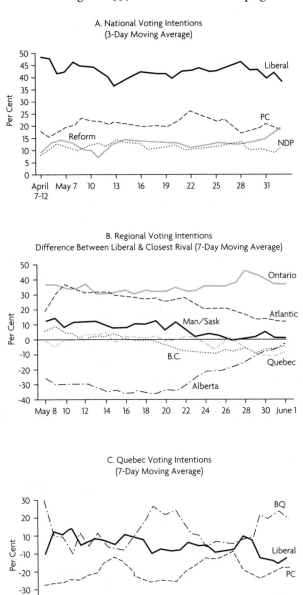

A. National Voting Intentions
(3-Day Moving Average)

B. Regional Voting Intentions
Difference Between Liberal & Closest Rival (7-Day Moving Average)

C. Quebec Voting Intentions
(7-Day Moving Average)

Table 8.1   Perceptions of Party Closest on Most Important
Issue by Week of Campaign, 1997 National Election Campaign Surveys

Party Closest	Week of Campaign				
	Two	*Three*	*Four*	*Five*	*Total*
Liberal	18%	18%	21%	21%	19%
PC	7	10	12	7	9
NDP	5	7	5	7	6
Reform	9	9	9	11	10
BQ	4	4	4	4	4
Other	•	•	1	1	1
None	33	30	30	25	29
No important issue	23	21	20	24	22
(N =)	(982)	(987)	(979)	(971)	(3,919)

• less than 0.5%.

but there were no really strong trends. Regional analysis reveals that the Liberals still had large leads in Ontario and the Atlantic provinces, and smaller ones in Manitoba and Saskatchewan where NDP support was increasing (see Figure 8.3B). In Alberta, the Liberals lagged far behind Reform, and in British Columbia and Quebec they faced stiff competition from Reform and the Bloc Québécois, respectively. In Quebec, it appeared that the Liberals also might be challenged by the Conservatives, who had begun to spark interest as the BQ campaign faltered (Figure 8.3C).

Although the issues were not clearly defined in the minds of many voters early in the campaign, the emerging picture was not especially favourable for a governing party. In this regard, Table 8.1 shows that almost one-quarter of our survey respondents could not identify a "most important election issue."[3] Among those who did, the Liberals were credited for their general management of the economy, but many people felt the government had not handled the unemployment problem effectively. Overall, less than 20 per cent identified a most important election issue and selected the Liberals as closest to them on that issue. In addition, in Alberta and especially in British Columbia, provinces where the Liberals had hoped to make inroads, the "three Rs" (deficit reduction, public-sector reduction, tax reduction) were working to the advantage of Reform, thereby dimming prospects of any serious Liberal gains.

Eight :: No Winners

Table 8.2 Party Competition on the Issues:
Liberals versus Nearest Competitor, by Region and Week
of Campaign, 1997 National Election Campaign Surveys

Region	Week of Campaign			
	Two	*Three*	*Four*	*Five*
Atlantic	0	+ 11	− 15	− 3
Quebec	− 2	0	+ 4	− 8
Ontario	+ 30	+ 29	+ 30	+ 36
Prairies	− 16	− 18	0	− 1
British Columbia	− 8	+ 8	+ 11	− 26

Note: Cell entries are percentage favouring Liberals on most important issue minus percentage favouring competing party with largest percentage on most important issue. Percentages calculated for voters mentioning a most important issue and selecting a party closest on that issue.

Mid-Campaign—Gaining (a Little) Ground

In the two weeks after the first French-language leaders debate, the Liberals retained a huge lead in Ontario, but elsewhere in the country other parties made headway (see Figure 8.3B). Reform remained strong in Alberta and was moving up in British Columbia, while Conservative support decreased, then increased in Quebec (Figure 8.3C) and, to a lesser extent, in the Atlantic provinces. NDP support increased in Nova Scotia and New Brunswick, as well as in the Prairies. The mix of election issues also clarified, as unemployment continued to be an important concern and national unity acquired some salience. The latter issue had its greatest resonance in Quebec where 20 per cent mentioned it. However, in Quebec and elsewhere, other issues, particularly deficit reduction and health care, were on the voters' minds. Opinions about which party was closest on the important issues differed sharply between Ontario and the rest of the country. Unlike voters in other regions, Ontarians opted strongly for the Liberals on the issues (see Table 8.2). More generally, the mid-campaign period witnessed widening regional differences in support for the parties, and based on their continuing dominance in Ontario, it was clear that only the Liberals had any chance of winning a parliamentary majority.

A Polity on the Edge

No Sure Thing

As election day approached, it became increasingly apparent that regional differences in party support might work to deny the Liberals their majority. In Quebec, they found themselves locked in a close battle with the Bloc. Separatist leaders Jacques Parizeau and Lucien Bouchard campaigned vigorously, attacking Prime Minister Chrétien for threatening to refuse to recognize the legitimacy of a narrow separatist victory in any future sovereignty referendum. The sharp divisions between the BQ and Liberals on national unity marginalized the Conservatives, who were trying, albeit unsuccessfully, to have the best of both worlds on the issue by appealing simultaneously to federalists and "soft nationalists." At the beginning of the last week of the campaign Conservative support in the province fell by almost 10 per cent (Figure 8.3C).

Ontario remained safe for the Liberals, but only because of the magnitude of their lead there. In the week before the election, Reform gained votes in the province after the party went negative by airing television commercials suggesting that it was time that Canada had a prime minister who was not a Quebecer. But, notwithstanding their 8 per cent gain, Reform remained 35 points behind the Liberals among Ontarians. In the West, despite last-minute forays by Prime Minister Chrétien to selected ridings, Reform and NDP support increased appreciably. The story was similar in the Atlantic provinces, where Liberal strength eroded as the Tories and New Democrats gained.

At the Polls

Although the Liberals ultimately prevailed, it was not until the British Columbia returns came in that Chrétien knew for certain that he was still the prime minister. In the Atlantic provinces, where the Liberals had won fully 31 of 32 seats in 1993, they carried only 11 in 1997. In contrast, the Conservatives captured 12 seats and the NDP gained eight in New Brunswick and Nova Scotia. Unlike the 1984 election when the John Turner-led Liberals had suffered major losses in central Canada as well as in the Maritimes, this time around the Liberals won the contest in and for the electoral heartland.

Eight :: No Winners

Their gains in Quebec translated into 26 seats (eight more than in 1993). The big story was in Ontario, where despite the late surge by Reform, the Liberals swept 101 of 103 seats. As for other parties, Liberal success in Quebec and a lacklustre campaign by party leader Gilles Duceppe notwithstanding, the BQ maintained its provincial majority, electing 44 MPs. Although the Conservatives also won five Quebec seats, in Ontario they managed to elect only a single MP. Reform and the NDP fared even worse, failing to win a single seat in the province.

PARTISANSHIP IN DECLINE

In 1993 the Bloc and Reform were seemingly well-positioned to make further advances, since their electoral successes had been accompanied by the growth of sizable, regionally concentrated, groups of party identifiers.[4] It did not happen. Indeed, the national percentage of Reform identifiers actually declined from 10 per cent to 5 per cent between 1993 and 1996. BQ partisanship was more volatile, falling to 33 per cent of the Quebec electorate in 1994, rising to 42 per cent at the time of the 1995 sovereignty referendum, and then dropping back to 25 per cent in 1996. The inability of the new parties to augment their partisan bases was not because Conservative and NDP identifications rebounded. Just the opposite. By 1996, their identifier groups had shrunk from 20 per cent to 13 per cent and from 11 per cent to 7 per cent, respectively. The Liberals also were unable to retain partisans. After increasing to 41 per cent in 1995, the Liberal group of identifiers decreased to 34 per cent in 1996. As the partisan bases of all the parties eroded in the year before the 1997 election, not surprisingly, there was a corresponding increase in the number of *non-identifiers*. For the second time since 1990, the non-identifier group reached a record high in 1996, with fully 30 per cent stating that they did not think of themselves as partisans of any of the federal parties.

Essentially, then, nothing had changed when the 1997 election was called; approximately one-third of the electorate identified with the Liberals, one-third identified with one of the opposition parties and one-third were non-identifiers. Although the latter group seemingly presented significant opportunities for one or more of the

Figure 8.4   The Dynamics of Party Identification during
the 1997 Federal Election Campaign (3-Day Moving Averages)

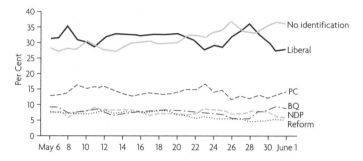

parties, all were singularly unsuccessful in "manufacturing partisans" during the 1997 campaign. Contradicting the venerable conventional wisdom that elections mobilize partisanship (e.g., Key, 1964: 484), the percentage of non-identifiers actually *increased* as the campaign progressed (see Figure 8.4). In its closing week, with the percentage of Liberal identifiers falling sharply, non-identifiers became the largest group in the electorate. The overall percentage of non-identifiers in our 1997 survey (30 per cent) is unprecedented for any election year since the first Canadian national election survey was conducted in 1965. Prior to 1997 the largest percentage of non-identifiers in any election year was 14 per cent (in 1993), and the average was 12 per cent.[5] The *de*mobilization of partisanship in 1997 was such that *all* parties—new and old alike—had proportionately fewer identifiers than four years earlier.

NONE OF THE ABOVE: ISSUES AND LEADERS

Issue-party linkages and party leader images are highly mutable forces that can drive voting behaviour in different directions in successive elections. But, the strength of these forces is not invariant, and in recent federal elections, issues, rather than leaders, have been relatively more important (Clarke et al., 1996: ch. 5). As is typically the case in federal elections, the country's economic performance was a salient issue in 1997. Our survey evidence shows that, nationwide, 55 per cent of those mentioning an issue selected some aspect of the economy as "most important." The big concern

Eight :: No Winners

Table 8.3 Perceptions of Most Important Issue and
Party Closest, 1997 National Election Campaign Surveys

Most Important Issue*		Party Closest (%)†						
		Liberal	PC	NDP	Reform	BQ	Other	None
Economic								
Deficit	10	**40**	10	1	20	3	1	26
Unemployment	32	24	13	11	8	4	1	**40**
Taxes	5	20	11	5	21	1	0	**42**
General Economy	8	**35**	8	6	17	4	1	30
Social								
Health Care	11	24	11	10	5	1	0	**49**
Education	3	11	8	7	13	3	0	**58**
Other Programs	3	23	6	21	9	3	3	**34**
Other								
National Unity	10	**30**	15	3	14	13	0	26
Pro-Quebec Independence	1	9	0	0	6	**69**	0	16
Government Accountability	3	13	11	9	22	3	4	38
All Other Issues	5	9	9	6	27	8	5	36
None, Don't Know	22	-	-	-	-	-	-	-

* Multiple mentions, percentage of respondents mentioning issue; † Horizontal percentages.
Note: Boldface indicates party preferred by majority or plurality of electorate on each issue.

was unemployment, cited by 32 per cent (see Table 8.3). Another
10 per cent were concerned about the deficit, 5 per cent referred to
taxes, and 8 per cent to the economy generally. Other prominent
issues were health care and national unity, cited by 11 per cent and
10 per cent, respectively.

A major problem facing the governing Liberals was that even
though they did better than their opponents, they still were not
favoured by majorities on *any* of the issues (Table 8.3). For example,
although the Liberals had enjoyed considerable success in reducing
the deficit and Finance Minister Martin claimed that the federal
government soon would enjoy a budget surplus, only 40 per cent of
those concerned about the issue believed the Liberals were closest to
them on it. Unemployment, in contrast, continued to be a serious
problem, but only 24 per cent of the much larger group exercised
about this issue endorsed the Liberals. The party also fared poorly

among persons citing threats to health care or other social programs. Nor did it do well among those worried about national unity. Although this issue historically had been a Liberal strong suit, only 30 per cent of those mentioning it as most important favoured the party.

The weakness of party-issue linkages is glaring when all issues are considered. Overall, as Table 8.1 shows, only 19 per cent chose the Liberals as closest to them on the issue they deemed most important. Comparable percentages for the other parties were: Reform, 10 per cent, Conservatives, 9 per cent, NDP, 6 per cent, and BQ, 4 per cent (see Table 8.1). Fully 29 per cent said *no party* was closest to them, and an additional 22 per cent said there *was no important issue.*[6] Thus, in 1997 the parties failed to convince one large group of voters that they were best suited to deal with important issues, and they failed to convince another large group that there were any important issues.

Leading the Vote?

It is "textbook knowledge" among party strategists and media pundits that an attractive leader is *the* key to success in Canadian elections. However, as in other areas of life, the empirical evidence is not always congruent with conventional wisdom. Studies of federal elections conducted over the past three decades indicate that party leader images do exert significant effects on voting behaviour, but their importance varies from one election to the next (see, e.g., Clarke et al., 1996: ch. 4). Many voters do not filter political news through the lens of durable partisanship, and media coverage of party leaders during election campaigns can be highly variable; today's hero may become tomorrow's villain. Moreover, the set of competing party leaders often changes in part or in whole from one election to the next. The result is that the impact of leader images on voting behaviour in any particular election is difficult to predict.

In 1997, the potential dynamism in leader images was largely unrealized, at least at the *national* level. As Figure 8.5 illustrates, feelings about the leaders of four of the five major parties (as summarized by 100-point thermometer scales)[7] moved within quite narrow ranges during the campaign. Three-day moving averages

Eight :: No Winners

Figure 8.5 Party Leader Thermometer Scores, 1997
Federal Election Campaign (3-Day Moving Averages)

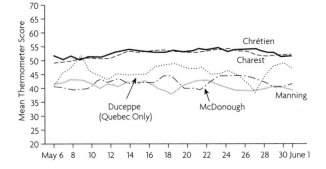

reveal that affection for Jean Chrétien varied from a low of 50 points (the neutral point on the scale) to a high of 54. Similarly, feelings about the Conservative, NDP, and Reform leaders—Jean Charest, Alexa McDonough, and Preston Manning—varied from 49 to 53 points, from 40 to 46 points, and from 38 to 43 points, respectively. Chrétien's and Charest's scores exhibited very weak upward trends (slightly less than .10 points per day), while Manning's moved gently downward. Feelings about BQ leader Gilles Duceppe were more volatile. His thermometer ratings varied from a high of 51 to a low of 38 and, like McDonough's, did not trend either upward or downward.

Campaign (non)dynamics aside, what is glaringly apparent is the absence of public enthusiasm for any of the party leaders. Nationally, only Jean Charest was more warmly received than his predecessor (Kim Campbell) had been in 1993, and only Charest (52) and Chrétien (53) had scores that edged above the neutral point on the 100-point scale (see Table 8.4). Average scores for McDonough and Manning were decidedly negative—42 in both cases. Duceppe's national mean score was a dismal 27 points, but even in Quebec, his rating among Francophones was only 47. Nor was he alone in this respect. There were big differences in feelings about Chrétien between Ontarians (60 points) and Francophone Quebecers (41 points), and similarly large differences obtained for McDonough and Manning—in both cases they were massively unpopular among Quebec Francophones. The only leader to generate positive feelings among this group was Jean Charest, although his mean score (53 points) can hardly be regarded as a ringing endorsement. More

Table 8.4   Party Leader Thermometer Scores by Region, 1993
National Election Survey and 1997 National Election Campaign Surveys

			Region			
Party		*— Quebec —*			*British*	
Leader	*Atlantic*	*French*	*Non-French*	*Ontario*	*Prairies*	*Columbia*	*Canada*
Liberal							
'93 Chrétien	65	41	76	62	57	57	56
'97 Chrétien	52	41	63	60	51	53	53
PC							
'93 Campbell	40	38	33	38	36	48	39
'97 Charest	54	53	63	53	50	47	52
NDP							
'93 McLaughlin	25	40	54	44	41	45	43
'97 McDonough	52	33	44	44	45	44	42
Reform							
'93 Manning	42	31	28	42	52	48	42
'97 Manning	37	25	34	44	45	44	42
BQ							
'93 Bouchard	20	60	20	16	16	18	28
'97 Duceppe	26	47	24	20	20	21	27

generally, in 1997, as in 1993, regional differences in people's feelings about party leaders tended to be variations on a theme of negativism.

REAL CHOICES AND POSSIBLE ONES

Modelling the Vote

To assess the determinants of electoral choice in 1997, we include issue and leader variables together with party identification and demographic characteristics in a multivariate model of the vote:

$$\text{VOTE} = \Phi(\beta_0 + \Sigma\beta_i\text{LEADER} + \Sigma\beta_j\text{ISSUE} + \Sigma\beta_k\text{PID} + \Sigma\beta_l\text{DEMO})$$

where: VOTE = vote for the Liberal, PC, NDP, Reform, or BQ parties; LEADER = thermometer scores for the party leaders; ISSUE = dummy variables measuring which party is closest on the most important election issue (persons saying no party is closest, or there is no important issue, constitute the reference category); PID = dummy variables measuring federal party identification (non-identifiers are the reference category); DEMO = demographic variables (age, annual family income, education, gender, region/ethnicity).[8] The β's are coefficients measuring the effects of various predictor variables. As in the analyses of voting behaviour discussed in earlier chapters, the dependent (voting) variables are dichotomies and, accordingly, we use binary probit to estimate these coefficients.[9]

Model estimates accord well with expectations. In the five vote models the coefficients for virtually all of the issue and leader variables are statistically significant and properly signed (see Table 8.5). For example, in the Reform analysis, choosing Reform as closest on the most important issue is positively associated with a vote for that party, and choosing another party is negatively associated with such a vote. Similarly, positive feelings about Preston Manning increase the probability of a Reform vote, and positive feelings about the leaders of other parties decrease that probability. The party identification variables also behave predictably, with identification with a party increasing the likelihood of voting for it, and identification with another party having the opposite effect. Again, and as long has been typical in analyses of voting behaviour in federal elections, many of the demographic variables do not exert statistically significant effects (see, e.g., Clarke and Stewart, 1992; Clarke et al., 1996: 94-98). Region/ethnicity is the principal exception; net of other considerations, residents of the Prairies or British Columbia were more likely than Ontarians (the reference category) to vote Reform, and Westerners and Quebec Francophones were less likely than Ontarians to vote Liberal. The models also perform well when judged in terms of their overall explanatory power. McKelvey R^2's vary from .62 (Conservative voting) to .78 (Liberal and Reform voting), and the percentages of cases correctly classified are very high, varying from 90.2 per cent in the case of the Liberals to 95.1 per cent for the NDP.

Table 8.5 Probit Analyses of Voting
Intentions, 1997 National Election Campaign Surveys

	Vote Intention				
Predictor Variables	*Liberal* b	*PC* b	*NDP* b	*Reform** b	*BQ*† b
Constant	− 0.70▲	− 2.25◆	− 0.99▲	− 2.10◆	− 1.70◆
Region/ethnicity:					
Atlantic	0.18	0.05	0.09	− 0.43	•
Quebec – French	− 0.43✚	0.49◆	− 0.81✚	•	1.22
Quebec – Non-French	0.00	0.32	•	•	•
Prairies	− 0.22▲	0.02	− 0.18	0.55◆	•
British Columbia	− 0.33✚	− 0.20	0.05	0.63◆	•
Age	− 0.00	0.01✚	− 0.00	0.00	− 0.01
Education	0.01	0.03	− 0.05	− 0.08	− 0.02
Gender	0.02	− 0.00	− 0.13	0.14	− 0.18
Income	− 0.08	0.07	0.03	0.12	− 0.01
Party closest, most important issue:					
Liberal	0.86◆	− 0.71◆	− 0.51✚	− 0.63◆	− 0.12
PC	− 1.16◆	1.06◆	− 0.57▲	− 0.46▲	− 0.64▲
NDP	− 0.84◆	− 0.38	0.88◆	− 1.31◆	•
Reform	− 0.99◆	− 0.67◆	− 0.92◆	0.86◆	•
BQ	− 1.07✚	− 0.62▲	− 0.41	•	0.56▲
Party leader affect:					
Chrétien	0.03◆	− 0.01◆	− 0.01◆	− 0.01◆	− 0.08
Charest	− 0.01✚	0.03◆	− 0.01✚	− 0.02◆	− 0.02◆
McDonough	− 0.01◆	0.00	0.03◆	− 0.01★	0.00
Manning	− 0.01◆	− 0.01✚	− 0.00	0.05◆	0.00
Duceppe	0.06▲	− 0.01▲	0.00	− 0.00	0.03◆
Federal party identification:					
Liberal	0.97◆	− 0.44◆	− 0.59◆	− 0.47✚	− 0.03
PC	− 0.70◆	0.98◆	− 0.45▲	− 0.19	0.65▲
NDP	− 0.96◆	− 0.65✚	1.23◆	− 0.65✚	0.94
Reform	− 0.71◆	− 0.13	− 1.28◆	0.68◆	•
BQ	− 1.66◆	− 1.09◆	− 1.03▲	•	1.82◆
McKelvey R^2 =	.78	.62	.67	.78	.69
% correctly classified =	90.2	91.4	95.1	94.9	90.6
Proportional reduction in error (λ) =	.76	.52	.61	.71	.77

◆ $p \leq .001$; ✚ $p \leq .01$; ▲ $p \leq .05$; one-tailed test.
* Quebec excluded; † Quebec only; • variable not included in analysis.

The preceding analyses demonstrate that, as in other federal elections, party-issue linkages, party leader images, and partisanship all significantly affected voting behaviour in 1997. As we did in our analysis of the voting in the 1993 federal election in Chapter Five, let us consider how the 1997 election might have turned out if these variables had assumed different values. We focus on three scenarios that had strong potential to affect the future development of the national party system and, indeed, the future of the country. The first scenario focuses on Liberal fortunes in British Columbia where Prime Minister Chrétien and his colleagues hoped to make a breakthrough and undercut Reform's claim that the Liberals represented only the interests of central and eastern Canada. The second scenario considers Reform voting in Ontario where the party must make significant inroads if it is to have realistic prospects of winning a federal election. The third scenario examines BQ voting, and how changes in factors affecting support for the party would have affected not only its fortunes, but also those of other parties and, perhaps, the future of Canada itself.

The scenarios are based on the results of the voting analyses presented above. We manipulate the values of the leader, issue, and party identification variables, while holding those of other variables constant. This enables us to calculate the probability of voting for a party when leader, issue, and partisanship variables are changed in ways that could have enhanced its support. We then employ these voting probabilities in a model of the relationship between the vote a party gets and the number of parliamentary seats it wins to assess the impact on the electoral fortunes of the Liberals in British Columbia, Reform in Ontario, and the Bloc in Quebec.[10]

We first consider Liberal voting in British Columbia, and study three hypothetical voters with characteristics typical of much of the B.C. electorate. One is a Liberal identifier, one does not identify with any federal party, and one identifies with Reform. Each has her age, education, and income set at average values. We begin by raising Prime Minister Chrétien's thermometer score from 53, its value in British Columbia in 1997, to 60, the score he recorded in Ontario. Aggregating the resulting voting probabilities for the three types of identifiers[11] shows that, by itself, this increase would have

Figure 8.6 Projections of Seats Won by Liberals in
British Columbia, Reform in Ontario, and the BQ in Quebec

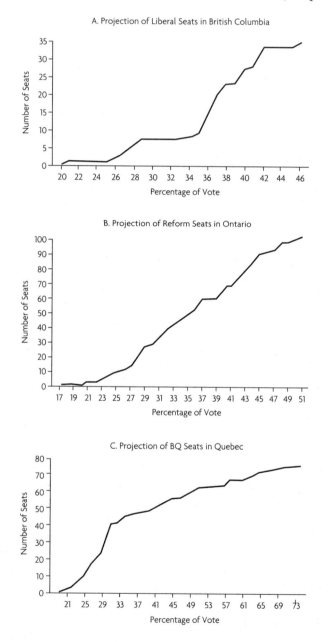

A. Projection of Liberal Seats in British Columbia

B. Projection of Reform Seats in Ontario

C. Projection of BQ Seats in Quebec

raised her party's vote from the 28.6 per cent it actually received to 34.1 per cent. As Figure 8.6A shows, this would have done virtually nothing to bolster the party's parliamentary representation (6 seats) in British Columbia because the Liberals needed to exceed the 35 per cent mark to make substantial seat gains. One plausible way of doing this would have been to combine heightened leader affect with slightly more favourable party-issue linkages. In fact, 19.1 per cent of British Columbians had chosen the Liberals as the party closest to them on the issue they though was most important. If this number had been only 5.9 per cent greater (such that one person in four favoured the Liberals on the issues) and Chrétien had enjoyed a thermometer score of 60, the Liberals would have received 38.4 per cent of the B.C. vote. This would have given the party fully 21 of 31 of the province's seats and a comfortable working majority in Parliament.

The second scenario considers Reform voting in Ontario. We again focused on three groups of voters (Liberal identifiers, non-identifiers, and Reform identifiers) with demographic characteristics identical to those of their British Columbia counterparts. Unfortunately for Reform's prospects, increasing Manning's thermometer score from its actual 44 in Ontario to the 60 received by Chrétien in the province would have produced only a minuscule increment in the Reform vote—from 18.8 per cent to 19.1 per cent. However, more favourable perceptions of the party on important issues would have helped Reform more. Raising Manning's thermometer rating to 60 points and also giving his party a 25 per cent share on the issues (rather than the 9 per cent it actually received), would have increased its vote to 25.1 per cent and given the party nine seats (see Figure 8.6B). However, a real breakthrough for Reform could have occurred if it could have increased its vote share from 25 per cent to 30 per cent. (Figure 8.6B). One way the party could have done this would have been to have even more voters favouring it on the issues. Another way would have been to increase its percentage of party identifiers. For example, if 20 per cent rather than 6 per cent of the Ontario electorate had been Reform identifiers, and the preceding leader and issue conditions had obtained, Reform would have garnered 30.5 per cent of the vote and 30 seats! This would have given Reform the breakthrough in Ontario that it craves, while reducing the Liberals to minority government status.

The third scenario illustrates another way in which the Liberals could have lost their parliamentary majority. This scenario considers factors affecting Bloc Québécois support in Quebec among three groups of voters, BQ identifiers, non-identifiers, and Liberal identifiers. The demographic characteristics of these voters are as described above. Recall that analyses of voting in the October 1995 sovereignty referendum presented in Chapter Six indicated that Quebecers feelings about party leaders have strong effects on their voting behaviour. Because of the unpopularity of BQ leader, Gilles Duceppe in 1997, we anticipated that simply raising his score to the level (60 points) enjoyed by his predecessor, Lucien Bouchard, would pay handsome dividends. This is indeed the case. In sharp contrast to British Columbia and Ontario where leader effects were modest, in Quebec increasing the BQ leader's thermometer rating would have boosted his party's vote by fully 16 per cent—from 38.3 per cent to 54.9 per cent. This, in turn, would have given the party 60 of Quebec's 75 parliamentary seats (Figure 8.6c), and denied the Liberals their majority. And, *ceteris paribus*, it would have left the BQ and Reform tied for the position of official opposition.

CONCLUSION: THE CONTINUING POLITICS OF DISAFFECTION AND DISENGAGEMENT

Protestations of party spin doctors notwithstanding, the 1997 federal election can be characterized as "a contest nobody won." The governing Liberals claimed to be winners, but this was true only in a narrow, technical sense. They retained power, but with a razor-thin, four-seat majority. The other old-line parties, the Progressive Conservatives and the NDP, declared that they had re-established their major party *bona fides*. Less biased observers would regard these assertions as far-fetched. Although both parties won the minimum number of seats to be recognized as official parliamentary parties, they remained pale shadows of their former selves. Except for gains in the Atlantic provinces, their performances echoed the disasters they had experienced four years earlier. As for Reform and the Bloc Québécois, 1997 was a disappointment. The BQ saw its vote and seat totals reduced, and it lost its position as the official opposition. Reform assumed that mantle, winning seven more seats than in 1993.

However, it failed to elect a single MP east of the Manitoba-Ontario border, thereby undercutting its claim to be a truly national party. It would appear that many voters also believed that they were losers, or so it might be inferred from the fact that only 67 per cent of them bothered to vote. This was the lowest turnout for any federal election in the twentieth century, and the third lowest turnout in Canadian history—only in 1891 (65 per cent) and 1896 (61 per cent) did fewer voters go to the polls. There were other indications of widespread dissatisfaction and disengagement. At the outset of the campaign voters questioned the need for the election, and a majority of those participating in our national surveys either denied that there were any important issues to be discussed, or claimed that no party was close to them on the issues they thought were most important. Neither were voters enthusiastic about any of the party leaders; nationally, feelings about *all* of the leaders tended to be either negative or, at best, lukewarm. Nor did these national numbers disguise enthusiasm for particular party leaders in various regions. Only in Ontario did a leader (Chrétien) receive an average thermometer rating that reached 60 on a 100-point scale. Scenarios based on our models of factors affecting voting behaviour indicate that these attitudes were consequential. Varying combinations of warmer feelings about party leaders, more positive party-issue linkages and larger groups of party identifiers could have paid handsome dividends for the Liberals in British Columbia, Reform in Ontario and the Bloc Québécois in Quebec. In fact, however, much of the electorate was in no mood to make favourable judgements about any party's leader or its stands on issues and, perhaps most striking, nearly one voter in three failed to identify with any of the federal parties.

More generally, these messages of dissatisfaction and disengagement suggest that Canadians are not about to return to the *status quo ante* and reinstate the party system that prevailed prior to 1993. However, the new party system, like its predecessor, lacks strong anchors in the mind of the electorate and perhaps may best be described as "in transit." Especially significant in this regard is that to date, neither the BQ nor Reform have been able to solidify, let alone expand, their partisan bases. Although the new parties continued to enjoy the benefits of having geographically concentrated voting strength, neither was able to establish large, stable groups of party identifiers. In fact, between 1993 and 1997, the Bloc lost nearly one-third of its identifiers and in the latter year less than three Quebecers in ten identified with it. Reform's performance was similarly uninspiring. Between 1993 and 1997, it lost identifiers in the Prairies and British Columbia and by the election only one voter in seven in the two regions identified with the party. Even in its Alberta stronghold, only one person in five was a Reform identifier in 1997. Perhaps more important, insofar as its goal of becoming a truly national party, our Ontario scenario suggests that even if Manning were to become a more popular leader, or if he were to give way to one, it would do virtually nothing to improve Reform's prospects in the province. The party still would require a major increase in its attractiveness on the issues or in the size of its partisan cohort to reap a politically consequential harvest of Ontario seats. Indicative of how formidable a task this would be is that less than one Ontarian in ten favoured Reform on the issues in 1997, and only one in 20 was a Reform identifier.[12]

It bears emphasis that in these regards Reform is not alone. In 1997 the number of voters rejecting a party identification reached the highest level since Canadian national election surveys were initiated in the mid-1960s. This extraordinary rejection of party labels is the latest manifestation of the more general erosion of partisanship over the past decade as a consequence of a rising tide of public discontent with the performance of *all* parties. This erosion has occurred in a context where many voters already lacked durable partisan attachments. The result in 1993 was the effective destruction of a long-lived national party system and its replacement by a new, regionally fragmented one. In 1997 voters offered a de facto ratification of this new system that "looks like Canada." However, it is readily apparent that this party system is not cast in concrete since large numbers of Canadians continue to be unhappy both with their parties and their politicians.

NOTES

1. Illustrative of the fragility of Liberal support in British Columbia, the party's vote intention share dropped by 25 per cent in the province (as compared to 9 per cent nationally) between November 1996 and January 1997 after Prime Minister Chrétien claimed during a CBC Town Hall appearance that he never had promised to eliminate the Goods and Services Tax.

2. Respondents were asked: "How do you think the general economic situation in this country has changed over the last 12 months? Would you say it has got a lot better, got a little better, stayed the same, got a little worse, got a lot worse?"

3. The question is: "In your opinion, what is the *most* important issue in the election?" Respondents mentioning an issue were asked: "Which party is closest to *you* on this issue?"

4. For non-Quebecers, the federal party identification is: (a) "Thinking of *federal* politics, do you usually think of yourself as a Liberal, Conservative, NDP, Reform, or what?" (b) [If party mentioned in (a)] "How strongly [party] do you feel—very strongly, fairly strongly, or not very strongly?" (c) [If "refused," "don't know," "independent," or "none" in (a)] Well, do you generally think of yourself as being a little *closer* to one of the *federal* parties than to the others?" (d) [If "yes" in (c)] Which party is that? For Quebecers, (a) is: "Thinking of *federal* politics, do you usually think of yourself as a Liberal, Conservative, NDP, Bloc Québécois, or what?" All respondents mentioning a party in (a) or (c) are considered to be party identifiers; those not mentioning a party in (a) and stating that they do not feel closer to a party in (c) are considered to be non-identifiers.

5. One might wonder if the 1997 non-identifier figure would be smaller if party identification were measured using post-election rather than pre-election data. Although we do not have 1997 post-election data, the three-day moving averages (Figure 8.4) indicate that the percentage of non-identifiers actually *increased* as election day approached. Also, in 1988, when PSC surveys were conducted before and after the election, the differences are small—14.8 per cent of the pre-election and 13.7 per cent of the post-election respondents are non-identifiers.

6. Since the surveys were conducted over the entire campaign, one might hypothesize that the overall weakness of party-issue linkages in 1997 is more apparent than real because voters interviewed early in the campaign may not have given much thought to the issues or which party they preferred on them. However, Table 8.1 reveals that date of interview is largely irrelevant. The percentages of persons saying no party is closest to them on the most important issue or that there is no important issue declines, but only slightly—from 56 per cent among week-two respondents to 49 per cent among their week-five counterparts.

7. The question is: "Think for a moment about a thermometer scale which runs from 1 to 100 degrees. Fifty is the neutral point. If your feelings are warm towards something, give it a score higher than 50, the warmer your feelings, the higher the score. If your feelings are cool towards something, give it a score less than 50. The cooler your feelings, the lower the score." After this preamble, respondents were asked to rate each of the party leaders. The order in which questions about various leaders was asked was randomized.

8. Age is measured in years; education is a five-category variable (elementary or less = 1; some secondary = 2; completed secondary/community college/technical school =3; some university = 4; completed university (B.A./B.Sc. or more) = 5); gender is scored woman = 2, man = 1); income is a three-category variable (under $35,000 = 1, $35,000-$74,999 = 2, $75,000 and over = 3).

9. If one assumes that a plausible reference point for electoral choice is the governing party (i.e., the Liberals), multinomial logit analyses yield results similar to the binary probit analyses reported here.

10. The seat projection model uses regional/provincial-level voting intention data to predict electoral seat distribution. The way the model is applied is to take the difference between a party's current percentage of the vote in a particular region/province and the party's percentage of the vote in the previous election. This difference is then assumed to be manifest at the riding level in every constituency in that region/province. Declines in support are measured against the total percentage of vote available to lose (support in previous election), whereas gains are measured against the total percentage of vote available to gain (100 per cent minus support in previous election). For example, if a party's support in the previous election was 50 per cent, and the latest polling data show this support to have dropped to 30 per cent, this represents a decline of 40 per cent of its support. Conversely, an increase from 50 per cent to 80 per cent represents a gain of 60 per cent of the total support possible to be gained. These differences, then, are assumed to be manifest at the riding level, so that in the former instance party support at every riding would decline by 40 per cent of its support in the previous election, while in the latter situation party support at every riding would increase by 60 per cent of its total available to be gained. Results for each riding are recalculated and "winners" declared. See Wearing (1994).

Here, the seat projection model is used to predict the number of seats that a party (the Liberals in British Columbia, Reform in Ontario, the BQ in Quebec) would have won had it obtained a different level of electoral support. We do this by varying the level of popular vote achieved by the party in question and simulating the impact of this change on support for other parties in the province. For example, during the campaign 34 per cent of Ontarians said they would consider voting Reform, but slightly less than 19 per cent actually did so. Among the 15 per cent who would consider voting Reform, but did not intend to do so, 59 per cent said they would vote Liberal, 30 per cent PC, 7 per cent NDP, and 4 per cent another party. Our assumption is that any additional Reform support would be drawn from other parties in these proportions, while any reduction in Reform support would have a similarly proportionate benefit. The seat projection model is re-run after each simulation to determine the disposition of seats at each level of Reform support.

11. The computed voting probabilities for the three groups of party identifiers are converted into a Liberal vote share by weighting these probabilities in terms of the relative sizes of the party identifier groups in the B.C. electorate. Analogous procedures are used to compute the expected vote shares for Reform and the BQ scenarios discussed below.

12. There is evidence that Reform has a sizable *potential* vote in Ontario; 34 per cent of Ontarians participating in the 1997 campaign surveys stated that they would consider voting for the party. However, all of the other parties have larger potential votes; fully 75 per cent said they would consider voting Liberal, 59 per cent would consider the PCs, and 44 per cent, the NDP. The pattern in the Atlantic provinces is similar: 30 per cent said they would consider voting Reform, but the percentages who would consider voting for the Liberals, PCs and NDP were 67 per cent, 70 per cent, and 60 per cent, respectively.

NINE

Opportunities

As observed in Chapter One, federalism has proved to be a profoundly ironic aspect of democratic government. Designed to overcome the centrifugal pressures of regionally correlated social cleavages, federal systems provide separatist movements with the institutional bases and statutory authority needed to achieve their aims. Since the Parti Québécois first contested a provincial election in 1970, Canada has provided a particularly illuminating example of this phenomenon. After becoming the government of Quebec in November 1976, the party worked for nearly four years to convince voters that independence was an attractive and viable option. The showdown between the PQ and its federalist adversaries finally occurred in May 1980 when the Péquistes held a referendum on their sovereignty-association proposal. The measure was soundly defeated, and the threat that Quebec would separate from Canada receded, but did not disappear. Fifteen years later history was repeated as another PQ government again used a provincial referendum to advance the cause of sovereignty. Although this second proposal also was rejected, the margin of defeat was extremely narrow. In both 1980 and 1995, the danger to Canada posed by the PQ flowed directly from the fact that the party was the democratically elected government of Quebec and, as such, could sustain the claim that it had the authority to hold a referendum on sovereignty. The decision to hold a referendum, the timing of the event, and the wording of the proposal put to the voters were all at the PQ's discretion. Although they raised objections, both the principal opposition party, the Quebec Liberals, and the federal government in Ottawa, were effectively powerless to prevent the referendums from being held on terms of the PQ's choosing.

MISSED OPPORTUNITIES

In the aftermath of the near miss in 1995, the fact that the Péquistes could not again use a referendum to jump-start the process of separating Quebec from the rest of Canada, if they were in opposition, rather than in government, was not lost on pro-Canada forces. The next provincial election therefore was seen as being extremely important. If the PQ were defeated, the spectre of separatism would be banished for up to at least five years, and possibly for much longer, should public support for the Péquistes recede. But how could a sufficiently large number of voters be persuaded to desert the PQ so that it might be ousted from power? Federalist strategists believed that a charismatic party leader could accomplish the task, and they judged that the leader of the national Progressive Conservatives, Jean Charest, was the man for the job. In reaching this conclusion they were strongly influenced by how voters had reacted to Charest during the 1997 federal election campaign. Quebec Francophones had ranked him as the most popular party leader, and his popularity among non-Francophones had been equalled only by that of Prime Minister Jean Chrétien. In a head-to-head comparison with BQ leader Gilles Duceppe, Charest had done well. As measured by relative placements on 100-point thermometer scales, 55 per cent of Francophones and fully 87 per cent of non-Francophones had preferred Charest to his BQ rival. Only 30 per cent of the former group, and only 5 per cent of the latter one, had preferred Duceppe. These numbers seemed to suggest that Charest had the personal magnetism needed to attract the major swing group in the Quebec electorate, the so-called "soft nationalists," and thereby assemble the coalition needed to defeat the PQ. Charest was asked to switch parties and become leader of the Quebec Liberals. He agreed to do so.

The plan to cast Charest as a "Captain Canada" who would drive the Péquistes into the political wilderness and save Canada thus was premised on the new Liberal leader's personal appeal. However, the premise was not as sound as it appeared. As just noted, Charest had been *relatively* popular during the 1997 federal election when compared to Duceppe. However, many advocates of a "Charest-to-the rescue" strategy failed to realize that his *absolute* level of popularity among Quebec Francophones at that time had not been

Nine :: Opportunities

Figure 9.1 Provincial Vote Intentions,
Quebec, September 1996–May1999

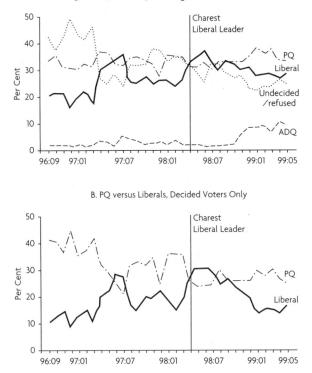

A. PQ, Liberals, and ADQ, Including Undecideds and Refusals

B. PQ versus Liberals, Decided Voters Only

especially high. Indeed, as we have seen in Chapter Eight, his average score on a 100-point feeling thermometer scale was 53, only slightly above the neutral point. Moreover, the appropriate comparison of leader popularity concerned the provincial, not the federal, political arena. Charest's principal rival in a forthcoming provincial election would not be Duceppe, but rather Lucien Bouchard, whose pulling power with voters had been demonstrated in the 1993 federal election and then again in the 1995 sovereignty referendum (see Chapters Five and Six). On the latter occasion Bouchard's thermometer score among Quebec Francophones had been much higher (64 points) than that of any other federal or provincial political leader. There was, then, every reason to believe that Bouchard would be a formidable opponent in a provincial election, and no reason to think that his popularity would be less than that of Charest among Francophones generally, or soft nationalists, in particular.

Nevertheless, it initially seemed that Charest might have a major impact. Even before he announced his decision to enter Quebec politics, rumours that he was about to do so had prompted a surge in Liberal support in public opinion polls (see Figure 9.1). Then, after he was acclaimed leader on March 26, 1998, the Liberals surpassed the PQ in the polls, and the percentage of undecided voters decreased. It appeared that the next provincial election would be a very close contest. The campaign officially began on October 28, 1998 with Premier Bouchard calling for voters to cast their ballots on November 30. When queried about his decision to go to the people, Bouchard did not soft-pedal his party's long-term commitment to sovereignty. He reaffirmed that commitment and promised to hold another referendum on the subject within a few years (CNEWS, 10/28/98). The Liberal response was confused and confusing. On the one hand, Charest declared that he would work to obtain special recognition for Quebec in a revised constitution. On the other, Prime Minister Chrétien announced that he saw no need for constitutional changes because Quebec's demands already had been satisfied (CNEWS, 10/28/98).

Sovereignty was not the only issue. Like other Canadians, Quebecers had suffered cuts in social programs in the mid-1990s, as both the federal and provincial governments attempted to put their financial houses in order by reducing the huge deficits that had accumulated over the preceding decade. Although the reductions in highly popular social services such as health care and education would seem to have been a natural issue for an opposition party, the Liberals' ability to exploit it was blunted by Charest's announcement that he planned to reduce taxes by 2.5 billion dollars and invigorate the economy by shrinking the size of the public sector (CNEWS, 10/20/98). Since that sector delivered those services and employed many Quebecers, the PQ was able to counter by arguing that the new Liberal leader was a thinly disguised ideological clone of Ontario premier, Mike Harris, who was busily prosecuting a painful neo-conservative agenda in that province. According to the PQ, Charest, like Harris, would purchase budget surpluses at the cost of social compassion and jobs. More generally, drawing attention to the economy was likely to be a mixed blessing for the Liberals.

Nine :: Opportunities

Although Quebec's unemployment rate remained a troublesome 10.5 per cent, the PQ government had achieved significant deficit reductions, and 37 per cent of Quebecers judged that economic conditions had improved during the party's term in office.[1] In contrast, only slightly over one person in four (26 per cent) thought the economy had deteriorated.

As the campaign progressed, polls showed the PQ enjoyed a sizable lead over the Liberals, with the small ADQ (Action Démocratique du Québec) party trailing far behind. A debate among the leaders held on November 17 provided an opportunity for Charest to close the gap, but he failed to seize it. Neither he nor Bouchard landed any "knockdown punches," as they sparred over the impact of the Liberals' proposed tax cuts and the cost of the parties' campaign promises. Charest reiterated the familiar claim that the threat of another referendum implied by re-election of the PQ would perpetuate political instability and thereby create uncertainty that would hurt the economy. Bouchard's response was equally familiar. The Premier emphasized that his vision of a sovereign Quebec entailed continuing economic partnership with Canada—independence would not mean isolation and impoverishment. The debates gave the voters precious little new information about the leaders or their policies, and the distribution of party support remained essentially unchanged.

At the beginning of the final week of the campaign, polls indicated that the PQ led the Liberals by about 10 per cent, a comfortable margin that would give the Péquistes a huge majority of seats in the National Assembly. The vote share forecast proved incorrect. Perhaps because of an ill-considered statement by former PQ Premier Jacques Parizeau on the Thursday before the election that the PQ would "milk Canada for all it was worth" and then separate (CNEWS, 11/26/98), or perhaps because of technical problems with the polls (Durand, Blais, and Vachon, 1999), the actual division of the vote was much closer than anticipated. When the ballots were counted, the Liberals had a slight lead over the PQ (43.7 per cent to 42.7 per cent), with the ADQ having 11.8 per cent. However, the Liberal edge in the vote did not give them a lead in seats. With their strength concentrated in Montreal, the Eastern Townships, and the area surrounding Hull, the Liberals won only 48 seats in comparison with the PQ's 76, with the remaining seat

Figure 9.2   Vote Intention by Language
Group, 1998 Quebec Provincial Election

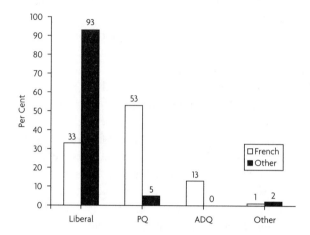

being captured by ADQ leader Mario Dumont. The PQ thus retained power, although its mandate was highly ambiguous. In his post-election news conference, Premier Bouchard provided his own interpretation: voters did not want another referendum immediately he said, but "I also know that when the conditions arrive for a winning referendum, that will be a different cup of tea" (CNEWS, 12/1/98). Most important, by reinstalling the PQ as a government with a comfortable majority in the National Assembly, the election had kept the threat of separatism alive.

At the Polls

A province-wide survey conducted immediately before the election enables us to investigate factors that influenced voting behaviour. Regarding socio-demographic characteristics, as in the 1995 sovereignty referendum, the vote varied sharply across language groups. As Figure 9.2 shows, Liberal support among non-Francophones was overwhelming, with fully 93 per cent of the decided voters reporting that they intended to vote Liberal, and only 5 per cent saying that they would vote PQ. In contrast, the PQ captured a majority (53 per cent) of the Francophone vote, with one-third (33 per cent) going to the Liberals. The other major demographic cleavage was age—among francophones, support for the Liberals was only 14 per

Nine :: Opportunities

Figure 9.3 Vote Intention by Age Group, 1998
Quebec Provincial Election, Francophones Only

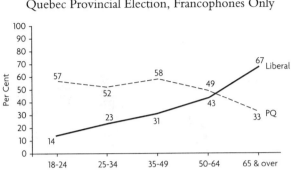

cent among the youngest (18-24) age group, but fully 67 per cent among the oldest (65 and over) one (see Figure 9.3). PQ support was not an exact mirror image as the party captured between 49 per cent and 57 per cent of the votes of all groups under the age of 65. However, among those 65 or older, Péquiste support was only 33 per cent. What these age gradients may portend for the future is a topic to which we will return later in this chapter.[2]

Leaders and Issues

As discussed above, the Liberals' strategy was premised on the assumption that Jean Charest had the personal magnetism needed to attract large numbers of Francophone voters, particularly so-called "soft nationalists" who vacillated on the sovereignty issue. In fact, as in the 1997 federal election, Charest was not warmly regarded by most Francophones, and they gave him an average score of only 45 points on a 100-point thermometer scale (Figure 9.4). Bouchard's average thermometer score among Francophones was much higher, 59 points. Nor did the Liberal leader best his PQ rival among persons who were undecided about sovereignty; as Figure 9.5 illustrates, the average thermometer scores for Charest and Bouchard among this group were 45 and 53, respectively. Charest did well only among Anglophones and persons opposed to sovereignty. Among the former group he outscored Bouchard by 66 to 29 points (Figure 9.4), and among the latter one, he led the PQ leader by 59 to 44 points (Figure 9.5).

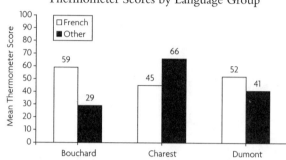

Figure 9.4 Average Party Leader
Thermometer Scores by Language Group

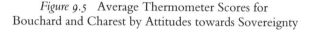

Figure 9.5 Average Thermometer Scores for
Bouchard and Charest by Attitudes towards Sovereignty

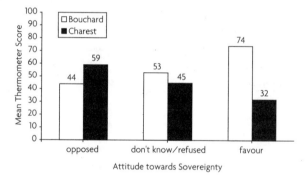

Leader images were not the only short-term forces at work. As is typical in Canadian elections, issues and, more particularly, linkages between parties and issues, had the potential to exert very significant effects. The 1998 election was not regarded by the voters as simply a disguised referendum on sovereignty. When asked what was the most important issue,[3] only 17 per cent cited sovereignty, whereas 31 per cent mentioned a specific economic issue or the economy generally, and 27 per cent referred to cuts in health care, education, or other social programs (Table 9.1). Another 17 per cent believed that there were no important issues. Voters were divided regarding which party they preferred on the issues they deemed most important. Although the Liberals enjoyed a large lead over the PQ among persons mentioning sovereignty (61 per cent to 26 per cent), and smaller ones among people concerned about reductions in social

Nine :: Opportunities

Table 9.1   Most Important Election
Issues, 1998 Quebec Provincial Election Survey

Issue	Most Important Issue*	Party Closest†			
		Liberal	*PQ*	*Other*	*DK/None*
Quebec sovereignty	17	**61**	26	4	10
Defend Quebec's interests	3	0	**100**	0	0
Economic:					
unemployment	11	21	**37**	14	29
deficit	7	11	**75**	8	6
other	13	**40**	25	13	22
Total Economic	31	26	**42**	12	21
Social:					
cuts in health, education, etc.	27	**38**	23	13	27
other	1	**33**	17	**33**	17
Leadership	3	21	14	0	**64**
All other issues	1	0	**71**	0	29
Don't know, no issues	17	—	—	—	—
Party closest (all issues)		29	28	8	**36**

*   percentage of respondents mentioning issue as most important;
†   horizontal percentages. *Note:* Boldface indicates party preferred by
majority or plurality of electorate on each issue.

programs (e.g., 38 per cent to 23 per cent on health care and education), they trailed the PQ by a substantial margin (26 per cent versus 42 per cent) among those citing economic issues. The overall result of these contrasting patterns of party preference was a virtual dead heat between the Liberals and the PQ on the issues—across the electorate, 29 per cent favoured the former party and 28 per cent favoured the latter one. This close division meant that neither major party could realize large *aggregate* gains via party-issue linkages. Also, other parties did not profit from the failure of the Liberals and the PQ to attract strong support on the issues. Only 7 per cent opted for the ADQ, and less than 1 per cent, preferred any other party. As in the 1997 federal election, the largest single group of voters (36 per cent) were those who said that they did not like any party on the issues or that there were no important issues.

The close aggregate division between the Liberals and the PQ on the issues does not foreclose the possibility that party preferences on the issues had significant *individual-level* effects on voting behaviour. Similar to the elections discussed in earlier chapters, both party-issue

A Polity on the Edge

Table 9.2   Voting Intentions by Feelings about
Party Leaders and Party Preference on Most Important Issue

A. *Percentages Voting Parti Québécois*

Party Preference on Most Important Issue

Relative Leader Affect	Other Party	None, Don't Know	Parti Québécois
Warmer feelings for other leader	3	5	58
Equal feelings for leaders	6	12	50
Warmer feelings for Bouchard	41	43	90

B. *Percentages Voting Liberal*

Party Preference on Most Important Issue

Relative Leader Affect	Other Party	None, Don't Know	Liberal
Warmer feelings for other leader	3	6	38
Equal feelings for leaders	22	11	65
Warmer feelings for Charest	60	87	96

linkages and feelings about the party leaders influenced voters' choices in the 1998 Quebec election. A preliminary indication of the strength of these effects may be obtained by tallying the percentages of PQ and Liberal voters for varying combinations of party preference on the issues and party leader preference (as measured by the 100-point thermometer scores). These calculations indicate that issue and leader preferences[4] made a big difference for PQ voting (Table 9.2A). For example, among persons who liked Bouchard better than another leader, the percentage voting PQ was only 41 per cent if a party other than the PQ was favoured on the issue deemed most important. However, the percentage casting a PQ ballot was fully 90 per cent among voters who liked Bouchard better than another leader and favoured the PQ on the most important issue. As an example of leader effects, consider persons who chose the Liberals as closest on the most important issue (see Table 9.2B). Among this group, the percentage voting Liberal increased from 38 per cent among those preferring another leader to Jean Charest, to 65 per cent who liked Charest and another leader equally, and to fully 96 per cent among those who preferred Charest to other leaders. The data in Table 9.2 also illustrate the combined strength of issue and leader effects. As just noted, among persons who endorsed a party on the issues and liked its leader better than his rivals, over 90 per cent or more intended to vote for that party. However, when another party was preferred on the issues and another leader was more attractive, the percentage intending to vote for the party in question fell precipitously—to only 3 per cent in both the PQ and Liberal analyses.

Modelling the Vote

The strength of leader and issue effects on the vote can be assessed more precisely using a multivariate model of voting behaviour. As in similar analyses in earlier chapters, this model includes variables measuring party preference on the issue selected as most important,[5] feelings about party leaders,[6] party identification,[7] and several socio-demographics (age, education, gender, income, and language).[8] Also included are variables tapping retrospective evaluations of economic conditions,[9] and attitudes towards sovereignty.[10] The survey data were gathered before the election, and a substantial number of respondents indicated that they were undecided how they would vote.[11] We accommodate these undecided voters by constructing two dependent variables, each of which has three categories. For the first dependent variable, these categories are: vote Liberal, undecided, and vote for another party; for the second one, the categories are: vote PQ, undecided, and vote for another party. These three-category variables are conceptualized as ordinal scales and, hence, ordered probit is an appropriate estimation technique (Long, 1997, ch. 5).

The probit analyses indicate that the models do a good job in explaining PQ and Liberal voting (as measured by the estimated R^2's and percentages of cases correctly classified), and that many of the predictor variables behave as anticipated. Considering the PQ analysis, identifiers with that party were more likely, and identifiers with other parties were less likely, than persons without a party identification to state that they would vote Péquiste (see Table 9.3). Party-issue linkages and leader images are significant as well. As expected, persons who favoured the PQ on the issue seen as most important were more likely to say they would cast a PQ

A Polity on the Edge

Table 9.3 Ordered Probit Analyses of Liberal
and PQ Voting in the 1998 Quebec Provincial Election

Predictor Variables	Vote			
	Liberal		Parti Québécois	
	b	s.e.	b	s.e.
Age	0.00	0.01	0.00	0.01
Education	− 0.10	0.08	− 0.05	0.10
Gender	0.13	0.15	− 0.12	0.16
Income	− 0.05	0.13	− 0.01	0.13
Language	− 0.20	0.28	0.08	0.36
Provincial party identification:				
Liberal	0.84♦	0.25	− 0.71♦	0.25
PQ	− 1.36♦	0.22	1.02♦	0.24
ADQ	− 0.54	0.36	− 1.02✚	0.38
Party leader affect:				
Bouchard	− 0.10▲	0.01	0.02♦	0.00
Charest	0.02♦	0.01	− 0.01▲	0.01
Dumont	− 0.01▲	0.01	− 0.01▲	0.01
Party closest, most important issue	0.56♦	0.15	0.40✚	0.12
Retrospective evaluations of the national economy	0.06	0.11	− 0.17	0.14
Support/oppose Quebec sovereignty	0.18	0.12	− 0.18	0.12
Average McKelvey R² =	0.78		0.71	
Average % correctly predicted =	77.0		71.2	
Average proportional reduction in error (λ) =	56.5		48.5	

♦ p ≤ .001;   ✚ p ≤ .01;   ▲ p ≤ .05; one-tailed test.

Note: b coefficients and associated standard errors are computed using
multiple imputation techniques for missing data described in King et al.
(1999). Ten data sets with imputed missing values are created for each
(Liberal and Parti Québécois) voting analysis.

ballot, as were those with positive feelings about party leader Lucien
Bouchard. In contrast, persons with positive feelings about the
leaders of other parties were less apt to favour the PQ. These patterns
are replicated in the Liberal case; a Liberal party identification,
perceptions that the Liberals are closest on the most important
issue, and positive feelings about the Liberal leader, Jean Charest,
all enhanced the likelihood of supporting the Liberals. In contrast,
identification with another party, perceiving another party as closest

Nine :: Opportunities

Table 9.4 Probit Analyses of Parti Québécois and Liberal
Party Identifications, 1998 Quebec Provincial Election Survey

	Party Identification	
Predictor Variables	*Parti Québécois* b	*Liberal* b
Age	0.00	0.01✚
Education	− 0.05	0.05
Gender	− 0.10	− 0.15
Income	0.28✚	0.07
Language	0.69✚	− 0.70◆
Retrospective evaluations of the national economy	0.28◆	− 0.01
Support/oppose Quebec sovereignty	0.80◆	− 0.73◆
Constant	− 2.53◆	− 0.86▲
McKelvey R^2 =	.43	.36
Percent correctly classified =	83.2	77.3
Proportional reduction in error (λ) =	.37	.18

◆ p ≤ .001; ✚ p ≤ .01; ▲ p ≤ .05.

on the most important issue, and positive feelings about other party leaders lessened Liberal support.

There are other similarities between the PQ and Liberal analyses. In both cases, none of the socio-demographic variables exerted significant effects, net of controls for other variables in the models. Also, neither economic evaluations nor attitudes towards sovereignty had a significant impact. The latter finding might be deemed counter-intuitive, but it is possible that feelings about sovereignty influenced voting behaviour *indirectly* by influencing other variables in the model, such as party identification and feelings about party leaders. Additional analyses support this conjecture. Table 9.4 shows that attitudes towards sovereignty strongly affected PQ and Liberal party identifications, net of economic evaluations and several socio-demographic characteristics. For example, in a scenario considering a hypothetical voter who is a Francophone, a man, and otherwise has average scores on other variables in the PQ party identification model, the probability of being a Péquiste identifier moves from .07 if he opposed sovereignty to .26 if he was undecided, and to .55 if he supported sovereignty.[12] A comparable scenario for Liberal

Table 9.5   Multiple Regression Analysis of Feelings about Lucien
Bouchard and Jean Charest, 1998 Quebec Provincial Election Survey

Predictor Variables	Bouchard *b*	Charest *b*
Age	− 0.21◆	0.15✚
Education	0.15	1.45
Gender	− 1.80	− 0.40
Income	− 0.20	− 0.30
Language	18.22◆	− 10.72◆
Retrospective evaluations		
of the national economy	5.21◆	0.42
Support/oppose Quebec sovereignty	11.41◆	− 12.64◆
Constant	35.11◆	44.28◆
Adjusted R^2 =	.35	.29

◆ p ≤ .001;   ✚ p ≤ .01.

partisanship shows that the probability of being a Liberal identifier
recedes from .47, if the voter opposed sovereignty, to .21, if he
was undecided, and to .06, if he favoured sovereignty. The impact
of attitudes towards sovereignty on feelings about party leaders
also were sizable. The estimated effects on the leader thermometer
score variables indicate that feelings about Lucien Bouchard were
23 points higher among voters who supported rather than opposed
sovereignty (see Table 9.5). In contrast, Jean Charest's thermometer
score was over 25 points lower among opponents than proponents
of sovereignty.

The analyses in Tables 9.4 and 9.5 also indicate that economic
evaluations indirectly influenced PQ (but not Liberal) voting by
affecting PQ partisanship and feelings about Premier Bouchard.
Other things equal, Bouchard's thermometer score was over 10
points higher among persons who judged that the economy had
improved than among those who believed that it had deteriorated.
Similarly, in a scenario with a voter who was undecided about
sovereignty and was otherwise similar to the one described above,
the probability of being a PQ identifier was twice as high (.31
compared to .15) among those who made positive rather than
negative judgements about the economy.

Taken together, these analyses indicate that PQ and Liberal voting
in the 1998 Quebec provincial election were affected by a variety

of forces, including many of the ones typically included in models of electoral choice in Canada. These "usual suspects" included partisanship, economic evaluations, perceptions of party closest on important issues, and party leader images. As argued above, the latter were particularly important in the 1998 Quebec context because of the decision of the Liberals to base their campaign strategy on the assumed charisma of Jean Charest. As we have seen, the assumption was not well-founded. Although Charest was extremely well-liked by Anglophones, he was not warmly received by the large Francophone majority. Moreover, Charest's chief rival, Lucien Bouchard—if not exactly the proverbial "800-pound gorilla"—was an "*homme formidable.*" In addition to being a skilled and experienced campaigner, Bouchard was much more popular than Charest among Francophones generally and, in particular, among Francophones who were undecided about the wisdom of the Péquistes' sovereignty option. Charest's weakness among the latter group was especially important given that the Liberal strategists had pinned their hopes on his ability to attract the support of so-called "soft nationalists."

The Liberals' leader-centred strategy was thereby flawed—Charest simply was not the charismatic politician they had assumed him to be. But, was the accompanying assumption that leader effects were very powerful elements in the set of forces driving electoral choice flawed as well? Evidence from analyses of voting in the 1995 sovereignty referendum and the 1997 federal election suggest that leader effects on voting behaviour can be quite powerful in Quebec and, as shown above, the leader thermometer variables all have significant and correctly signed effects in the analyses of PQ and Liberal voting. But, just how strong were these effects? What level of popularity would have enabled Charest to attract the votes of persons who had not made up their minds on sovereignty? Was there any possibility that, however popular, he could draw appreciable support among persons who favoured sovereignty? How important was Bouchard's popularity for the decision to vote PQ?

To answer these questions, we constructed scenarios using the results of our multivariate models of voting behaviour (see Table 9.3). Our hypothetical voter again was a Francophone male with average scores on the age, education, income, and economic evaluation variables. We assessed the impact of varying levels of popularity for Bouchard and Charest by computing PQ and Liberal

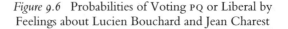

Figure 9.6 Probabilities of Voting PQ or Liberal by
Feelings about Lucien Bouchard and Jean Charest

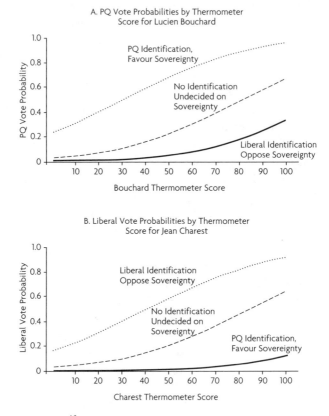

vote probabilities[13] as their thermometer scores are increased from 1 to 100 points. These probabilities were computed for three key groups of voters in the Quebec electorate: PQ identifiers who favoured sovereignty, non-identifiers who were undecided about sovereignty, and Liberal voters who opposed sovereignty.[14]

Considering PQ voting first, one sees that feelings about Bouchard made a large difference in the probability of voting Péquiste among those voters who were PQ identifiers and favoured sovereignty (see Figure 9.6A). Among these voters the probability of a PQ vote increased rapidly as feelings about Bouchard became increasingly positive. At his mean thermometer rating (55 points in the electorate as a whole), the probability of voting PQ was .68. The probability of a PQ vote also increased by a substantial amount among non-identifiers who were undecided about sovereignty. However, Bouchard's thermometer score had to be fully 82 points before this probability exceeded .5. A score of 82 is far above the highest rating (68 for Pierre Trudeau in 1968) ever accorded any federal or provincial party leader. Among Liberal identifiers opposing sovereignty, feelings about Bouchard did little to make a PQ vote a realistic possibility. Even if he had recorded the highest possible thermometer score (100 points), the probability that such a voter would opt for the PQ remained a dismal .33.

The probability curves for Charest resemble those of his PQ adversary (see Table 9.6B). Among his core supporters, i.e., Liberal identifiers who opposed sovereignty, the probability of voting Liberal was .55 if the hypothetical voter described above had an average level of affect (48 points across the entire electorate) for Charest. However, this probability climbed rapidly as affect for the Liberal leader increased, and reached .75 if feelings about him were one standard deviation above average. It is the probability curve for the non-identifiers who were undecided about sovereignty that was the real "killer" for Charest and the Liberals. This group, which contains many of the so-called soft nationalists that the Liberals had targeted in devising their campaign strategy, was quite impervious to Charest's appeal at realistic levels of popularity. For example, if a person in this group had average feelings about Charest (48 points), the probability of voting Liberal was only .19. Even if that person had felt as warmly (68 points) about Charest as an average voter had felt about Trudeau 30 years earlier, the likelihood of a Liberal vote remained far below .5 (.34). Indeed, it would have taken an unprecedented level of popularity (81 points) to push the Liberal voting probability for persons in this group above .5. Finally, the bottom curve in Figure 9.6B shows that Charest effects among PQ identifiers who favoured sovereignty were trivial. Even if a voter in this group was wildly enthusiastic about the Liberal leader and gave him a 100-point thermometer rating, the probability of that voter casting a Liberal vote was only .12. Among voters with average feelings (48 points) for Charest, that probability was vanishingly small (< .01).

The numbers displayed in Figure 9.6B thus forcefully argue that there were distinct limits to the Liberals' leader-centred strategy as operationalized in the person of Jean Charest. Charest's personal drawing power, like that of his rival, Lucien Bouchard, was strongest in his party's core constituency. In Charest's case, this group consisted of Liberal identifiers who opposed sovereignty. Among the key swing group—non-partisans who were undecided about sovereignty—Charest's appeal and its ability to attract votes was decidedly modest. Charest himself seemed to recognize that more than personal appeal would be needed; recall that he stated at the outset of the campaign that if he became premier, he would press for constitutional change. But recall also that Prime Minister Chrétien had undercut him by publicly voicing opposition to further attempts to revise the constitution. By publicly gainsaying his provincial colleague, Chrétien had missed a very important opportunity to give Charest the appearance of being able to pursue a range of constitutional options between sovereignty and the status quo. The former may frighten many soft nationalists but, as observed in Chapter Six, the latter has precious little appeal.

Boxed in by the prime minister on the constitution, Charest had to make other policy appeals. It may be argued that he boxed himself in further when he decided what these appeals would be. Specifically, by stating that he would combine tax cuts with reductions in the public sector, Charest seemed to ignore a campaign maxim that has served Liberals very well over the years, namely, "campaign from the left, then govern from the right." Although lower taxes always have appeal, the prospect of accommodating them by reductions in the civil service was transformed by PQ spin doctors into threats to social programs. These possibilities were causes for apprehension among those voters who already were exercised by the reductions in budgets for health care and education that had occurred during the PQ's term in office. The net effect was to give the Liberals, the principal opposition party, an edge on the social issues, but an edge that conceivably could have been much larger. Then, as we have seen, in raising the topic of the economy by calling for tax reductions, Charest invited voters to focus on a policy area where only one person in four thought things had deteriorated under the PQ's stewardship. He thus was calling attention to a set of issues where the PQ had an overall advantage, hardly an effective way to harvest votes.

In sum, Charest and his party did not have the firepower needed to win an election. A single-member plurality electoral system combined with their concentrated base of support made it difficult to translate votes into seats efficiently. In retrospect, winning the election was bound to be a very tough task for the Liberals. Our analyses suggest it would have required a combination of truly exceptional leader attractiveness and powerful issue appeals to dislodge the PQ. For the reasons discussed above the Liberals lacked this combination, thereby missing an opportunity to set Quebec and Canadian history on a path quite different from the one envisaged by Bouchard and his Péquiste colleagues.

THE SCOPE OF OPPORTUNITY

A United Canada versus a Sovereign Quebec

The 1998 Quebec election, like the 1995 sovereignty referendum, left the futures of Quebec and Canada undecided. Several province-wide surveys of the Quebec electorate conducted between October 1996 and April 1999 enable us to study public beliefs, attitudes, and opinions that will be crucial in deciding those futures. Most important, of course, are orientations towards sovereignty and independence. The former are measured using the aforementioned question on vote intentions in a future sovereignty referendum, whereas the latter are measured by asking people if they prefer that Quebec stay in Canada or become an independent country.[15] These two questions appeared jointly in ten surveys with a combined sample size of 6,757 valid responses. Taken together, they provide the data needed to investigate the scope of political opportunity for separatist and federalist forces in contemporary Quebec.

Cross-tabulating responses to the sovereignty and independence questions reveals that slightly over 46 per cent of Quebecers oppose both sovereignty and independence, whereas only 30.8 per cent favour both options (see Table 9.6). These numbers lend comfort to federalists, but they are not the whole story. There are groups who either favour sovereignty while being undecided about or opposed to independence (8.1 per cent), or favour independence while being undecided about or opposed to sovereignty (2.2 per cent). Persons in the first of these groups clearly indicate that they would vote "yes" in a future sovereignty referendum, while those in the second

Table 9.6 Combinations of Voting Intention in a Future
Sovereignty Referendum and Attitudes towards Quebec
Independence, Combined October 1996-April 1999 Quebec Surveys

Vote in Future Sovereignty Referendum	Attitudes Towards Independence		
	Stay in Canada	*Undecided, Don't Know*	*Become Independent*
Against sovereignty	46.2	*1.3*	**1.0**
Undecided, don't know	*4.5*	*6.9*	**1.2**
In favour of sovereignty	**5.0**	*3.1*	**30.8**

$$\chi^2_4 = 6307.632, p = .000; \tau_b = .78$$

Note: Cell entries are percentages of total sample, N = 6757.

one must be considered probable "yes" voters. Altogether, the total
pro-sovereignty/independence group can be estimated as 41.1 per
cent of the electorate (the sum of the boldface numbers in Table
9.6). This leaves a third group of potential sovereignty/independence
recruits, namely people who state that they are undecided about
both options, or oppose one of them, while being undecided about
the other. This group (the italicized numbers in Table 9.6) comprises
12.7 per cent of the electorate. In sum, neither the pro-Canada nor
the pro-sovereignty/independence groups constituted a majority in
the 1996-99 surveys, and more than one person in 10 remained
undecided about what would be a desirable future for Quebec and
Canada (see Figure 9.7).

Consistent with the analyses of
voting in the 1995 sovereignty
referendum and the 1998 provincial election, these attitudes are
strongly correlated with language
and age. Fully 85 per cent of non-
Francophones, but only 40 per
cent of Francophones, are in the
pro-Canada group, whereas 9 per
cent of the former group and 46
per cent of the latter one are in
the pro-sovereignty/independence
group (see Table 9.7). The age
gradient is steep, with the per-

Figure 9.7 Attitudes towards
Sovereignty and Independence
October 1996-April 1999 Surveys

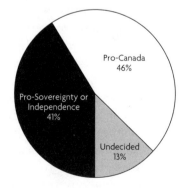

Nine :: Opportunities

Table 9.7   Pro-Canada and Pro-Sovereignty/
Independence Groups by Socio-Demographic Characteristics,
Combined October 1996–April 1999 Quebec Surveys

Socio-Demographic Variables	Pro-Canada	Undecided, Don't Know	Pro-Sovereignty/ Independence
Age:			
18-24	39	9	52
25-34	43	13	44
35-49	41	13	46
50-64	52	13	35
65 & over	63	16	21
Education:			
Less than high school	45	17	38
Graduated high school	44	13	44
Some university	47	9	44
Graduated university	52	11	38
Gender:			
Men	46	10	44
Women	47	16	38
Income:			
Under $35,000	45	15	40
$35,000–$74,900	45	13	42
$75,000 or more	52	7	41
Language:			
French	40	14	46
Other	85	7	9

Note: Horizontal percentages.

centage of pro-Canada persons increasing from 39 per cent in
the youngest (18-24 year old) age group to 63 per cent in
the oldest (65 years of age and older) one. In contrast, pro-
sovereignty/independence orientations decrease from 52 per cent of
those in the 18 to 24 age bracket to only 21 per cent of those 65 or
older. Also consonant with earlier analyses, correlations with other
demographic variables are quite weak. For example, there is virtually
no difference in the percentages of men and women in the pro-
Canada group, and the size of the pro-sovereignty/independence
group differs by only 6 per cent—44 per cent for men and 38 per
cent for women. Educational and income differences are similarly
small (see Table 9.7).

Table 9.8 Beliefs about Quebec and Canada by Language
Group, Combined October 1996–April 1999 Quebec Surveys

Statement about Quebec and Canada	Francophones			Other		
	agree	*undecided*	*disagree*	*agree*	*undecided*	*disagree*
A. Quebec pays more taxes	**56**	26	18	**31**	30	39
B. Constitution can't be changed	**48**	20	33	**47**	17	36
C. Quebec often humiliated by ROC	**53**	11	36	**22**	11	68
D. ROC doesn't understand Quebec	**52**	13	35	**34**	11	55
E. Canada protects French language	39	12	**49**	73	10	**17**
F. Quebecers not different	59	6	**38**	72	5	**23**
G. Personal finances suffer	39	18	**43**	71	14	**15**
H. Fortunate to live in Canada	86	4	**10**	95	3	**2**

Balance of pro-sovereignty/independence and pro-Canada responses:

Mean	0.04	– 3.19
Standard deviation	2.87	3.63

Note: Horizontal percentages; boldface numbers indicate pro-sovereignty/independence responses.

Opinions About Quebec-Canada Relationships

The October 1996-April 1999 surveys contain a battery of eight
"agree-disagree" statements designed to measure Quebecers opinions about Canada or relationships between Quebec and Canada
that might influence their orientations towards sovereignty and
independence. Responses to these statements again reveal large
differences between Francophones and non-Francophones. Majorities of Francophones agreed that Quebec pays more in taxes to
Canada than it receives in return, that Quebec often has been
humiliated by the rest of Canada, and that the rest of Canada does
not understand Quebec, whereas majorities or sizable pluralities
of non-Francophones disagreed with each of these statements (see
Table 9.8). Large differences between the two language groups also
characterized opinions about how they would fare economically
in an independent Quebec—a plurality of Francophones (43 per
cent) disagreed with the statement that they would be personally
worse off, whereas a large majority of non-Francophones (71 per
cent) agreed. Similarly, 49 per cent of Francophones disagreed
that Canada has done a good job protecting French language and
culture, whereas 73 per cent of non-Francophones agreed. As well, a

Nine :: Opportunities

sizable difference obtained in opinions about whether Quebecers are different from other Canadians—72 per cent of non-Francophones as compared to 59 per cent of Francophones agreed that Quebecers are not very different from their fellow citizens in other parts of the country. The two statements where the language groups did not differ concern possibilities for constitutional change and the desirability of living in Canada. Both groups were quite evenly divided regarding whether the constitution can be changed to Quebec's satisfaction, with 48 per cent of Francophones and 47 per cent of non-Francophones agreeing that it is unlikely that such changes can be achieved. Overwhelming majorities of both groups agreed that they were fortunate to live in Canada. Overall, the average number of negative responses concerning Canada or relations between Quebec and Canada (of a possible eight) was 3.49 for Francophones and 1.92 for non-Francophones.

Within both the Francophone and non-Francophone language communities, responses to the statements about Canada and Quebec-Canada relationships exhibit a consistent age pattern. In every case, younger persons are more likely to offer responses conductive to supporting sovereignty or independence. In some cases, these age differences are relatively modest; for example, 48 per cent of the 18-24-year-old Francophones and 36 per cent of those 65 or older agreed that the constitution cannot be changed in ways that would satisfy Quebec, and 50 per cent of the former group and 42 per cent of the latter one agreed that the rest of Canada does not understand Quebec (data not shown). Other differences are much larger. Thus, 56 per cent of the 18-24-year-old Francophones but only 25 per cent of the 65-or-older group disagreed with the proposition that Canada has done a good job protecting French language and culture, and 53 per cent of the former group and 23 per cent of the latter one disagreed with the notion that their personal finances would deteriorate if Quebec became independent. The number of pro-sovereignty/independence responses to the eight statements among Francophones declined from an average of 3.72 among the youngest (18-24) age cohort to 2.48 among the oldest (65 and over) cohort. Among non-Francophones the comparable figures are 2.20 for the 18-24-year-olds and 1.41 for the 65-or-over group. In sum, in every age group Francophones are much more likely to express pro-sovereignty/independence views than non-Francophones, but

Figure 9.8 Self-Identification by Language
Group, October 1996-April 1999 Surveys

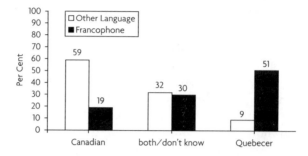

in both language communities there are discernible age differences, with younger persons being more likely to express such opinions.

Canadians or Quebecers?

As observed in Chapter One, previous research has demonstrated that identification of oneself as a Canadian or a Quebecer is an important determinant of political community support. The October 1996-April 1999 surveys consistently show massive differences between Francophones and non-Francophones in these self-identifications.[16] Across the entire period, 51 per cent of Francophones, but only 9 per cent of non-Francophones, identify themselves as Quebecers (see Figure 9.8). In sharp contrast, 19 per cent of Quebecers, but fully 59 per cent of non-Francophones identify themselves as Canadians.

Similar to the data on other political orientations presented above, there are very sharp age gradients in self-identifications among Francophones. As illustrated in Figure 9.9, the percentage of persons identifying themselves as Quebecers declines steadily from 67 per cent among those in the 18-24 age bracket to 28 per cent among those in the 65 and older group. Purely Canadian self-identifications among Francophones are not dominant in any age group, but rise from 15 per cent among the 18-24 age cohort to 30 per cent among those 65 or older. Similarly, the percentage of Francophones expressing dual (Canadian and Quebecer) identifications increases from 18 per cent to 42 per cent across these age groups. Within the non-Francophone group, the pattern is very different. Here, there is a preponderance of Canadian self-identifications in every group,

Nine :: Opportunities

Figure 9.9   Self-Identification by Age Group,
Francophones, October 1996-April 1999 Surveys

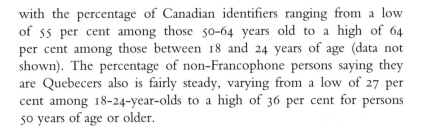

with the percentage of Canadian identifiers ranging from a low of 55 per cent among those 50-64 years old to a high of 64 per cent among those between 18 and 24 years of age (data not shown). The percentage of non-Francophone persons saying they are Quebecers also is fairly steady, varying from a low of 27 per cent among 18-24-year-olds to a high of 36 per cent for persons 50 years of age or older.

Modelling Attitudes towards Sovereignty/Independence

A multivariate analysis enables us to assess the impact of self-identifications,[17] opinions about Canada and the relationship between Quebec and Canada,[18] age cohort, language, and various other demographic variables (education, gender, income)[19] on orientations towards sovereignty/independence. Above, we have identified three groups—persons who are consistently pro-Canada, those who state that they are undecided about sovereignty or independence, and those who favour sovereignty or independence or both for Quebec. Rather than simply assuming that these three groups may be arrayed along a unidimensional pro-Canada pro-sovereignty/independence continuum, we will use a multinomial logit analysis (Long, 1997, ch. 6) to determine if the predictor variables are able to discriminate the declared undecided group from the pro-Canada one. The rationale for this analysis stems from the hypothesis articulated by some observers that a large majority of survey respondents who say they are "undecided" or "don't know" when asked their opinions about sovereignty or independence in public opinion surveys are really "frightened federalists," i.e., they are pro-Canada, but are reluctant to express this view during the course of a telephone conversation with a stranger. By using the pro-Canada group as the reference category and estimating separate sets of parameters for the undecided and pro-sovereignty/independence categories, the multinomial logit procedure provides leverage for testing this hypothesis.

The multinomial logit model includes the predictor variables listed above, as well as month of interview to control for short-term trends in attitudes towards sovereignty/independence over the period during which the data were collected (October 1996–April 1999). The results (see Table 9.9, column two) reveal that all of the opinions about the relationship between Quebec and Canada exert significant effects on the likelihood of membership in the pro-sovereignty/independence group, as does self-identification as a Quebecer rather than a Canadian. Net of these effects, age and education also are influential; compared to the reference age cohort (those 65 or over), all younger age groups and less well-educated persons are more likely to favour sovereignty/independence. Most of these predictor variables also are significant for the undecided category (Table 9.9, column one), and in every case the signs on the coefficients are in the direction one would expect if declared undecideds are, in fact, an intermediate category between the pro-Canada and the pro-sovereignty/independence groups. For example, self-identification as a Quebecer rather than a Canadian increases the probability of being in the undecided rather than the pro-Canada category. Undecideds also are more likely than pro-Canada persons to believe that the costs of federalism outweigh the benefits, that Quebec often has been humiliated by the ROC, that the ROC does not understand Quebec, that Canada has not done a good job in protecting French language and culture, and that Quebec is different than the ROC. In addition, undecideds are more likely to disagree that they would be worse off financially if Quebec were to become independent, and to deny that they are fortunate to live in Canada.

The multinomial logit analyses thus indicate that the undecideds have self-identifications and attitudes towards the relationship between Quebec and the ROC that are significantly different from those in the pro-Canada group. As an additional check

Table 9.9 Multinomial Logit Analysis of Attitudes towards Sovereignty/
Independence, Combined October 1996–April 1999 Quebec Surveys

	Attitudes towards Sovereignty/Independence*	
Predictor Variables	Undecided *b*	Pro-Sovereignty or Independence *b*
Age Group:		
18-24	− 0.07	0.91◆
25-34	0.27▲	0.54◆
35-49	0.38✚	0.75◆
50-64	0.10	0.31▲
Education	− 0.23◆	− 0.22◆
Gender	0.50◆	0.02
Income	− 0.16▲	− 0.04
Language (Francophone v. other)	0.74◆	0.76◆
Self-identification (Quebecer v. Canadian)	0.34◆	0.99◆
Costs outweigh benefits of federalism	0.23◆	0.52◆
Constitution cannot be changed	− 0.03	0.14◆
Quebec often humiliated by ROC	0.18◆	0.43◆
ROC does not understand Quebec	0.22◆	0.31◆
Quebec language & culture not protected	0.16◆	0.31◆
Quebec not different from rest of Canada†	0.12✚	0.22◆
Worse off if Quebec sovereign†	0.77◆	1.37◆
Fortunate to live in Canada†	0.70◆	1.14◆
Month of interview	− 0.19◆	− 0.02◆
Constant	− 0.83✚	− 0.05

Estimated R^2 = .36
% correctly classified = 74.3
Proportional reduction in error (λ) = .448

◆ $p \leq .001$;　✚ $p \leq .01$;　▲ $p \leq .05$; one-tailed test.
* Respondents with pro-Canada attitudes are the reference group; N = 6663.
† Scoring of variable reflexed.

on this conclusion, one may temporarily set aside the pro-
sovereignty/independence group and perform a binary logit analysis
distinguishing between the pro-Canada and undecided groups(see
Long, 1997: 162-63). The results (not shown) again reveal a
large number of significant and correctly signed coefficients, and
indicate that the several predictors taken as a group are statistically
significant (likelihood ratio χ^2_1 = 853.90, p < .001). A similar analysis
where the pro-Canada group is temporarily discarded and the

Figure 9.10   Probability of Favouring Sovereignty/
Independence by Personal Economic Condition in Independent
Quebec and Self-Identification as Canadian or Quebecer

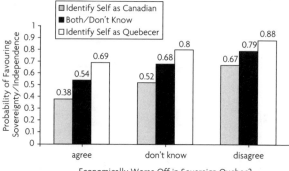

model is used to distinguish between the undecideds and the pro-sovereignty/independence group also indicates that the undecideds are a distinct category. Once more, coefficients for most predictors are statistically significant and correctly signed and, taken as a group, they are statistically significant (likelihood ratio $\chi^2_1 = 771.96$, p < .001). Thus, these analyses reaffirm the message that neither the pro-Canada nor the pro-sovereignty group is in a majority in contemporary Quebec.

The results of the multinomial logit analysis can be used to investigate factors that are particularly important for moving voters into or out of the pro-sovereignty/independence category. For this purpose, we construct scenarios in which predictor variables of interest are manipulated while other variables are controlled. Specifically, we consider a young (18-24-year-old) Francophone woman and examine the effects of changes in self-identification and judgements about her financial condition if Quebec were to become independent (the person is otherwise average in her demographic characteristics and opinions about the relationship between Quebec and the ROC). Focusing on these two variables enables us to test hypotheses discussed in earlier chapters that such identities and cost-benefit analyses are fundamentally important determinants of political community support. The emphasis placed on these propositions is not confined to the realm of academic discourse. Rather, encouraging Quebecers to think of themselves as Canadians and convincing them that maintaining Quebec's membership in the Canadian federation makes economic good sense for themselves and their families long have been major components of federalist strategies for defeating the PQ and its sovereignty project.

The scenarios indicate that these hypotheses are indeed well-founded. Figure 9.10 displays the probabilities of being in the pro-sovereignty/independence group for nine combinations of self-identification and judgments about the financial consequences of Quebec independence. If, as in our scenario, a young Francophone woman identifies with Canada and believes that she would be worse off financially in an independent Quebec, her probability of being in the pro-sovereignty/independence group is only .38 (see Figure 9.10). However, if she identifies herself as a Quebecer while continuing to believe that independence would impose financial hardships, her probability of being in the pro-sovereignty/independence group climbs to .69. Economic evaluations are important as well. If she identifies herself as a Canadian but disagrees with the idea that independence spells economic adversity, the likelihood of being in the sovereignty/independence camp is .67. The joint effects of self-identification and economic evaluations are powerful. A young Francophone woman who identifies herself as a Quebecer and does not think that she would suffer economically if Quebec were to leave Canada has a .88 probability of being in the pro-sovereignty/independence group.[20]

In a second set of scenarios, we manipulate self-identifications, judgements about the economic consequences of independence, and opinions regarding the possibility of changing the constitution in ways that would satisfy Quebec. The ongoing struggle to achieve such constitutional revisions has been one of the central themes in Canadian political history in the last three decades of the twentieth century. And, as discussed in earlier chapters, the failure of the Meech Lake and Charlottetown accords reinvigorated separatist sentiments and bolstered support for the Bloc Québécois and Parti Québécois in the early and mid-1990s. The willingness of successive generations of leading federal politicians including prime ministers Trudeau and Mulroney to invest huge amounts of political capital in repeated efforts to achieve a constitutional settlement acceptable to Quebecers testifies to the strength and pervasiveness of the assumption that such a settlement would do much to deflate support for separatism. But is the assumption well founded?

A Polity on the Edge

Table 9.10 Probabilities of Being in Pro-Sovereignty/
Independence Group by Belief in Possibility of Constitutional
Renewal, Controlling for Self-Identification and Perceived
Personal Financial Situation in an Independent Quebec

A. *Identifies Self as Canadian*

	Constitutional Change Cannot Be Achieved		
	Disagree	*Don't Know*	*Agree*
Financially Worse Off in Independent Quebec			
Agree	.36	.40	.44
Don't know	.51	.55	.59
Disagree	.65	.69	.72

B. *Identifies Self as Both Canadian and Quebecer or Doesn't Know*

	Constitutional Change Cannot Be Achieved		
	Disagree	*Don't Know*	*Agree*
Financially Worse Off in Independent Quebec			
Agree	.52	.56	.60
Don't know	.66	.70	.73
Disagree	.78	.81	.83

C. *Identifies Self as Quebecer*

	Constitutional Change Cannot Be Achieved		
	Disagree	*Don't Know*	*Agree*
Financially Worse Off in Independent Quebec			
Agree	.67	.71	.74
Don't know	.79	.82	.84
Disagree	.87	.89	.91

Our scenarios suggest that, other things equal, *the importance of constitutional change may well be exaggerated.* Consider again a young Francophone woman who both identifies herself as a Quebecer and rejects the proposition that independence and financial hardships go hand-in-hand. If that person also believes that constitutional changes that would satisfy Quebec are impossible, the probability of being in the pro-sovereignty/independence group is extremely high, .91 (see Table 9.10). This probability decreases only slightly, to .87, if she thinks such changes are possible. As a second example, consider a young Francophone woman who identifies as a Quebecer, but believes independence spells economic hardship. Such a person has a .74 probability of being pro-sovereignty/independence if she thinks constitutional renewal is possible, and this probability declines only moderately, to .67, if she concludes that such renewal is not possible. As a third and final example, consider a young person who identifies herself as a Canadian but rejects the notion that she would suffer financially in an independent Quebec. The likelihood that she would be pro-sovereignty/independence is .72 if she does not believe constitutional renewal is feasible. However, this likelihood remains sizable, .65, if she thinks that meaningful constitutional revisions are possible. More generally, the patterns in the data in Table 9.11 tell us that, depending on what combination of self-identification and economic evaluation is being considered, beliefs about possibilities of constitutional change shift the probability of being in the pro-sovereignty/independence group by two to eight points. These effects are not politically trivial given the close balance of pro-Canada and pro-sovereignty/independence orientations in contemporary Quebec, but they are dwarfed by those associated with self-identifications and economic evaluations.

The Dynamic of Opportunity

The preceding analyses of survey data gathered since the autumn of 1996 suggest that the outcome of a sovereignty referendum held in the near future is highly uncertain. Neither the pro-Canada group nor the pro-sovereignty group constitute a majority of the electorate and, although the former group is larger than the latter one, the gap between them is quite modest. Thus, as in 1995, the same kinds of short-term forces that influence voting behaviour in federal and provincial elections, such as impressions of provincial and federal party leaders and evaluations of performance of the provincial and federal governments in economic and other policy areas, could be expected to play pivotal roles in a sovereignty referendum. The very nature of these forces makes it impossible to forecast how

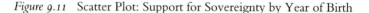

Figure 9.11   Scatter Plot: Support for Sovereignty by Year of Birth

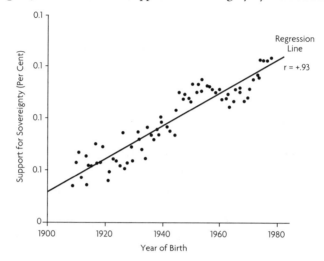

they might play out—party leaders come and go, and public reactions to governmental performance will be powerfully affected by future economic trends and conditions that are shrouded in uncertainty. But what about the more distant future? Are there longer-term underlying forces driving support for sovereignty upward or downward? Although uncertainty is necessarily magnified over longer time horizons, this question may be addressed by considering the potential impact of demographic change on the outcome a future referendum.

Data presented above documented a striking age gradient in political attitudes among Quebecers—younger people are much more likely than older ones to say that they would vote "yes" in another referendum. We may illustrate the aggregate strength of this relationship by regressing the percentage supporting sovereignty on year of birth. Employing data from nearly 26,000 interviews conducted since September 1996, this analysis indicates that support for sovereignty increases by about .6 per cent across successive annual birth cohorts. The correlation between the two variables is very strong (+.93), and most of the points defined by the percentage of each birth cohort supporting sovereignty cluster quite tightly around the regression line (see Figure 9.11). There are two possible explanations for such a powerful relationship—explanations that suggest two quite different possible futures for Quebec and Canada.

276

Nine :: Opportunities

The Life-Cycle Hypothesis

One explanation involves what social scientists call life-cycle effects. A life-cycle explanation would maintain that strong support for sovereignty among young Quebecers reflects the kinds of political attitudes and beliefs that are attractive to such persons, coupled with age-related differences in judgements concerning risk exposure. In general, it is a familiar observation that younger people are the ones most likely to reject the status quo and espouse extremist political movements (e.g., Dalton, 1996: ch. 4). As people become older, they gradually become more averse to risk, adopting a more conservative outlook and rejecting the impulsive, radical views of their youth. In the Quebec case, these age-related differences in attitudes towards risk suggest that young persons would be relatively easy to recruit to the sovereignist cause because most of them have minimal investments in the existing economy and society. The possible risks of sovereignty do not frighten them because they have relatively little to lose. Perhaps equally important, they believe they have a great deal of time to recoup any losses they might incur. In contrast, because older people generally have both more at stake and less time to recover, sovereignty involves greater risks. This is particularly true for seniors who live on fixed incomes and depend on Ottawa for old-age pensions.

Essentially, the life-cycle hypothesis suggests that levels of support for sovereignty will be relatively static across age cohorts over time, but dynamic within them as they move through the electorate. In years to come, successive groups of young voters entering the electorate will continue to support sovereignty in proportions of, say, 2:1, whereas older voters will support federalism by a similar margin. As younger people gain life experience, they will re-evaluate the risks of sovereignty and, based on this cost-benefit calculus, many will reject it in favour of having Quebec remain in Canada. Moreover, not only will voters become federalists as they age, but demographic trends, i.e., low birth rates and increasing longevity, will lessen the overall impact of successive new generations of radical youth. On this basis alone, aggregate levels of support for sovereignty are likely to decline by about 0.2 per cent annually for the next 20 years, all other things being equal.

The hypothesis that sovereignty is largely a product of attitudes and beliefs adopted in youth and then discarded as impractical or reckless as one becomes older may describe tendencies at work among Quebecers and other electorates, but does not satisfactorily explain long-term patterns one sees in the Quebec case. Most important, it cannot explain the rise in support for sovereignty over the last 20 years or the outcomes of the 1980 and 1995 referendums. As just noted, demographic trends have run contrary to what the life-cycle hypothesis would predict. In 1980, 43 per cent of the Quebec electorate was under 34 years of age, whereas in 1995 only 35 per cent fell into that age category. Compared with 1980, the electorate in 1995 was considerably older and, according to the life-cycle hypothesis, should have been less radical than the one in 1980. However, although demographic conditions were much more congenial to the separatist cause in 1980 than in 1995, the two referendum outcomes were exactly the opposite to what should have occurred if the life-cycle hypothesis was the dominant explanation of forces affecting the balance of pro and con attitudes towards sovereignty. In 1980, 40 per cent of Quebecers voted for sovereignty, whereas over 49 per cent did so 15 years later. Perhaps these outcomes simply reflected the fact that long-term life-cycle effects were swamped by short-term forces running in very different directions in the two referendums. Certainly, the configuration of such forces was different in the two contests, and some of them, for example, party leader images, were more congenial to the cause of sovereignty in 1995 when the widely disliked Jean Chrétien was prime minister than in 1980 when the highly popular Pierre Trudeau led the country.

The Socialization Hypothesis

An alternative hypothesis concerning the relationship between age and sovereignty is that support for sovereignty is largely a function of basic political values and, for the most part, people are unlikely to change these values as they age (see, e.g., Nevitte, 1996). According to this hypothesis, an individual's *actual age* is not the primary consideration when considering the probability of voting for sovereignty. Rather, the timing of a person's birth or, more

Nine :: Opportunities

Figure 9.12 Support for Quebec Sovereignty by Age Group

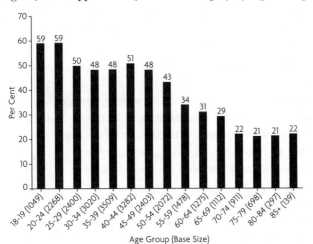

accurately, the historical period during which a person undergoes formative political socialization experiences, has a crucial effect on attitudes towards sovereignty. To illustrate, Figure 9.12 presents support for sovereignty as measured by voting intentions in a future referendum across 15 narrow age bands ranging from 18-19 years of age to 85 and older. These narrow age bands draw attention to significant differences in support from one group to the next. If support for sovereignty is driven primarily by life-cycle considerations as discussed above, it is easy to explain why 59 per cent of 20-24-year-olds support sovereignty whereas only 50 per cent of those 25-29 years old do so—many of those in the 20-24-years age group are still in school and have not established a strong stake in existing socio-economic and political arrangements. In contrast, the 25-29 age group contains relatively more people who have assumed the responsibilities that come with starting careers and families. Such people likely have begun to reconsider some of the views they held in college or university, and sovereignty may be deemed impractical in light of these new responsibilities. But, what explains differences among adjacent groups in the middle-age brackets, e.g., the 50-54 age group as compared with the 55-59 age group? Support for sovereignty among these two groups is significantly different—43 per cent of the 50-54-year-olds (N = 2,072) say they would vote "*oui*," whereas only 34 per cent of

55-59-year-olds (N = 1,478) would do so (see Figure 9.12). This
sizable difference between two adjacent middle-aged groups is well
outside the margin of error for samples of this size, and is at odds
with the life-cycle hypothesis.

If the political socialization hypothesis is correct, what differenti-
ates these two groups is not a few years of age *per se*, but rather
the historical period when their formative socialization experiences
occurred. Although the age at which such experiences take place
may vary, it can be argued that they tend to happen when people
are starting to participate in the electoral process, i.e., when they are
between 18 and 21 years old. Those who are between 50 and 54 in
our surveys would have reached voting age between 1961 and 1965.
This was a period of rapid political and social change in Quebec; the
province was in the throes of the Quiet Revolution and influential
politicians, intellectuals, and media figures were voicing demands
that Quebecers should end their historic political and economic
domination by English Canada and become *"maître chez nous."* By
contrast, persons between 55 and 59 years of age were the last of
what may be called the "Duplessis generation." Their formative
political socialization experiences took place in the middle and late
1950s, towards the end of a political era of relative quietude. These
differing historical contexts of socialization are consistent with the
significant differences in support for sovereignty among these two
successive middle-aged birth cohorts.

As additional evidence of the proposition that attitudes towards
sovereignty tend to reflect differences between "political generations," Figure 9.13 presents data on referendum voting intentions
by periods of initial political socialization as just defined. The figure
illustrates that there were three significant periods when support
for sovereignty across adjacent age cohorts increased by at least
10 points. As just noted, the Quiet Revolution era of the early
and mid-1960s produced a substantial increase in the number of
sovereignists. There also is a large increase in sovereignist sentiments
among those reaching the age of majority in the early 1990s,
when the successive failures of the Meech Lake and Charlottetown
accords focused attention on English Canada's rejection of Quebec's
"traditional" demands, particularly recognition of the province as
a distinct society. Also noteworthy is that the period around the
end of the Great Depression and the beginning of World War II

Nine :: Opportunities

Figure 9.13   Support for Quebec Sovereignty
by Period of Initial Socialization

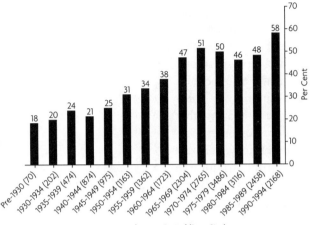

Socialization Period (Base Size)

is associated with a significant increase in support for sovereignty. More detailed analyses show men reaching the age of majority during this era are considerably more inclined to be sovereignists than are women. These findings may suggest that the impact of the conscription crisis—where Quebec opposed the proposition that young men would be drafted into the Canadian armed forces for duty overseas by a margin of 3:1 and the rest of Canada supported it in almost the same proportions—echoes in public political attitudes more than a half-century later.

These periods of "humiliation" or "enlightenment" often are cited by students of Quebec politics as critical events, so it would not surprise us if they were to play important roles in shaping the values of particular generations of Quebecers. However, there is one such event that is noticeably absent—the patriation of the constitution without Quebec's consent in 1981. If, as many sovereignists claim, this was another in a long series of affronts inflicted on Quebec by English Canada, one would expect the group undergoing formative political socialization experiences at the time would show substantially greater support for sovereignty than the group immediately preceding it. In fact, there is no evidence that the appeal of sovereignty is stronger among persons entering the electorate during the period when the constitution was being patriated. As Figure 9.13 shows, support for sovereignty actually is lower among the 1980-84 and 1985-89 age cohorts than among the 1970s and 1990s ones. Indeed, the 1980s cohorts are the only groups coming of age over the past 60 years for which such a significant decline is apparent.

The decrease in support for sovereignty among the 1980s cohorts suggests that neither Pierre Trudeau nor Brian Mulroney were entirely accurate in their prescriptions for the country. Trudeau was correct to argue that patriation of the constitution would not be perceived as an insult to Quebec. However, he was wrong if he believed that the existence of a new constitution, by itself, would be enough to stem the long-run rise of sovereignist

Table 9.11 Predicted Support for Sovereignty in 1980 and 1997 by Age Group

| | Support for Sovereignty | |
Age Group	1980	1997
18 to 19	54	70
20 to 24	55	65
25 to 29	55	54
30 to 34	48	55
35 to 39	40	54
40 to 44	33	56
45 to 49	30	55
50 to 54	27	44
55 to 59	23	37
60 to 64	21	31
65 to 69	21	29
70 to 74	21	25
75 to 79	21	22
80 and over	21	21
Total	39	51

sentiments. The ongoing replacement of older, and much more federalist, groups of voters by younger, more sovereignist, ones slowed but did not stop in the 1980s, and it eventually produced a situation in which the sovereignists could realistically entertain the possibility of winning a referendum. Trudeau also was naive to assume that defeat of the Meech Lake Accord would not play into the separatists' hands and advance the clock towards separation by boosting the strength of separatist feeling among young persons coming of age in the early 1990s. Brian Mulroney, in contrast, was prescient in realizing that some sort of accommodation to Quebec had to be made in order to make the separatist option less appealing. *Ceteris paribus*, in the absence of a substantial federal offer Quebec would have half its population wanting to separate within 20 years. However, initiating a process of constitutional negotiations was a dangerous gamble, because success was by no means guaranteed and, if the socialization hypothesis is correct, failure could be extremely consequential. The widely publicized inability of the federalist forces to win agreement on a package of constitutional revisions designed to diffuse sovereignist sentiments could strengthen support for sovereignty, particularly among young Quebecers. The result would be to enhance the likelihood that processes of demographic replacement eventually would produce a sovereignist majority in the province. To use his own metaphor, Mulroney's decision to try to get a new deal on the constitution was a roll of the dice that would put the future of Canada in jeopardy.

1980 Revisited

If the political beliefs and values associated with sovereignty are as enduring as the socialization hypothesis suggests, vote intentions in a future referendum should allow us to recreate past ones with a reasonable degree of accuracy. We test this conjecture by simulating attitudes towards sovereignty at the time of the 1980 referendum. This involves using current levels of support for sovereignty among age cohorts, eliminating persons who reached voting age after 1980 and "bringing back to life" those who have since died. We assume that the latter individuals would support sovereignty in roughly the same proportions as people currently 80 years or older. Table 9.11 shows present support for sovereignty within each age group and predicted support during the 1980 referendum. By multiplying the support levels for each age group by the number of people in that group, it is possible to produce an aggregate figure for the province as a whole *circa* 1980. This exercise indicates that the *"oui"* side would have obtained 39 per cent of the referendum vote in 1980. In fact, it received 40 per cent.

The Future

If it is possible to simulate the past using current referendum voting intentions, it also should be possible to simulate the future. For example, someone who was 23 years old at the time of the 1980 referendum was 40 in 1997 and will be 63 in 2020. At present, just 33 per cent of 63-year-olds support sovereignty, but, according to the socialization hypothesis, 52 per cent of them will do so in 2020, all other things being equal. We also assume that Quebecers will continue to enter the electorate with 64 per cent supporting sovereignty and that, as they age, they will maintain their preference for sovereignty. Such a scenario clearly indicates that the chances of a separatist victory are improving, not declining, as older voters leave the electorate and are replaced by younger ones for whom sovereignty is a legitimate and increasingly popular option.

What do trends in support for sovereignty generated by these assumptions portend for the near and most distant future? The dotted line in Figure 9.14 displays the predicted trend line of support for sovereignty into the first two decades of the twenty-first century. Also shown is the projected trend in the proportion of Quebecers who believe that Quebec should become an independent country. This latter line may be interpreted as the lower bound on "*oui*" voting. As documented earlier in this chapter, the vast majority of persons who endorse the idea of independence are ardent supporters of sovereignty, and it may be assumed that they would be unlikely to change their views and vote "*non*" in a referendum. The third line on Figure 9.14 may be seen as an upper boundary on "*oui*" voting. It represents the average level of support in 1996, the highest level of support that the sovereignist forces have enjoyed for a sustained period of time. It seems unlikely that the percentage of "*oui*" voters can advance much beyond this level, but it also is unlikely to fall below the lower level established by the percentage favouring independence. Rather, buffeted in the short-term by varying mixes of pro- and anti-sovereignty events and conditions, it can be expected that support for sovereignty will ebb and flow around an underlying upward trend within these boundaries.

During the last four years of the millennium, sovereignists lost some momentum—and the trend for the "*oui*" side was downward, while the "*non*" side managed to make gains. By the spring of 1999, support for sovereignty stood at 42 per cent of decided voters, down 13 points from the autumn of 1996. However, this decline is neither unexpected nor outside the bounds of what is predicted by the socialization model displayed in Figure 9.14. It would be astonishing if the PQ government were able both to address the deficit problems that have beset Quebec and simultaneously to maintain support for sovereignty at the adrenalin-pumping levels that stood immediately after the 1995 referendum. The fact that support for sovereignty has fallen roughly proportionately among all age groups indicates that the

Nine :: Opportunities

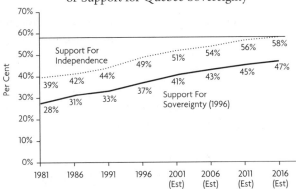

Figure 9.14 Estimated Boundaries
of Support for Quebec Sovereignty

waning of enthusiasm in recent years is a product of period-specific short-term forces, rather than a sea change in the factors that affect how persons in different age groups feel about the issue.

The trends summarized in Figure 9.14 suggest that the next 10 years will be ones of considerable uncertainty, since underlying levels of support for sovereignty will approach 50 per cent. During this period volatile short-term forces, which may make a difference of only a few percentage points on either side of the long-term trend line, will be the deciding factors between victory and defeat in a third referendum. Another sovereignist defeat would likely put the issue in cold storage for several years. However, holding a third referendum during the PQ's current mandate may be the party's last chance for some time to achieve a *"oui"* majority. Certainly, if the PQ is defeated in the next provincial election—which must be held by November 2003—sovereignty will be taken off the political agenda for up to five years. Moreover, in all likelihood the highly popular PQ leader, Lucien Bouchard, will leave office before that date. Whether his successor will be able to generate the high levels of enthusiasm among the Quebec electorate needed to help the PQ win a future sovereignty referendum is unknown. Such short-term forces and the contingencies created by the results of future elections aside, it is likely the PQ's struggle to win a sovereignty referendum will be facilitated by the long-term trends in public attitudes documented above.

CONCLUSION: PROBLEMATIC PROSPECTS

Over the past three decades, the struggle between federalists and their sovereignist adversaries for the hearts and minds of Quebecers has been played out in the confines of Canada's evolving federal democracy. In the aftermath of the 1995 referendum, both sides recognized that control of the Quebec provincial government was extremely important. If the Liberals could oust the PQ from power and form a majority government, the threat of a *"oui"* majority in a third sovereignty referendum could be averted for as much as five years. In their efforts to win the 1998 Quebec provincial election, federalist forces relied on a tried if not true strategy in Canadian elections, namely the personal magnetism of a new party leader. The strategy was simple and flawed. Significantly less popular among Francophones than PQ chieftain Lucien Bouchard, the new Liberal leader, Jean Charest, was unable to harvest large numbers of votes from the pivotal group of voters who did not identify with any of the provincial parties and were undecided about the merits of a sovereign Quebec. Nor was Charest able to overcome his popularity deficit with a package of policies and issues that would appeal to such voters. Confronted with a popular rival leader and a mixed response to their issue appeals, the Liberals nevertheless were able to gain a wafer-thin plurality of the popular vote. However, their vote was concentrated in a few geographic areas and, as a result, the single-member plurality electoral system gave the PQ a solid majority in the National Assembly. The Liberals had missed their opportunity to become the government of Quebec.

The Parti Québécois also missed a significant opportunity in the election. They had maintained their grip on the reins of power, but they did not obtain a plurality, let alone a majority, of the popular vote. Given that Bouchard had opened the campaign with an announcement that the quest for a sovereign Quebec was still very much on the PQ agenda, the ambiguous election outcome was interpreted by all concerned as meaning that another sovereignty referendum was not an option, at least in the short run (CNEWS, 10/28/98). Federalists spun the result as signifying that the PQ lacked a popular mandate to hold a referendum and, for their part, Bouchard and his Péquiste colleagues instantly recognized that this interpretation carried political weight, and it would be impossible to proceed with a referendum in the near future. However, as Bouchard commented shortly after the ballots had been counted, the longer term was something else again.

The extraordinarily close divisions of the votes in the 1995 sovereignty referendum and the 1998 provincial election thus left the sovereignty question—and the futures of Quebec and Canada—unresolved as the twentieth century drew to a close. This result is very much in keeping with the division of the electorate on the issue. Large quantities of survey data gathered over the 1996–99 period show that neither federalism nor sovereignty had majority support in the electorate as a whole. Although Anglophones were massively opposed to the sovereignty option, the Francophone community was deeply divided. Self-identifications and economic judgements strongly influenced these attitudes, with persons who identified themselves as Quebecers rather than Canadians, and those who believed that they would not necessarily be worse off economically if Quebec were to become independent, being much more likely to be sovereignists. In contrast, beliefs about the ability of Ottawa, Quebec, and the other provinces to reach agreement on constitutional revisions that would satisfy Quebec's aspirations have much weaker effects. The latter finding suggests that a future constitutional deal *per se* may not hold the key to swinging Quebec opinion decisively in favour of remaining a part of Canada.

Lurking everywhere in Quebec public opinion is the age correlation. With metronome regularity, the complex of beliefs, attitudes, and behaviours associated with support for and opposition to sovereignty differed across age groups in the electorate. In many instances, these relationships were strong, with younger Francophones manifesting orientations supportive of sovereignty. Older persons, particularly those 65 and over, in contrast, were massively opposed. Disentangling life-cycle effects, age-cohort-related socialization effects, and period effects is notoriously difficult (see, e.g., Glenn, 1977), but a close reading of the data strongly suggests that—possible life-cycle effects aside—these age relationships index generational differences in socialization experiences. There appears to be an ongoing trend for successive generations of young Quebecers entering the electorate to be much more supportive of sovereignty than the older generations they are replacing.

Recognizing that all extrapolations of trends should carry a large "other things equal" caveat, the present analyses thus suggest that Canada's long-term prospects are problematic. If current age-related patterns in support for sovereignty persist and are indeed driven in large part by socialization effects, there is a substantial probability that the sovereignist side eventually can win a referendum—even in a situation where short-term forces are not particularly favourable. It may take 20 years, but the inevitability of generational change will make the prospect of a referendum victory by the "*oui*" side more and more likely as time goes on. Of course, it remains possible federalists might be able to turn the tide of change in their direction. If they can lower the rate of socialization into the sovereignist camp (currently at about 60 per cent), generational change will begin to work in the federalists favour, rather than against them. However, it may be too late to begin this process which, ideally, should have been started 35 years ago. Even if federalists were able to lower the socialization rate to 20 per cent, the glacial nature of generational change means that it would be another 25 years before the underlying rate of support for sovereignty would begin to decline appreciably. This is because, initially, the "new federalists" would merely replace the "old federalists" who have similar opinions on the issue. It is not until the "Quiet Revolution" voters begin to die that substantial changes in socialization would begin to have an effect. The prospect of a sovereign Quebec has been a defining feature of the Canadian political experience for several decades, and it is likely to remain so for the foreseeable future.

NOTES

1. The economic evaluation question is: "How do you think the general economic situation in this country has changed over the last 12 months? Would you say it has got a lot better, got a little better, stayed the same, got a little worse, got a lot worse."

2. Other socio-demographic differences in voting were considerably smaller, e.g., 56 per cent of Francophone men intended to vote PQ, as compared to 48 per cent of Francophone women. Thirty-two per cent of the former group and 35 per cent of the latter one intended to vote Liberal.

3. The most important election issue question is: "Thinking again about the upcoming election on November 30, in your opinion, what is the most important issue in this election?" Respondents mentioning an issue were then asked "Which party is closest to you on this issue?" and "How important will this issue be to you in deciding how to vote in the election?"

4. Leader preferences are measured by comparing scores on the 100-point thermometer scales.

5. The variable in the PQ vote analysis is constructed as: prefer PQ on most important issue = +1, prefer no party or there is no important election issue = 0, prefer other party = -1. This variable is weighted by the self-perceived importance of issue concerns as a determinant of the vote scored as: very important = +3, somewhat important = +2, not very important/no party closest/no important issue = +1. The resulting variable ranges from +3 to -3. For the Liberal vote analysis, the variable is constructed in the same way, except that prefer Liberal on most important issue is scored +1.

6. Leader feelings are measured using the 100-point thermometer scales.

7. Party identification is measured as a series of dummy (0-1) variables with no identification as the reference category. Note that only provincial party identification is available for use in these analyses.

8. Age is measured in years; education is: grade school or no formal education = 1, some secondary school = 2, completed secondary school = 3, some or completed community college = 4, some or completed university to B.A. level = 5, some or completed graduate/professional school = 6; gender is: men = 0, women = 1; (annual family) income is: less than $35,000 = 1, $35,000 to $74,999 = 2, $75,000 or more = 3; language is: French = 1, other = 0.

9. Economic evaluations are scored: economy got a lot or a little better = 3, economy stayed the same = 2, economy got a little or a lot worse = 1.

10. Attitudes towards sovereignty are measured using vote intention in a future sovereignty referendum. Persons intending to vote "yes" are scored +1, those intending to vote "no" are scored -1, and those saying they are undecided are scored 0.

11. Missing values for the several variables in these analyses are estimated using the multiple imputation techniques implemented in the Honaker et al. (1999) AMELIA program. See also King et al. (1998).

12. Regarding the calculation of probabilities for the binary probit model, see Long (1997: 64-71).

13. The calculation of probabilities for the ordered probit model is described in Long (1997: 130-33).

14. Attitudes towards sovereignty are measured using vote intention in a future referendum. See note 10 above.

15. The independence question is: "Ultimately, would you prefer Quebec to stay in Canada or become an independent country?"

16. The self-identification question is: "Do you generally think of yourself as a Canadian, a Quebecer or what?" The terms "Canadian" and "Quebecer" are rotated in successive interviews.

17. Persons identifying themselves as Canadians are scored -1, those identifying themselves as both Canadians and Quebecers or are unsure are scored 0, and those identifying themselves as Quebecers are scored 1.

18. For the following statements, "agree" responses are scored +1, "don't know" responses are scored 0, and "disagree" responses are scored -1: (a) costs outweigh benefits of federalism, (b) constitution cannot be changed, (c) Quebec often humiliated by ROC, (d) ROC does not understand Quebec. For the following statements, "disagree" responses are scored +1, "don't know" responses are scored 0, and "agree" responses are scored -1: (e) Quebec language and culture protected by Canada, (f) Quebec not different from rest of Canada, (g) financially worse off if Quebec becomes independent; (h) fortunate to live in Canada.

19. The age-cohort variables are a series of 0-1 dummy variables with the 65-and-over age group serving as the reference category. The scoring of the education, gender, income, and language variables is described in note 8 above.

20. Another statement that taps perceptions of instrumental considerations bearing on pro-Canada versus pro-sovereignty/independence orientations is whether respondents consider themselves fortunate to live in Canada. Similar to economic evaluations, these perceptions have large effects on the probability of adopting one of these orientations. For example, among persons who identify themselves as Canadians, the probability of being pro-sovereignty/independence climbs from .38 for those who agree that they are fortunate to live in Canada to .83 for those who disagree with this statement. Among those who identify themselves as Quebecers, the comparable probabilities are .69 and .95, respectively.

TEN

On the Edge

REPRISE

We have tried to explain why Canada is a polity "on the edge," why the continued viability of one of the oldest members of the democratic club is problematic. Our focus has been on six pivotal events during a 10-year period that individually and collectively have contributed to the country's current situation.

The first of these events was the 1988 federal election, a contest dominated by debate concerning the advisability of Canada entering into a free trade agreement with the United States. In important respects, the election resembled the first (1980) Quebec sovereignty-association referendum. In both cases, one of the contesting parties characterized the issue at stake as one that went to the heart of what Canada is about, whereas the other represented the choice as far less momentous—more than politics as usual, but certainly not one affecting the future of Canada as a political community. In the 1988 election, the less consequential characterization offered by Brian Mulroney and the Progressive Conservative Party was accepted at least de facto by the Canadian public. The PCs were returned to office and they interpreted their victory as a mandate to implement the FTA. Unfortunately, the economic benefits that the PCs claimed would flow from the free trade agreement did not materialize in the short run. Soon after the pact was passed, the economy faltered and Prime Minister Mulroney and his government were unable to resuscitate it. The PCs campaign slogan that they were best equipped to "manage change" was contradicted by the reality of a deepening recession. Many voters blamed the Mulroney government for their plight, and support for the prime minister and his party plummeted.

We have argued that the country's economic difficulties and the attendant negative political fallout for the federal government figured in Mulroney's decision to hold a national referendum in October 1992 on the Charlottetown Constitutional Accord. The referendum was the second important event examined in this volume. From the prime minister's point of view, passage of the Accord would be good for the country, his party, and himself. Although he campaigned vigorously on behalf of the referendum proposal, issuing dire warnings that the Accord was Canada's "last, best hope for survival," it was decisively rejected by an unhappy electorate. Besides being a stinging rebuff to Mulroney and his government, the demise of the Accord was a major setback for federal constitutional strategists. The hope was that passage of the agreement would defuse separatist sentiments in Quebec that had been reinvigorated by the failure of an earlier attempt at constitutional renewal, the Meech Lake Accord.

Defeat of the PC government's second constitutional proposal was soon followed by defeat of the government itself. The 1993 federal election, our third concern, was an unmitigated disaster for the Tories. Every Conservative candidate across the country, but two, went down to defeat. Nor did voters confine their wrath to the governing party; rather, another old-line party, the NDP, also was virtually eliminated from Parliament. Displacing the PCs and New Democrats were two new parties, Reform in the West and the Bloc Québécois in Quebec. Both new parties enjoyed striking successes in their regional strongholds, with the Bloc capturing enough seats to become the official opposition. The irony of an avowedly separatist party claiming the title of "Her Majesty's Loyal Opposition" served only to underscore the seriousness of the country's crisis of national integration—a crisis that continued before, during, and after the 1995 Quebec sovereignty referendum. The referendum is the fourth major event considered.

Elected as the provincial government of Quebec in September 1994, the Parti Québécois quickly began to pursue its long-sought goal of independence. The centrepiece of the PQ's strategy—as it had been in the late 1970s—was a referendum proposal to initiate a process by which Quebec would become politically sovereign. This proposal, voted on in October 1995, was defeated by the narrowest of margins. Perhaps equally important for the country's future, the referendum's near passage did nothing to soften the attitudes of millions of people inside and outside of Quebec. There was no groundswell of support for a constitutional compromise that would keep Canada intact. Nor was there a meaningful grassroots dialogue between Quebecers and their fellow citizens elsewhere in Canada, and the famous "two solitudes" metaphor has continued to describe communication between the two groups since the referendum.

The fifth and sixth events were the 1997 federal election and the 1998 Quebec provincial election. In an important sense, both events were "contests nobody won." Like the sovereignty referendum two years earlier, the 1997 election seemed yet another exercise in collective frustration. Its principal result was to certify the reality of a new regionally fragmented national party system. The Liberals were returned to power, but with a much reduced parliamentary majority, and PC and NDP fortunes revived only slightly. Although Reform won enough seats to displace the Bloc Québécois as the official opposition in Parliament, its ability to represent itself as a truly national party and potential alternative government rang hollow given its failure to elect a single MP east of the Ontario-Manitoba border. Similarly, the BQ's reduced vote and seat totals undercut its claim to be the voice of Quebec in federal politics.

The 1998 Quebec provincial election also returned a weakened governing party to office. Unlike the federal Liberals, the Parti Québécois retained a large majority of seats, but its ability to claim a mandate to further its drive for sovereignty was seriously inhibited by its inability to gain a plurality, let alone a majority, of the popular vote. Nevertheless, by remaining the government, the Péquistes continued to hold the strategic high ground from which they could purse their dream of a sovereign Quebec.

PERSISTENT PROBLEMS: THE ECONOMY AND QUEBEC

Brian Mulroney was a leading actor in three of the political dramas on which we have focused. In retrospect, it is apparent that the period of his stewardship as prime minister was one that called for a series of very difficult decisions. However, governing in trying times is not an unique experience. Although it may provide Mulroney with precious little comfort, even a cursory reading of Canadian political history reveals that the lot of *every* prime minister, like that of Gilbert and Sullivan's policeman, at times is not a happy one. That is because from John A. Macdonald to Jean Chrétien prime ministers have had to face, Janus-like, the recurrent problems of the economy and Quebec. Each of these problems makes governing difficult. Together—particularly when their effects are concatenated over a brief time period—they can push the Canadian polity "to the edge."

During the past half-century successive prime ministers and the governments they led have attempted to address the two problems differently. In the immediate postwar period, Mackenzie King's Liberal government opted for continentalism, tying the country's economy closer to that of its giant southern neighbour and hoping thereby to maintain and, if possible, to increase war-created prosperity. King also perpetuated a number of symbolic policies, such as having a "Quebec lieutenant" to tie Quebec to the rest of Canada and, more particularly, to the Liberal Party. King's efforts were continued by his successor, Louis St. Laurent, who also oversaw the expansion of an assortment of federally funded social programs intended to narrow regional economic disparities and stabilize the distribution of an expanding population. It can be argued that, for his part, John Diefenbaker tried to finesse both problems by emphasizing the importance of a national identity predicated on his evocative, if imprecise, notions of an "unhyphenated Canadian" and a "vision of the North," coupled with a bill of rights and the "compassionate conservatism" of increasingly generous social programs. It was during the Diefenbaker years that the Quebec Liberal government of Jean Lesage began the Quiet Revolution that was to transform life in "la belle province" and initiate a process of redefining Quebec's relationship with the rest of Canada. Nearly 40 years later, the outcome of that process remains far from certain.

Other than for a brief Conservative interregnum in 1979, Liberal governments under Lester Pearson and Pierre Trudeau held sway federally for over two decades after Diefenbaker and the Conservatives were defeated in the 1963 federal election. Both Pearson and Trudeau recognized Canada's changing economic and political realities but responded to them in different ways. Despite an increase in economic nationalism in his party and in the country at large, Pearson continued to pursue the continentalist policies favoured by his predecessors, whereas Trudeau tried by various means to loosen the American grip on the Canadian economy. Regarding Quebec, Pearson was willing to accommodate Quebecers' desire for greater autonomy and the restructured, decentralized federal system that would inevitably result. Trudeau, in contrast, was loathe to accept the idea of an asymmetrical federalism in which Quebec would be recognized as a province *"pas comme les autres,"* and Quebecers would be treated differently from other Canadians. He would not accede to special status for Quebec in a revised confederation, or attempt to satisfy Quebec while simultaneously placating other provinces by devolving many important powers from the federal to the provincial levels of government. Rather, he focused on implementing language policies that would make the "French fact" manifest throughout the country and, thereby, make Quebecers feel at ease everywhere in Canada (McRoberts, 1997). He also showed a marked distaste for the seemingly never-ending series of *ad hoc* compromises he perceived to be the principal results of federal-provincial first ministers' conferences in which prime ministers were forced to deal with the provincial premiers as if they were the heads of sovereign states. Rather, what was needed, in Trudeau's view, was a new constitution, which would bring a degree of stability, if not outright closure, to the open-ended nature of federal-provincial relations and which would contain a bill of rights entrenching the civil rights and liberties of all Canadians. His goal of a new constitution was finally realized in 1982. The problem was that the Parti Québécois government of Quebec refused to sign on.

Meanwhile, problems of stagflation—low rates of growth coupled with varying combinations of high rates of inflation and unemployment—continued unabated throughout much of the 1970s and early 1980s. The ill-health of the economy and the public's hope that the Progressive Conservatives and their new leader, Brian Mulroney, might reinvigorate it, were largely responsible for the PC victory in the September 1984 federal election. Three of the events on which we have focused in this book were products of the Mulroney years that followed: the 1988 free trade election, the 1992 national referendum on constitutional renewal, and the 1993 federal election. The latter event was a political earthquake that reconfigured the national party system and destroyed any prospects that the PCs would govern Canada again in the foreseeable future.

THE BROKERAGE TRIANGLE: LEADERS, ISSUES, PARTIES

Brian Mulroney left office with abysmally low approval ratings and, in the ensuing years, he often has been vilified by academic commentators and media pundits as the person responsible for the constitutional and economic problems that bedevilled Canada in the latter part of the twentieth century. However, it is possible that a future generation of historians may well treat Mulroney much better than the "chattering classes" have in recent years. Indeed, future historians may contend that, in terms of breadth of vision, he and his fellow Quebecer, Pierre Trudeau, were the foremost prime ministers of the century. In support of their contention, these historians might observe that if Pierre Trudeau wanted to resolve the Quebec problem by making the French fact manifest throughout Canada, Mulroney understood this first required getting Quebec back into Canada. Thus, instead of considering a major aircraft maintenance contract going to Montreal rather than to Winnipeg to be the first of many bad decisions on his part, it may instead be seen as a well-reasoned judgement designed to cement his *bona fides* with Quebecers without seriously eroding his western base of support—a decision that would help convince sceptics in Quebec that he really was a "Boy from Baie Comeau" rather than another blue-suited Tory representative of the Anglo establishment who would willingly sell out the interests of his native province. In gaining the trust of Quebecers, Mulroney would generate the political capital needed to pursue the "mega-constitutional" projects (Russell, 1993) that would integrate Quebec into Canada's national political community.

Future historians also may point to the doggedness with which Mulroney pursued his vision of Quebec coming home to Canada. That the Meech Lake Accord did not succeed, they may contend, was largely the result of factors beyond his control, notably the failure of the agreement to secure ratification by the Manitoba legislature. If Manitoba had approved, the pressure on Newfoundland Premier Clyde Wells to ratify would have been too great to ignore. It could be further argued that if only (a sizable "if only" to be sure)

Ten :: On the Edge

Meech Lake had been ratified and the constitutional issue resolved, there would not have been a Bloc Québécois, and the Reform Party would have been a much less potent threat to the PCs in the West. Although the recessionary economy likely would have cost the Tories the 1993 election, the national party system would not have imploded.

Finally, with regard to methods by which the constitutional issue might be resolved, future historians may point out that having refused to throw in the towel after Meech Lake, and after having cobbled together the Charlottetown Accord, Mulroney was sufficiently in tune with public sentiment in late-twentieth-century Canada to understand that a fundamental agreement on the constitution would not be recognized as legitimate unless and until it received the electorate's approval in a national referendum. Thus, although it may be the case that a major political benefit of holding a referendum would be to divert public attention from, and hopefully reduce public ire over, his government's management of the ailing economy, nonetheless Mulroney's principal goal was to legitimize a compromise solution to the country's continuing constitutional crisis by employing an instrument of participatory democracy.

With regard to Mulroney's other principal goal of employing neo-conservative programs to secure prosperity, he became (admittedly, at first, not entirely by choice) the champion of the free trade agreement, which, it might be argued, set the stage for the country's economic recovery in the mid-1990s. Perhaps equally important was his decision to slaughter one of neo-conservatism's most sacred cows by *raising* rather than *lowering* taxes. Future historians may argue that Mulroney's decision to enact a widely detested value-added tax (the GST) was an act of political courage that would eventually enable his Liberal successor, Jean Chrétien, to enjoy introducing balanced (and even the luxury of surplus) budgets while simultaneously proposing measures to restore cuts in highly popular social programs. That is on the one hand.

On the other, Mulroney's future critics might respond that political courage and political wisdom are not synonymous, and his willingness to (in his words) "roll the dice" resulted in a series of decisions that proved disastrous for his party and country. As observed in Chapter Seven, just as Mulroney's decision not to award the CF-18 contract to Winnipeg began the erosion of his western base and enabled Reform to get off the ground, his decision to hold the 1992 referendum on constitutional renewal breathed new life into a sagging Bloc Québécois. The referendum's decisive defeat then set the stage for the Bloc to win a majority of Quebec's seats in the 1993 federal election. The Bloc's electoral victory decimated the PCs in Quebec, and thereby profoundly changed the contours of the national party system. Absent a sizable number of seats in the province, the PCs ability to win a future federal election was markedly reduced. Moreover, the presence of a strong BQ meant that the Liberals were the only remaining viable pro-Canada electoral option in Quebec at either the federal or provincial levels of government.

Nor were these Mulroney's only miscalculations. Critical historians might further note that poor choices for the cabinet following the PC election victory in 1984 resulted in a series of miscues and scandals that caused Tory support to plummet and remain low for most of his first term in office. In addition, such critics might observe that Mulroney's subsequent decision to go forward with the massively unpopular GST soured an electorate already vexed by what would become a deep and protracted recession. It also appalled many of his advisors who, rather than applauding his political resolve, condemned his economic rashness bordering on stupidity for raising instead of lowering taxes when the economy was in the doldrums. More importantly, the public's perception—despite his oft-repeated claim to lead a party that could manage change—that, in fact, it could not, and, in particular, that it could not revive a stagnant economy, were major factors in that party's near extinction when the votes were counted in 1993. Indeed, by becoming a virtual "poster boy" for the seeming inability of a party to govern effectively during almost a decade in office, Mulroney may well have significantly eroded the public's affection for and confidence in political parties more generally—an erosion that has serious consequences in any mature democracy, especially one with the integration problems confronting Canada.

It often is argued that a stable and effective party system and a stable and effective democracy go hand in hand. Changes in mass communication generally and in the use of television in particular, have caused candidates for major elective offices to function as a kind of prism through which the public views and evaluates the political process. This is especially true of perceptions of the leaders of political parties, whether governing or opposition. A second prism or perceptual screen through which parties and their leaders and policies are viewed and judged is provided by voters' psychological identifications with parties. Indeed, early studies argued that such identifications constituted an "unmoved mover" in the public mind—a long-term force that did much to shape perceptions of party leaders and political issues.

Although partisan attachments are influential determinants of electoral choice in Canada, survey evidence indicates such attachments tend to be weak and unstable. The flexibility of partisanship, in turn, means that highly mutable party leader images and party-issue linkages typically have important effects on voting in federal and provincial elections. The direction and strength of these short-term forces vary over time and space. For example, throughout Pierre Trudeau's tenure as Liberal leader, public reactions to him had powerful effects on voting behaviour. However, the nature of these effects changed over time. In 1968, during his first campaign as Liberal leader, Trudeau was an extremely popular, even charismatic, figure, whose appeal transcended regional and ethno-linguistic cleavages in the electorate. Much had changed by the time he waged his last campaign in 1980. Although feelings about him still had strong effects on electoral choice, he was regarded as a veritable prince of darkness by many voters in the West. The impact of Jean Chrétien's image has been rather different. In 1997, his popularity in Ontario helped the Liberals win 101 of that province's 103 parliamentary seats, while the relative coolness of the rest of the country towards him was a factor that reduced his party's parliamentary majority to a razor-thin edge. But evidence presented in Chapter Eight suggests that the magnitude of the Chrétien effect in that election should not be overestimated. For example, even if he had been as popular in British Columbia—a province in which the Liberals expected to do well—as he was in Ontario, it still would have done little to increase the number of B.C. seats (six) his party won in 1997. In contrast, if only 6 per cent more British Columbians had favoured the Liberals on the *issues*, they would have captured 21 of the province's 31 seats and thereby obtained a comfortable working majority in Parliament.

A Polity on the Edge

Getting voters to prefer a party on the issues has been no easy thing in recent Canadian elections. Many voters do not view parties through the lens of strongly tinted partisan glasses that would colour their perceptions of the issue positions and the competence of competing parties. Forging ties between parties and issues also is inhibited by rapid changes in the issue agenda. For example, although the Canada-U.S. free trade agreement dominated the issue agenda during the 1988 election campaign, it was virtually forgotten by parties, press, and voters by the time of the next (1993) election. The transience of election issues may be partly a function of the "democratization" of information/communication processes. Technological innovations beginning with television in the 1950s and extending to copiers, fax machines, personal computers, e-mail, the Internet, and Web sites in recent years have meant that a multiplicity of issues can be formulated and spun to the voting public by the media, social movements of every kind, so-called single-issue groups, conventional interest groups, self-styled experts in the academic and corporate worlds, individual "true believers" of various persuasions, government bureaucracies, and, of course, political parties. Traditionally, democratic theory assigns parties the task of defining, from this veritable cacophony of self-interested claims for attention, the set of issues that voters will consider during an election.

As numerous earlier studies have observed, Canadian parties typically try to maximize their prospects of electoral success by building (i.e., "brokering") coalitions of supporters with varied interests by selectively articulating issues that have very broad appeal (see, e.g., Clarke et al., 1996). To this end, issues generally are cast in valence (e.g., "the issue is a healthy economy") rather than positional terms (e.g., "low-income voters deserve a 5 per cent tax cut"). During a campaign the leaders of one party may excoriate a policy proposed by another party, and then adopt that same policy if they win the election. Winning parties also may adopt major policies after an election about which they may not have said word one during the campaign. Finally, since issues that do not resonate with voters are quickly discarded by the parties, there is precious little continuity in the salience of particular issues from one election to the next. The result is that party discourse on the issues tends to have a disjointed and ad hoc quality.

Ten :: On the Edge

Although requisite data on public opinion in earlier decades are not available, surveys conducted in the 1990s indicate that voters are not blind to how parties treat issues, and their distaste for these practices has contributed to the massive negativity they express about political parties. Unhappiness with the perceived cynicism of a brokerage-politics approach to issues also may explain why national party leaders have found it difficult to construct linkages between parties and issues in voters' minds in recent elections. In addition, the brokerage-politics approach to issues may help explain why many voters have only vague ideas of what, if anything, the several parties have to say about specific issues, let alone how parties' issue positions and concerns are articulated to more broadly defined ideological frameworks. In turn, the conjunction of negative evaluations and hazy images created by constant maneuvering in multi-dimensional and highly mutable issue spaces helps explain why many Canadians lack strong and stable psychological attachments with political parties. There is, then, a mutually reinforcing syndrome of weak and unstable partisan attachments, transient issue agendas and party-issue linkages, and brokerage electioneering strategies, on the one hand, and voter cynicism and discontent with parties, leaders, and the larger political order, on the other.

It is, of course, the case that Canada is not the only country in which the political parties are charged with similar sins of omission and commission. In the United States, for example, Republican presidents such as George Bush have been criticized by their most committed partisans for campaigning from the right, especially in primary elections, but governing from the left. Somewhat similarly, liberal Democrats have contended that Democratic presidents such as Jimmy Carter and Bill Clinton have been guilty of just the opposite—of campaigning from the left but governing from the right. And, in Britain (other than for the Conservative governments led by Margaret Thatcher) similar kinds of complaints have been made about Conservative and Labour Party leaders from Harold Macmillan to Tony Blair. To the above may be added a more recent, but now very familiar, complaint that party leaders in mature democracies govern on the basis of focus groups and opinion polls rather than being guided by an issue compass magnetized by fundamental ideological principles.

Notwithstanding the tendency of political parties and their leaders in other democracies to be charged with and perhaps be guilty of the same shortcomings as their Canadian counterparts, it may be less the case of who does and does not commit these transgressions, than of how often they are committed. In this regard, critics of Canadian parties have contended that all parties are guilty, but the Liberal Party which has governed the country for the greater part of the twentieth century, is most culpable (see, e.g., Meisel, 1975; Whitaker, 1977). Whether the Liberals merit this dubious distinction is debatable. What is not open to question is the charge that, over time, the federal parties have been either unable or unwilling to generate, campaign on, and then follow through with coherent packages of major policies that transcend regional differences grounded in economic and cultural particularisms. In the 1960s and 1970s, such policy packages frequently were defined by critics in terms of appeals to class interests that would cut across regional and ethno-linguistic cleavages (e.g., Porter, 1965). In the 1980s and 1990s, this emphasis on the ameliorative effects of a class-based issue discourse by the parties was supplemented and, even supplanted, by analyses articulating rights-based claims of such groups as Aboriginal peoples, immigrants, gays, lesbians, the physically challenged, and visible minorities (e.g., Gwyn, 1995; Sniderman, Fletcher, Russell, and Tetlock, 1996). What has not changed is the belief that political parties do not address important issues with constructive policies. Many Canadian voters join observers in the academy and the media in pressing the charge. And, as our survey evidence on Reform Party members presented in Chapter Seven emphasizes, issue- and policy-based appeals can be powerful political attractors—motivating people to become members of an insurgent political party, and propelling them to work actively on that party's behalf, even when there is no prospect of individual rewards for their service.

LESSONS FOR THE NEW MILLENNIUM

In this study we have been concerned with the question of why one of the world's oldest democracies continues to experience integration problems that other mature democracies either have experienced in less acute form or else have successfully resolved. In the first chapter we hypothesized that the most recent crisis of integration is a product of the concatenation within a 10-year period of six events, all of them concerned in one way or another with the economy or Quebec. Individually, each of these events both spurred the crisis and shaped its evolution. In combination, they overturned a long-lived national party system and posed a very serious challenge to the larger political order.

Consider the intertwined fates of the economy, Quebec, and the national parties and their leaders. It is reasonable to conjecture that, despite the outcome of the 1992 national referendum on constitutional reform, Brian Mulroney, rather than Kim Campbell, would have led the Conservatives in the 1993 federal election if the economy had not been in a serious recession during much of Mulroney's second term as prime minister. As we have suggested, it is conceivable that the 1992 constitutional referendum might never have been held if the economic picture had been appreciably brighter at the time. And, even if the Charlottetown Accord *had* been rejected in a referendum and the Tories *had* been turned out of office in 1993, they still would not have been virtually wiped out as a parliamentary party. Alternatively, it might even be argued that if Mulroney's earlier attempt to resolve the country's constitutional problems, the Meech Lake Accord, had been successful, he would have remained as party leader, and his party would have had a fighting chance to win in 1993. The success of Meech Lake would have had another important effect of making it unlikely that Lucien Bouchard would have abandoned the PCS to form the Bloc Québécois. Absent the BQ, and with a leader lionized for resolving the long-standing constitutional impasse by forging a historic agreement between Ottawa, Quebec, and the other provinces, the PCS electoral prospects would have been much improved. Although the recessionary economy might still have proved their undoing, defeat was not guaranteed, and decimation was highly improbable.

Similarly, if the 1992 referendum on constitutional renewal had not been held, it is reasonable to speculate that the national party system would not have fragmented and the 1995 Quebec sovereignty referendum would not have been held. It was the massive rejection of the Charlottetown Accord that revived separatist forces in

Quebec. The BQ used the referendum defeat as a springboard to wage its successful 1993 federal election campaign. Then, the BQ's success helped to pave the way for the PQ to return to power in the 1994 provincial election. In turn, the latter victory was the necessary prerequisite for the 1995 sovereignty referendum.

Still another reasonable supposition is that a principal reason Prime Minister Chrétien called the 1997 national election after only three and one-half years in power was the prospect of strengthening his hand against the separatists. Securing a new mandate, with a large majority of parliamentary seats and a strong showing in Quebec, would do exactly that. As noted in Chapter Nine, support for sovereignty in public opinion polls had decreased after the 1995 sovereignty referendum and, nationally, the polls seemed to indicate that the Liberals were poised to win another election whenever they should decide to call one. A resounding victory that swept a large cohort of Liberal MPs from Quebec into office would severely damage the BQ, and help to position the Liberals to defeat the PQ in the next Quebec provincial election—and as long as the PQ were out of power, the threat of another sovereignty referendum was non-existent.

It was the failure of this scenario to play out that encouraged Lucien Bouchard to hold a provincial election the following year, and to acknowledge that, if returned to office, the PQ would continue to pursue its sovereignty agenda. Although the PQ won a majority of National Assembly seats in that election, it narrowly lost the popular vote. Had it done so more decisively, the correlation of federalist and separatist forces would certainly have been altered, thereby improving at least the short- and medium-term prospects for the continuation of Canada in its current form.

What lessons can we draw from these events? In our view there are five. The first is that despite the best efforts over the years of a great many intelligent and dedicated people, in and out of government, to formulate constitutional options that would finally resolve the complex, emotional issue of Quebec's place in the federal system, none has succeeded. Moreover, even the fact that the country was teetering on the brink of disintegration in October 1995 did not precipitate a process of compromise and reconciliation. Nor can this failure be attributed solely to the presence of a PQ provincial government in Quebec that has no interest in reaching accommodation with political élites representing the rest of Canada. It is striking that surveys before and after the 1995 sovereignty referendum revealed very few changes in public attitudes, either in Quebec or elsewhere, in the wake of the event.

More generally, it seems that constitutional tinkering, however rational, intelligent, and well-intended, is unlikely to resolve majority-minority political conflicts grounded in differences in language usage, widely shared, strongly held cultural values, and differing interpretations of key historical experiences. Analyses of Quebecers attitudes towards sovereignty and independence presented in Chapter Nine indicate that although expectations of the likelihood of reaching a compromise on the constitution affect these attitudes, their influence is much weaker than community self-identifications as a Quebecer or a Canadian. It also bears emphasis that community self-identifications are not the only factors that govern the choice between an independent Quebec and a united Canada. Judgements regarding the financial costs of independence for oneself and one's family also are very important and, like self-identifications, their effects greatly outweigh those generated by beliefs about the possibility of constitutional renewal.

Second, the use of referendums to secure popular agreement on major socio-cultural or political-economic problems is problematic in democracies, especially those like Canada that are characterized by deep-seated, reinforcing social cleavages. A useful political theorem is that the more complex the issue, the more difficult it will be to achieve a consensus on how best to deal with it. In particular, the Canadian attempts to reach agreement by devising multi-faceted "bundled" referendum proposals that give every voter something to like may have failed because such proposals also give every voter something to dislike. A lemma to this theorem is that the disposition of political élites and mass publics to complex referendum proposals will differ. A successful logroll that achieves élite accommodation on a diverse package of constitutional reforms may be exactly the recipe for creating a referendum proposal that will fail when it is submitted to the public (Johnston et al., 1996).

Our studies of Canadian referendums also suggest that referendum issues can rarely, if ever, be non-partisan in a democracy. Regardless of whether a government intended it, voters will view the issue in question as government constructed and sponsored. And, they are likely to vote "yes" or "no" partly on the basis of how they feel about the governing party and its leader. The larger politico-economic context in which a referendum occurs is thus very important. In particular, holding a referendum during a recession is an invitation for discontented voters to hold *their own* referendum, with the subject being the government's (mis)management of the economy rather than the official referendum proposal. Other political actors are relevant as well. In cases where governing and opposition parties take different positions on a referendum proposal, voters feelings about opposition parties and their leaders will influence referendum choices.

The above difficulties notwithstanding, growing public support in contemporary mature democracies for devices of direct democracy makes a strong normative and, perhaps irresistible, political case for referendums on fundamental issues. In a number of these democracies, including Canada, it now would be virtually impossible to make a basic decision affecting a country's future without referring it to the electorate for approval. The conundrum that Brian Mulroney faced in having the élite-generated Meech Lake constitutional agreement derailed by élite-level politics in two provinces and the 1992 referendum proposal on the subsequent Charlottetown constitutional agreement rejected by a disaffected electorate is one that is likely to beset the political leaders of other mature democracies. The stories of the two failed Canadian constitutional accords emphasize the twinned difficulties that the politics of élite accommodation and the politics of direct democracy now pose for leaders trying to achieve significant structural reforms designed to bolster political community.

Third, in democracies with populations characterized by deep-seated and reinforcing social, cultural, or regional cleavages, parties with serious aspirations of winning elections will have almost inevitably to engage in the coalition-building arts of "brokerage politics." The alternative is to practice a "principled" style of electioneering that emphasizes position rather than valence issues. Many of the former divide rather than unify, thus enhancing the probability that no single party will be able to win a majority of parliamentary seats. This probability very likely would be magnified if Canada were to abandon its electoral system for any of the currently popular proposals for some form of proportional representation (see, e.g., Milner, 1999). The resulting coalition governments will be more "representative" of at least some segments of the voting public in that parties in the coalition will draw support almost exclusively from those groups in the electorate for which a party's issue positions have strong resonance. However, because such coalitions are prone to pernicious combinations of ideological incoherence, policy stalemate, and political instability, this enhanced representation likely will be at the cost of a significant measure of governmental effectiveness.

That said, the demise of Canada's long-standing "two-party-plus" national party system (Epstein, 1964) and its replacement by a regionally fragmented one emphasizes the need for parties to strive to build winning coalitions without engaging in the usual pathologies of brokerage politics, such as saying one thing during a campaign and doing another after the election; of denigrating opponents and then adopting their policy proposals; and of adopting major policies never raised as issues during an election campaign. To the late V.O. Key Jr.'s (1968: 17) famous aphorism that "voters are not fools," we would add the caveat, "nor do they appreciate being taken for one." In Canada, negative evaluations of, and disaffection from, political parties, chronic and increasing weakness and instability of partisan attachments, and mounting distaste with "politics as usual" suggest that it is folly on the part of party leaders to believe otherwise. The Canadian case is not unique—there is evidence from numerous contemporary mature democracies that public support for political parties is trending downward, as cynicism with politics and politicians and disengagement from the existing political order rises (e.g., Dalton, 1996: chs. 9-10).

Getting beyond traditional modes of brokerage politics to a style and substance of politics that at once satisfies escalating public demands for broader representation, enhanced participation, and effective governance is a major challenge confronting mature democracies as the twenty-first century begins. In the Canadian case at least, it will not be easy to meet this challenge. At any point in time power-seeking politicians have strong incentives under current electoral arrangements to play the traditional brokerage game. Not doing so is an almost certain recipe for electoral defeat. Once in power, governing parties enjoy considerable freedom to renege on campaign promises or introduce major policies not discussed during a campaign because the brokerage electioneering strategies that emphasize a changing mix of valence issues foster a politics of very short time horizons and extreme voter myopia. Operating on the tried-and-true maxim that "a week is a long time in politics," governing parties and their leaders are encouraged to look after their own best interests "here and now." Possible long-term adverse consequences for the party system or polity in which it is embedded are rationally neglected by such self-interested political actors. Whether the incentive structure that fosters this "tragedy of the party system" (see Ostrom, 1991; see also Kollman, Miller, and Page, 1992) can be changed without creating new, equally serious, problems remains to be seen (see, e.g., Courtney, 1999).

The fourth lesson concerns how inter-linked domestic and international economic forces can affect the prospects of political (dis)integration. Above we noted that every prime minister at some time has had to deal with the politically vexing problem of the economy and the even more vexing, emotionally laden issue of Quebec. With the adoption of the Canada-U.S. free trade agreement (FTA) and the subsequent North American free trade agreement (NAFTA), it seems clear that the fundamental direction of Canadian economic policy has been set for the foreseeable future. Providing a neo-conservative answer to the economic question reinforces historically close economic ties between Canada and United States—as the American economy goes, so will the Canadian. Although many Canadians might prefer more degrees of freedom in this regard, most of them have at least tacitly accepted the argument that the enormous changes that globalization has brought make this an almost inevitable course of action.

In retrospect, it is apparent that there was an important, but largely neglected, aspect of the great debate on free trade in the 1988 federal election campaign. Neither the PCs, who strongly supported the FTA, nor the Liberals, who vigorously opposed it, articulated a coherent analysis of the agreement's implications for Canadian *unity*. One of the important findings about voting behaviour in the 1995 sovereignty referendum, and of support for sovereignty/independence in the post-referendum period, concerns the impact of Quebecers perceptions of the economic benefits and costs of citizenship in a sovereign Quebec and a united Canada. Assessments of the risks of sovereignty are closely related to voters expectations of the future well-being of the Canadian economy and the economy of a sovereign Quebec. Both of these economies are, or would be, strongly influenced by membership in, or exclusion from, NAFTA. During the 1995 sovereignty referendum campaign, spokespersons for the federal government issued veiled, and not-so-veiled, threats that a sovereign Quebec would be blocked from entering NAFTA by the Canadian government.

Whether such an attempt would be made, and whether it would be successful, is not presently known. But the larger message is lesson four—the attractiveness of independence movements is partially, but substantially, a function of benefit-cost and associated risk calculations. In the twenty-first century, such calculations will be made not only with reference to relationships with a political system from which exit is being contemplated, but also with reference to potential relationships with larger transnational politico-economic entities. In the Canadian case, the latter entity is NAFTA, for European countries, it is the European Union. Judgements regarding the likely economic successes or failures of such organizations create powerful "pressures from above" that can be expected to influence the attitudes and behaviour of members of groups (such as Quebecers) who are contemplating the consequences of membership in alternative political communities.

The fifth and final lesson concerns the possibility of the disintegration of Canada and other democracies, mature and emerging. In the spring of 1995, some observers recalled the decisive defeat of the PQ sovereignty-association proposal in the 1980 referendum, and argued that history would repeat itself. If Premier Parizeau and his new Péquiste government dared to hold another referendum, they would suffer a crushing rejection at the polls. But, recognizing the inevitability of another defeat, they very likely would not proceed. These forecasts proved to be drastically wrong—despite the barrage of media commentary that sharply discounted their chances of winning, the Péquistes held their nerve, held the referendum, and the proposal came within a fraction of 1 per cent of passing.

What would happen if a future sovereignty proposal receives majority support is unknown; the passage of a sovereignty proposal is not tantamount to a unilateral declaration of independence. It is not necessarily the case that Ottawa would even agree to open negotiations concerning the terms under which Quebec would become sovereign. Nor is it known how ardent pro-Canada groups in Quebec such as Aboriginal peoples, Anglophones, and persons of non-French and non-Anglo-Celtic ethnic origins would behave, or how Canadians in other provinces would react. It is possible to sketch a variety of plausible scenarios concerning how events would unfold after the passage of a sovereignty referendum (see Young, 1998). Some of these scenarios involve peaceful processes of negotiation leading to sovereignty association or outright independence, whereas others feature varying combinations of spiralling economic uncertainty, protracted political stalemate, even escalating violence. As Young (1998) emphasizes, no one knows how to assign probabilities to such disparate alternatives; massive uncertainty surrounds what would happen if Quebec votes *"oui"* in a future sovereignty referendum.

But, what is the likelihood that a sovereignty proposal actually would be approved, should another referendum be held? Public opinion polls conducted since the 1995 referendum show that support for sovereignty has receded somewhat. For those favouring a united Canada, that is, of course, good news. But, there also is a more ominous, if less obvious, message for pro-Canada forces in the recent survey data. As documented in Chapter Nine, younger Quebecers are *much more likely* to support sovereignty and full independence than are older persons. Assuming that this sharp age gradient reflects, to a substantial extent, generationally related socialization processes, suggests that inexorable demographic forces are quietly eroding the size of the group of likely *"non"* voters. As older pro-Canada Quebecers are replaced by successive cohorts of young, pro-sovereignty persons, the likelihood of a *"oui"* majority in a future referendum increases. Should present age-related differences in support for sovereignty continue, the size of the group disposed to favour sovereignty will become so large that even adverse short-term forces might not be able to thwart a *"oui"* majority in a future referendum campaign.

Since the possibility of a *"oui"* majority in a future sovereignty referendum is decidedly non-trivial, the end of Canada—a country judged by people around the world as a premier example of a prosperous and successful mature democracy—in its current form is also a very real possibility. In our judgement, should Quebec achieve some form of sovereignty-association or even full independence, this should not—indeed, must not—be viewed as the apocalypse. Ex-premier Parizeau's intemperate post-referendum remarks notwithstanding, there is abundant evidence that a sovereign Quebec would not be a repressive, authoritarian regime; rather it would join the growing ranks of new democracies. But, unlike the vast majority of these political systems, the new Quebec would have economic, social, and political cultural resources comparable to those of existing *mature* democracies. An independent Quebec therefore very likely would become one of the smaller economically prosperous and politically stable Western democracies such as Austria, the Netherlands, and the Scandinavian countries. There also is every reason to believe that, absent Quebec, Canada would continue to be a highly affluent, socially tolerant, and politically inclusive democracy. Sir Wilfrid Laurier claimed that the twentieth century would belong to Canada. In important respects, he was close to the mark. Over the past 100 years Canada has made enormous economic, social, and political progress, and has become one of the most admired countries on earth. Tolerance, civility, and compromise constitute the best of the Canadian political tradition. If Quebecers and other Canadians insist that these democratic virtues continue to be practiced in the context of the heated politics of Quebec sovereignty, Laurier's inspirational conjecture can define the twenty-first century realities of Quebec and the rest of Canada, whether they are together or apart.

APPENDIX

Data Sources

Numerous large-scale surveys of the Canadian electorate provide the data analysed in this book. The principal ones are: (1) national cross-sectional and interlocking panel surveys conducted in 1983, 1984, 1988, 1990, 1992, 1993, 1995, 1997; (2) a panel survey of the Quebec electorate conducted immediately before and after the 1995 sovereignty referendum; (3) monthly surveys of the Quebec electorate carried out during the September 1996-May 1999 period; (4) a mail questionnaire sent to members of the Reform Party in the autumn of 1993. The 1983 survey also contains a panel component composed of persons interviewed in the 1979 and 1980 national election surveys. Fieldwork for all of the surveys except the 1992 referendum survey was conducted by Canadian Facts, Toronto, Ontario. The 1992 survey was carried out by the Carleton University Survey Centre. Principal funding for the several studies was provided by research grants to Harold D. Clarke and Allan Kornberg from the National Science Foundation (U.S.). Supplementary funding was provided by the Canadian Embassy, Washington, D.C., the Provost's Fund, Duke University, and the University of North Texas. Technical information regarding the surveys is available from the authors upon request. Several of the data sets may be obtained from the ICPSR Data Archive, University of Michigan, Ann Arbor, the ISR Data Archive, York University, Toronto, and the Essex Data Archive, University of Essex, Colchester, England. These data sets also may be downloaded from Harold Clarke's Web site: www.psci.unt.edu/hclarke/

Other survey data were gathered in the 1965, 1968, 1974, 1979, 1980, and 1984 Canadian national election studies, the 1977, 1979, and 1981 Quality of Life studies, and studies carried out at the time of the 1980 Quebec sovereignty-association referendum. The 1965 election study was conducted by Philip Converse, John Meisel, Maurice Pinard, Peter Regenstreif, and Mildred Schwartz, and the 1968 study was carried out by John Meisel. The principal investigators for the 1974, 1979, and 1980 election surveys and the 1980 Quebec sovereignty referendum survey were Harold D. Clarke, Jane Jenson, Lawrence LeDuc, and Jon Pammett. Ronald Lambert, Steven Brown, James Curtis, Barry Kay, and John Wilson were principal investigators for the 1984 election study. The Quality of Life project was carried out by Tom Atkinson and others. Allan Kornberg and Joel Smith were principal investigators for the "Three Cities" study carried out at the time of the 1980 Quebec sovereignty referendum. The 1965-84 election survey data are available from the ICPSR and ISR Data Archives, and the Quality of Life survey data are available from the ISR Data Archive.

Trends in public opinion were measured using data from monthly or quarterly public opinion polls conducted by the Canadian Institute of Public Opinion (CIPO) and the Decima organization. The Centre for the Study of Public Opinion, Queen's University, supplied the Decima data, and the CIPO data were obtained from the Leddy Library, University of Windsor.

References

Aldrich, John H., and Forrest D. Nelson. 1984. *Linear Probability, Logit, and Probit Models*. Beverly Hills, Calif.: Sage.

Archer, Keith. 1987. "A Simultaneous Equation Model of Canadian Voting Behaviour," *Canadian Journal of Political Science* 20: 553-72.

Archer, Keith, and Faron Ellis. 1994. "Opinion Structure of Party Activists: The Reform Party of Canada," *Canadian Journal of Political Science* 27: 277-306.

Banting, Keith, and Richard Simeon. 1983. *And No One Cheered: Federalism, Democracy and the Constitution Act*. Toronto: Methuen.

Bean, Charles R. 1994. "European Unemployment: A Survey." *Journal of Economic Literature* 32: 573-619.

Belknap, George, and Angus Campbell. 1952. "Political Party Identification and Attitudes Toward Foreign Policy," *Public Opinion Quarterly* 15: 601-23.

Bell, David, and Lorne Tepperman. 1979. *The Roots of Disunity: A Look at Canadian Political Culture*. Toronto: McClelland & Stewart.

Black, Edwin R. 1975. *Divided Loyalties: Canadian Concepts of Federalism*. Montreal and Kingston: McGill-Queen's University Press.

Black, Edwin R., and Alan C. Cairns. 1966. "A Different Perspective on Canadian Federalism," *Canadian Public Administration* 9: 27-44.

Blake, Donald E. 1982. "The Consistency of Inconsistency: Party Identification in Federal and Provincial Politics," *Canadian Journal of Political Science* 15: 691-710.

Bliss, Michael. 1991. "Canadianizing American Business: Roots of the Branch Plant," in A.I. Silver, ed., *An Introduction to Canadian History*. Toronto: Canadian Scholars Press.

Bloom, Howard S., and H. Douglas Price. 1975. "Voter Response to Short-Run Economic Conditions: The Asymmetric Effects of Prosperity and Recession," *American Political Science Review* 69: 1240-54.

Bollen, Kenneth. 1989. *Structural Equations with Latent Variables*. New York: Wiley Interscience.

Bothwell, Robert. 1998. *Canada and Quebec: One Country Two Histories*. Vancouver: University of British Columbia Press.

Boyer, Patrick. 1992. *Direct Democracy in Canada: The History and Future of Referendums*. Toronto: Dundurn Press.

Brulé, Michel. 1992. "France After Maastricht," *The Public Perspective* (November/December): 28-30.

Budge, Ian, Ivor Crewe, and Dennis Farlie, eds. 1976. *Party Identification and Beyond*. New York: Wiley.

Butler, David, and Austin Ranney, eds. 1978. *Referendums: A Comparative Study of Practice and Theory*. Washington: American Enterprise Institute.

Cain, Bruce, John Ferejohn, and Morris Fiorina. 1987. *The Personal Vote: Constituency Service and Electoral Independence*. Cambridge: Harvard University Press.

Cairns, Alan C. 1971. "The Judicial Committee and Its Critics," *Canadian Journal of Political Science* 10: 695-726.

———. 1983. "Constitution-Making, Government Self-Interest, and the Problem of Legitimacy," in Allan Kornberg and Harold D. Clarke, eds. *Political Support in Canada: The Crisis Years*. Durham, NC: Duke University Press.

Campbell, Angus, Philip E. Converse, Warren E. Miller, and Donald E. Stokes. 1960. *The American Voter*. New York: Wiley.

Campbell, Angus, Gerald Gurin, and Warren E. Miller. 1954. *The Voter Decides*. Evanston, Ill.: Row, Peterson.

Carty, R. Kenneth, ed. 1992. *Canadian Political Party Systems: A Reader*. Peterborough, Ont.: Broadview Press.

Clarke, Harold D., Nitish Dutt, and Allan Kornberg. 1993. "The Political Economy of Attitudes towards Polity and Society in Western European Democracies," *Journal of Politics* 55: 998-1021.

Clarke, Harold D., Jane Jenson, Lawrence LeDuc, and Jon H. Pammett. 1979. *Political Choice in Canada*. Toronto: McGraw-Hill Ryerson.

———. 1996. *Absent Mandate: Canadian Electoral Politics in an Era of Restructuring*, 3rd ed. Toronto: Gage.

Clarke, Harold D., and Allan Kornberg. 1992. "Support for the Canadian Federal Progressive Conservative Party Since 1988: The Impact of Economic Evaluations and Economic Issues," *Canadian Journal of Political Science* 25: 29-54.

———. 1993. "Evaluations and Evolution: Public Attitudes towards Canada's Federal Political Parties, 1965-1991," *Canadian Journal of Political Science* 26: 287-312.

———. 1994. "The Politics and Economics of Constitutional Choice: Voting in Canada's 1992 National Referendum," *Journal of Politics* 56: 940-62.

———. 1996. "Choosing Canada? The 1995 Quebec Sovereignty Referendum," *PS: Political Science and Politics* 29: 676-82.

———. 1996. "Partisan Dealignment, Electoral Choice and Party-System Change in Canada," *Party Politics* 2: 455-78.

Clarke, Harold D., Allan Kornberg, Faron Ellis, and Jonathan Rapkin. 1999. "Not for Fame or Fortune: Membership and Activity in the Canadian Reform Party," *Party Politics* 6: 75-94.

Clarke, Harold D., and Allan McCutcheon. 1998. "Mixed Markov Latent Class Models for the Dynamics of Party Identification," paper presented at the Annual Meeting of the Midwest Political Science Association, Chicago, April 23.

References

Clarke, Harold D., and Marianne C. Stewart. 1987. "Partisan Inconsistency and Partisan Change in Federal States: The Case of Canada," *American Journal of Political Science* 31: 383-407.

———. 1992. "Canada," in Mark Franklin, Tom Mackie, Henry Valen, et al., *Electoral Change: Responses to Evolving Social and Attitudinal Structure in Western Countries.* Cambridge: Cambridge University Press.

———. 1996. "Economists and Electorates: The Subjective Economy of Governing Party Support in Canada," *European Journal of Political Research* 29: 191-214.

Clarke, Harold D., Marianne C. Stewart, and Gary Zuk, eds. 1989. *Economic Decline and Political Change: Canada, Great Britain, the United States.* Pittsburgh: University of Pittsburgh Press.

Clarke, Harold D., et al. 1992. *Controversies in Political Economy: Canada, Great Britain, the United States.* Boulder, Colo.: Westview Press.

Converse, Philip E. 1976. *The Dynamics of Party Support.* Beverly Hills, Calif.: Sage.

Converse, Philip E., and Georges Dupeux. 1966. "Politicization of the Electorate in France and the United States," In Angus Campbell, Philip E. Converse, Warren E. Miller, and Donald E. Stokes, eds., *Elections and the Political Order.* New York: Wiley.

Cook, Ramsay. 1995. *Canada, Quebec and the Uses of Nationalism,* 2nd ed. Toronto: McClelland & Stewart.

Cooper, Barry, Allan Kornberg, and William Mishler, eds. 1988. *The Resurgence of Conservatism in Anglo-American Democracies.* Durham, NC: Duke University Press.

Cornellier, Manon. 1995. *The Bloc.* Toronto: Lorimer.

Courtney, John C. 1999. "Electoral Reform and Canada's Parties," in Henry Milner, ed. *Making Every Vote Count.* Peterborough, Ont.: Broadview Press.

Crewe, Ivor. 1981. "Electoral Participation," in David Butler, Howard R. Penniman, and Austin Ranney, eds., *Democracy at the Polls: A Comparative Study of Competitive National Elections.* Washington: American Enterprise Institute.

Dalton, Russell J. 1996. *Citizen Politics,* 2nd ed. Chatham, NJ: Chatham House.

Dalton, Russell J., Scott C. Flanagan, and Paul Allen Beck, eds. 1984. *Electoral Change in Advanced Industrial Democracies: Realignment or Dealignment?* Princeton, NJ: Princeton University Press.

Downs, Anthony. 1957. *An Economic Theory of Democracy.* New York: Harper and Row.

Durand, Claire, André Blais, and Sébastien Vachon. 1999. "Why Did the Polls Go Wrong in the 1998 Quebec Election? Or Did They?" paper presented at the 54th Annual Conference of the American Association for Public Opinion Research (AAPOR) St. Petersburg Beach, Fla., May 13-16.

Easton, David. 1965. *A Systems Analysis of Political Life.* New York: Wiley.

Eldersveld, Samuel J. 1964. *Political Parties: A Behavioral Analysis.* Chicago: Rand McNally.

Epstein, Leon D. 1964. "A Comparative Study of Canadian Parties," *American Political Science Review* 58: 46-60.

Flanagan, Thomas. 1985. "The Manufacture of Minorities," in Neil Nevitte and Allan Kornberg, eds., *Minorities and the Canadian State.* Oakville, Ont.: Mosaic Press.

———. 1995. *Waiting for the Wave: The Reform Party and Preston Manning.* Toronto: Stoddard.

Franklin, Mark N., Cees van der Eijk, and Michael Marsh. 1995. "Referendum Outcomes and Trust in Government: Public Support for Europe in the Wake of Maastricht," *West European Politics* 18: 102-17.

Franklin, Mark N., Michael Marsh, and Lauren McLaren. 1994. "Uncorking the Bottle: Popular Opposition to European Unification in the Wake of Maastricht," *Journal of Common Market Studies* 32: 455-72.

Friedman. Thomas L. 1999. *The Lexus and the Olive Tree.* New York: Farrar, Straus, Giroux.

Frizzell, Alan, Jon H. Pammett, and Anthony Westell. 1989. *The Canadian General Election of 1988.* Ottawa: Carleton University Press.

———. 1994. *The Canadian General Election of 1993.* Ottawa: Carleton University Press.

Frizzell, Alan, and Anthony Westell. 1985. *The Canadian General Election of 1984.* Ottawa: Carleton University Press.

Gagnon, Alain G., and Brian Tanguay, eds. 1989. *Canadian Parties in Transition.* Toronto: Nelson.

Gibbins, Roger. 1994. *Conflict and Unity: An Introduction to Canadian Political Life*, 3rd ed. Toronto: Nelson.

Glenn, Norval D. 1977. *Cohort Analysis.* Beverly Hills, Calif.: Sage.

Gratton, Michael. 1988. *So, What Are the Boys Saying? An Inside Look at Brian Mulroney in Power.* Toronto: Paperjacks.

Gwyn, Richard. 1995. *Nationalism Without Walls: The Unbearable Lightness of Being Canadian.* Toronto: McClelland & Stewart.

Held, David. 1987. *Models of Democracy.* Stanford, Calif.: Stanford University Press.

Hinich, Melvin, Michael C. Munger, and Scott DeMarchi. 1998. "Ideology and the Construction of Nationalism: The Canadian Election of 1993," *Public Choice* 97: 401-28.

Honker, James, et al. 1999. *AMELIA: A Program for Missing Data.* Cambridge, Mass.: Harvard University, Department of Government.

Irving, John A. 1959. *The Social Credit Movement in Alberta.* Toronto: University of Toronto Press.

Jeffrey, Brooke. 1993. *Strange Bedfellows, Trying Times: October 1992 and the Defeat of the Powerbrokers.* Toronto: Key Porter Books.

Jenson, Jane. 1976. "Party Loyalty in Canada: The Question of Party Identification," *Canadian Journal of Political Science* 8: 543-53.

Johnston, Richard, André Blais, Henry E. Brady, and Jean Crête. 1992. *Letting the People Decide: Dynamics of a Canadian Election.* Stanford, Calif.: Stanford University Press.

Johnston, Richard, André Blais, Elisabeth Gidengil, and Neil Nevitte. 1996. *The Challenge of Direct Democracy: The 1992 Canadian Referendum.* Montreal and Kingston: McGill-Queen's University Press.

Joreskog, Karl, and Dag Sorbom. 1988. *LISREL 7: A Guide to the Program and Applications.* Chicago: SPSS Inc.

Key, V.O., Jr. 1955. "A Theory of Critical Elections," *Journal of Politics* 17: 3-18.

———. 1964. *Politics, Parties, and Pressure Groups*, 5th ed. New York: Crowell.

———. 1968. *The Responsible Electorate.* New York: Vintage Books.

References

King, Gary, James Honaker, Anne Joseph, and Kenneth Scheve. 1998. "Analyzing Incomplete Political Science Data: An Alternative Algorithm for Multiple Imputation," paper presented at the annual meeting of the American Political Science Association, Boston, September.

Kollman, Ken, John H. Miller, and Scott E. Page. 1992. "Adaptive Parties in Spatial Elections," *American Political Science Review* 86: 929-37.

Kornberg, Allan. 1970. "Parliament in Canadian Society," in Allan Kornberg and Lloyd D. Musolf, eds., *Legislatures in Developmental Perspective*. Durham, NC: Duke University Press.

Kornberg, Allan, and Harold D. Clarke. 1992. *Citizens and Community: Political Support in a Representative Democracy*. New York: Cambridge University Press.

Kornberg, Allan, and Harold D. Clarke, eds. 1983. *Political Support in Canada: The Crisis Years*. Durham, NC: Duke University Press.

Kornberg, Allan, Harold D. Clarke, and Marianne C. Stewart. 1979. "Federalism and Fragmentation: Political Support in Canada," *Journal of Politics* 41: 889-906.

Kornberg, Allan, and Samuel J. Hines. 1977. "Parliament's Role in the Integration-Modernization of Canadian Society, 1865-1876," in Albert Eldridge, ed., *Legislatures in Plural Societies*. Durham, NC: Duke University Press.

Kornberg, Allan, William Mishler, and Joel Smith. 1975. "Political Elite and Mass Perceptions of Party Locations in Issue Space: Some Tests of Two Positions," *British Journal of Political Science* 5: 161-85.

Kornberg, Allan, Joel Smith, and Harold D. Clarke. 1979. *Citizen Politicians-Canada: Party Officials in a Democratic Society*. Durham, NC: Carolina Academic Press.

Knopff, Rainer. 1985. "The Statistical Protection of Minorities: Affirmative Action Policy in Canada," in Neil Nevitte and Allan Kornberg, eds., *Minorities and the Canadian State*. Oakville, Ont.: Mosaic Press.

Lambert, Ronald D., James E. Curtis, Steven D. Brown, and Barry J. Kay. 1987. "Social Class, Left/Right Political Orientations, and Subjective Class Voting in Provincial and Federal Elections," *Canadian Review of Sociology and Anthropology* 24: 526-49.

Laxer, James, and Robert Laxer. 1977. *The Liberal Idea of Canada: Pierre Trudeau and the Question of Canada's Survival*. Toronto: Lorimer.

Laycock, David. 1994. "Reforming Canadian Democracy? Institutions and Ideology in the Reform Party Project," *Canadian Journal of Political Science* 27: 213-48.

LeDuc, Lawrence, Harold D. Clarke, Jane Jenson, and Jon H. Pammett. 1984. "Partisan Instability in Canada: Evidence From a New Panel Study," *American Political Science Review* 78: 470-84.

LeDuc, Lawrence, and Jon H. Pammett. 1995. "Referendum Voting: Attitudes and Behaviour in the 1992 Constitutional Referendum," *Canadian Journal of Political Science* 28: 3-34.

Lewis-Beck, Michael. 1988. *Economics and Elections: The Major Western Democracies*. Ann Arbor, Mich.: University of Michigan Press.

Lipset, Seymour Martin. 1968. *Agrarian Socialism: The Cooperative Commonwealth Federation in Saskatchewan*. New York: Doubleday.

———. 1990. *Continental Divide: The Values and Institutions of the United States and Canada.* New York: Routledge.

Long, J. Scott. 1997. *Regression Models for Categorical and Limited Dependent Variables.* Thousand Oaks, Calif.: Sage.

Lower, Arthur R.M. 1958. "Theories of Canadian Federalism--Yesterday and Today," in Lower et al., eds., *Evolving Canadian Federalism.* Durham, NC: Duke University Press.

Lumsden, Ian. 1970. *Close the 49th Parallel etc.: The Americanization of Canada.* Toronto: University of Toronto Press.

MacDermid, Robert H. 1989. "The Recall of Past Partisanship: Feeble Memories or Frail Concepts," *Canadian Journal of Political Science* 22: 363-75.

Macpherson, C.B. 1953. *Democracy in Alberta: The Theory and Practice of a Quasi-Party System.* Toronto: University of Toronto Press.

Mayo, Henry. 1960. *An Introduction to Democratic Theory.* New York: Oxford University Press.

McNaught, Kenneth. 1969. *The Pelican History of Canada.* London: Penguin.

McRoberts, Kenneth. 1988. *Quebec: Social Change and Political Crisis,* 3rd ed. Toronto: McClelland & Stewart.

———. 1995. *Beyond Quebec: Taking Stock of Canada.* Montreal and Kingston: McGill-Queen's University Press.

———. 1997. *Misconceiving Canada: The Struggle for National Unity.* Toronto: Oxford University Press.

McRoberts, Kenneth, and Patrick Monahan, eds. 1993. *The Charlottetown Acord, the Referendum, and the Future of Canada.* Toronto: University of Toronto Press.

Meisel, John. 1975. *Working Papers on Canadian Politics,* 2nd ed. Montreal and Kingston: McGill-Queen's University Press.

———. 1991. "Decline of Party in Canada," in Hugh G. Thorburn, ed., *Party Politics in Canada,* 6th ed. Scarborough, Ont.: Prentice Hall.

———. 1991. "The Dysfunctions of Party," in Hugh G. Thorburn, ed., *Party Politics in Canada,* 6th ed. Scarborough, Ont.: Prentice Hall.

Miller, Warren E., and M. Kent Jennings. 1986. *Parties in Transition: A Longitudinal Study of Party Elites and Party Supporters.* New York: Russell Sage.

Milner, Henry, ed. 1999. *Making Every Vote Count.* Peterborough, Ont.: Broadview Press.

Mishler, William, and Harold D. Clarke. 1990. "Political Participation in Canada," in Michael S. Whittington and Glen Williams, eds., *Canadian Politics in the 1990s,* 3rd ed. Toronto: Nelson.

Monahan, Patrick J. 1991. *Meech Lake: The Inside Story.* Toronto: University of Toronto Press.

Morton, William. 1950. *The Progressive Party in Canada.* Toronto: University of Toronto Press.

Nevitte, Neil. 1996. *The Decline of Deference: Canadian Value Change in Cross-National Perspective.* Peterborough, Ont.: Broadview Press.

Norpoth, Helmut, Michael Lewis-Beck, and Jean-Dominique Lafay. 1991. *Economics and Politics: The Calculus of Support.* Ann Arbor, Mich.: University of Michigan Press.

Ostrom, Elinor. 1991. *Governing the Commons: The Evolution of Institutions for Collective Action.* New York: Cambridge University Press.

References

Pammett, Jon H. 1987. "Class Voting and Class Consciousness in Canada," *Canadian Review of Sociology and Anthropology* 24: 269-89.

Petterson, Per Arnt, Anders Todal Jenssen, and Ola Listhaug. 1996. "The 1994 EU Referendum in Norway: Continuity and Change," *Scandinavian Political Studies* 19: 257-81.

Pierce, Roy, Henry Valen, and Ola Listhaug. 1983. "Referendum Voting Behavior," *American Journal of Political Science* 27: 43-63.

Pinard, Maurice. 1971. *The Rise of a Third Party: A Study in Crisis Politics.* Toronto: Prentice Hall.

Porter, John. 1965. *The Vertical Mosaic: An Analysis of Social Class and Power in Canada.* Toronto: University of Toronto Press.

Preston, Richard. 1972. *The Influence of the United States on Canadian Development.* Durham, NC: Duke University Press.

Quinn, Herbert F. 1963. *The Union Nationale: A Study in Quebec Nationalism.* Toronto: University of Toronto Press.

Russell, Peter H. 1992. *Constitutional Odyssey: Can Canadians Be a Sovereign People?* Toronto: University of Toronto Press.

———. 1993. "The End of Mega Constitutional Politics in Canada?" *PS: Political Science and Politics.* 27: 33-37.

Schickler, Eric, and Donald Philip Green. 1997. "The Stability of Party Identification in Eight Western Democracies," *Comparative Political Studies* 30: 450-83.

Schwartz, Mildred A. 1974. *Politics and Territory: The Politics of Regional Persistence in Canada.* Montreal and Kingston: McGill-Queen's University Press.

———. 1983. "Political Support and Group Dominance," in Allan Kornberg and Harold D. Clarke, eds., *Political Support in Canada: The Crisis Years.* Durham, NC: Duke University Press.

Sigurdson, Richard. 1994. "Preston Manning and the Politics of Postmodernism in Canada," *Canadian Journal of Political Science* 27: 249-76.

Smith, Joel, and Allan Kornberg. 1983. "The Quebec Referendum: National or Provincial Event?"in Allan Kornberg and Harold D. Clarke, eds., *Political Support in Canada: The Crisis Years.* Durham, NC: Duke University Press.

Smith, Peter J. 1987. "The Ideological Origins of Canadian Confederation," *Canadian Journal of Political Science* 20: 3-29.

Smiley, Donald V. 1980. *Canada in Question: Federalism in the Eighties,* 3rd ed. Toronto: McGraw-Hill Ryerson.

Sniderman, Paul, Joseph F. Fletcher, Peter H. Russell, and Philip E. Tetlock. 1996. *The Clash of Rights: Liberty, Equality, and Legitimacy in Pluralist Democracy.* New Haven: Yale University Press.

Stein, Michael B. 1973. *The Dynamics of Right-Wing Protest: A Political Analysis of Social Credit in Quebec.* Toronto: University of Toronto Press.

Stevenson, Garth. 1989. *Unfulfilled Union: Canadian Federalism and National Unity,* 3rd ed. Agincourt, Ont.: Gage Publishing.

Stevenson, H. Michael. 1987. "Ideology and Unstable Party Identification in Canada: Limited Rationality in a Brokerage Party System," *Canadian Journal of Political Science* 20: 813-50.

Stewart, Marianne C., and Harold D. Clarke. 1997. "Partisan Inconsistency and the Dynamics of Party Support in Federal Systems: The Canadian Case," *American Journal of Political Science* 41: 97-116.

van der Eijk, Cees, Mark N. Franklin, et al. 1996. *Choosing Europe: The European Electorate and National Politics in the Face of Union.* Ann Arbor, Mich.: University of Michigan Press.

Wallas, Graham. 1981. *Human Nature in Politics.* New Brunswick, N.J.: Transaction Books.

Watkins, Mel. 1968. "A New National Policy," in Trevor Lloyd and Jack McLeod, eds. *Agenda 1970: Proposals for a Creative Politics.* Toronto: University of Toronto Press.

Wearing, Peter. 1994. "It Don't Mean a Thing if It Ain't Got That Swing: A Model for Predicting Elections." *Canadian Journal of Marketing Research* January: 66-70.

Weinberg, Gerhard L. 1994. *A World at Arms: A Global History of World War II.* Cambridge: Cambridge University Press.

Whitehorn, Alan. 1994. "The NDP's Quest for Survival," in Alan Frizell, Jon H. Pammett, and Anthony Westell, eds. *The Canadian General Election of 1993.* Ottawa: Carleton University Press.

Wilson-Smith, Anthony. 1995. "A House Divided." *Maclean's* November 13: 14-16.

Woolstencroft, Peter. 1994. "'Doing Politics Differently': The Conservative Party and the Campaign of 1993," in Alan Frizzell, Jon H. Pammett, and Anthony Westell, eds., *The Canadian General Election of 1993.* Ottawa: Carleton University Press.

Whitley, Paul F., et al. 1994. "Explaining Party Activism: The Case of the British Conservative Party," *British Journal of Political Science* 24: 79-94.

Young, Robert A. 1998. *The Secession of Quebec and the Future of Canada,* revised and expanded edition. Montreal and Kingston: McGill-Queen's University Press.

Young, Walter D. 1969. *The Anatomy of a Party: The National CCF 1932-1961.* Toronto: University of Toronto Press, 1969.

Zakuta, Leo. 1964. *A Protest Movement Becalmed: A Study of Change in the CCF.* Toronto: University of Toronto Press.

Zaller, John. 1992. *The Nature and Origins of Mass Opinion.* Cambridge: Cambridge University Press.

Author Index

Subject Index

socio-demographic characteristics 201-02, 209-12
Regional cleavages 25, 27, 31,
39, 41-44, 162-68, 245,
302, 306-07
differences in voting
behaviour 59, 94-99
different perceptions of
Charlottetown Accord
94-105, 112-17
different perceptions of free
trade agreement 19-20,
25-27, 57, 59, 77-79
different perceptions of
political parties 19-20,
57, 112-14, 133-35, 231
See also Societal cleavages
Reisman, Simon 54
Resource issues 43
Royal commissions and policy
innovation 53

St. Laurent, Louis 31, 294
Saskatchewan 95, 212
Social Credit Party (Socreds) 28,
187
Socialism 22
Social issues 21-22
Social programs 22, 30, 33, 157,
248, 252-53, 297
Societal cleavages 23, 25-27, 31,
57, 70-71, 105, 245, 301,
305-07
Sovereignty. *See* Quebec:
1980 sovereignty
referendum, 1995
sovereignty referendum
Stagflation 32, 43, 72, 295

See also Inflation;
Unemployment
Support for Canada
in Quebec 46, 180-82
in the rest of Canada 180-82
Support for national political
authorities 76, 154, 173,
175-81
in Quebec 179-81
in the rest of Canada 179-81
Support for national political
regime 46
for civil service 154, 173
for judiciary 154, 173
for parliament 154, 173
in Quebec 164-65
in rest of Canada 164-65

Tariffs 21-22, 27, 205
Taxes, policy 69-70, 248, 262,
297
Thatcher, Margaret 33, 54, 301
Tories. *See* Progressive
Conservative Party
Trans Canada Airlines 28
Trudeau, Pierre 31, 42-43,
47-48, 52, 57, 62, 95, 144,
294-99
Turner, John 18, 48-49, 52-56,
58, 62-63, 140

Unemployment 19, 22, 27, 28,
32, 41, 43, 49, 53, 68, 72,
135, 221, 229, 249
See also Elections: 1984 federal election, 1993 federal
election
Union Nationale 29, 42
United Farmers Parties 29

This book was
composed in
Adobe Bembo
and Font Bureau
Agenda using
Adobe InDesign
software.